TROUBLING ADOPTION
Heartbreak and Hope

Cath Lambert

P

First published in Great Britain in 2026 by

Policy Press, an imprint of
Bristol University Press
University of Bristol
1–9 Old Park Hill
Bristol
BS2 8BB
UK
t: +44 (0)117 374 6645
e: bup-info@bristol.ac.uk

Details of international sales and distribution partners are available at policy.bristoluniversitypress.co.uk

© Bristol University Press 2026

DOI: 10.51952/9781447371977

British Library Cataloguing in Publication Data
A catalogue record for this book is available from the British Library

ISBN 978-1-4473-7194-6 hardcover
ISBN 978-1-4473-7195-3 paperback
ISBN 978-1-4473-7196-0 ePub
ISBN 978-1-4473-7197-7 ePdf

The right of Cath Lambert to be identified as author of this work has been asserted by them in accordance with the Copyright, Designs and Patents Act 1988.

All rights reserved: no part of this publication may be reproduced, stored in a retrieval system, or transmitted in any form or by any means, electronic, mechanical, photocopying, recording, or otherwise without the prior permission of Bristol University Press.

Every reasonable effort has been made to obtain permission to reproduce copyrighted material. If, however, anyone knows of an oversight, please contact the publisher.

The statements and opinions contained within this publication are solely those of the author and not of the University of Bristol or Bristol University Press. The University of Bristol and Bristol University Press disclaim responsibility for any injury to persons or property resulting from any material published in this publication.

Bristol University Press and Policy Press work to counter discrimination on grounds of gender, race, disability, age and sexuality.

Cover design: Liam Roberts
Front cover image: Stocksy/Alan Shapiro

Contents

List of figures		iv
Acknowledgements		v
1	What is adoption?	1
2	The role of archives in adoption narratives	26
3	Developing alternative knowledges and ways of knowing	46
4	Re-thinking attachment theory and adoption	73
5	Telling adoption stories in new ways	96
6	The emotional complexities of adoption	116
7	Interdependence in adoption policy and practice	140
8	A manifesto for change	168
Notes		187
References		189
Index		210

List of figures

3.1	Art of Attachment film installation and engagement space at VDT's studio, New England House, Brighton	55
3.2	Art of Attachment clay crafts	56
3.3	Art of Attachment origami crafts	57
3.4	Art of Attachment origami crafts	57
3.5	BTC Power of Words workshop: tree branch with hand-drawn labels and leaves showing overall display	68
4.1	Still image of table scene from Art of Attachment film installation (2021)	83
4.2	Still image of Annette and Toni partnering, split screen, from Art of Attachment film installation (2021)	86
5.1	BTC Power of Words workshop: labels written by participants hung on tree: *Hard to find the right words*	104
5.2	BTC Power of Words workshop: label written by participants hung on tree: *What was written was not true*	105
5.3	BTC Power of Words workshop: label written by participants hung on tree: *Just a surrogate*	107
5.4	BTC Power of Words workshop: labels written by participants hung on tree: *I am supposed to be a mom*	108
6.1	Origami heart produced by participant in Art of Attachment workshops: *If you never recover, I understand*	128
7.1	BTC Power of Words workshop label: *I don't feel like I should be a mom*	149
7.2	BTC Power of Words workshop label: *I'm not good enough*	150
7.3	BTC Power of Words workshop label: *I can't use my words*	160

Acknowledgements

Thanks to the many people who have been there with support and sustenance of all kinds during the research and writing of this book. I have benefitted from critical feedback from Professor Hannah Jones and from an anonymous reviewer. I am hugely grateful to Dr Charlotte Vincent at Vincent Dance Theatre (VTD) for scholarly, creative and emotional collaboration and companionship. I also owe special thanks to the Breathe, Trust, Connect (BTC) team who welcomed me into their service and were generous with their time and ideas. The collaborative Art of Attachment research workshops with VDT were funded by an ESRC Impact Grant. Fieldwork with BTC was supported by a University of Warwick Research Development Fund strategic award. The year-long ethnography with BTC would not have happened without generous research leave provided by the University of Warwick. To the parents accessing support from BTC: thank you for sharing your stories with me. I hope this book does them justice and contributes to bringing about much needed change.

1

What is adoption?

Introduction

What is adoption? The answer to this question depends on who you ask. Most people know that adoption means a child cannot live with their family of origin and so they become part of another family. Most people do not give much more thought to practical and legal details or ethical implications unless their lives are touched by adoption. Many lives *are* touched by adoption. What adoption means, what it looks and feels like, can be understood and narrated in innumerable ways. The mother having her baby taken from her hours after she has given birth; the child in her adoptive family home looking at photographs of her birth family; the young adult finding out they were adopted as a baby and have another family they know nothing about; the adoptive parent wondering how to quell the distress of the newly arrived toddler who calls him dad but is a stranger; the social worker assessing a family struggling to adequately care for their child; the grandparents, knowing their adopted daughter cannot safely parent her new baby, wondering if they are able to provide kinship care at this stage of their lives; the Judge, issuing a court order that a child be permanently placed with a different family. All these people, and countless more, have very different feelings and experiences, knowledges and understandings about what adoption is. They have different adoption stories.

Not many of these stories are told, or heard, and some of them are barely tellable. Dominated by powerful state and popular discourses certain narratives about adoption proliferate, often unchallenged. They tend to portray adoption as a positive story, enabling children to have a permanent home and enabling people who wish to parent to make a family through adoption. The complexities and paradoxes of adoption, the profound and lasting losses and griefs, are much less easily heard and told. People who have been adopted, and families who have lost their child/ren to adoption, have more limited means to speak or be heard (Deblasio, 2021; Merritt, 2024). There is little scope for different actors within adoption (birth/first families,[1] child and adult adoptees, adoptive parents, social workers, policy makers) to exchange knowledge and learn from each other, leading to distinct and barely compatible languages and knowledges being utilised. This is damaging at an experiential and emotional level, leaving groups and individuals invalidated. It also has negative consequences for policy reform.

Across the world, contemporary adoption is increasingly being recognised as in need of reform (Pösö et al, 2021). Evidence points to unjust processes of state intervention in contexts of economic and social crisis, and failure to invest and explore alternatives in systems that sustain patterns of intergenerational trauma (Broadhurst and Mason, 2013, 2020; McSherry et al, 2022). At the same time, adoption is still widely upheld as a legitimate, sometimes valorised, way in which to make and do family. These contradictory impulses make adoption an increasingly fraught area of critical investigation. At this time of increased scrutiny for adoption, there is urgent need to enable people's stories and experiences to be told and rendered intelligible within relevant political spaces. This book addresses this need by demonstrating possibilities for generating and sharing marginalised stories and experiences. Bringing academic, creative and practice-based approaches together, the evidence and discussion in *Troubling Adoption* demonstrates how careful, trauma-informed research can enable expression and exchange of knowledges that need and deserve to be heard and validated in wider discussions around adoption. At the heart of the book is recognition that contemporary adoption, in the many diverse national and transnational forms it takes, is neither working well nor ethically defensible.

Defending and sustaining adoption policy depends on longstanding and powerful narratives and knowledges about what adoption is, why it is necessary, and the experiences and outcomes for all people involved. *Troubling Adoption* takes some of these narratives and knowledges to task. It does so through critique, building on others' work, but also through the production and analysis of empirical material, generated through collaborative work I have undertaken with creative and social care practitioners, involving parents who have lost their child/ren to adoption. *Troubling Adoption* aims to make visible invisible experiences and knowledges, and as such it develops a conceptual and methodological framework for 'seeing' and 'knowing' that which may be 'unseen' and 'unknown'. The methodology is not just a means to an end, but the process of knowledge production is central to the book's argument. The methodological approach draws on my previous work on live sociological method (Lambert, 2018; see also Back and Puwar, 2012; Paton and Jackson, 2025). Detailed discussion around the methodological framing and specific methods used to generate and analyse data is offered in Chapter 3 but I outline them here:

- A series of research workshops conducted as part of Art of Attachment: a film installation and engagement space devised by Charlotte Vincent, Artistic Director of Vincent Dance Theatre (VDT).[2] Involving social workers and other professionals and students interested in family intervention, these free creative workshops, facilitated by VDT staff,

explored themes of loss and attachment through in-depth engagement with Art of Attachment on film[3] alongside practical, craft-based creative activities. Data from these workshops comprises fieldnotes; transcripts of participants' voices in the workshops; photographic documentation of paper and clay-based craft outputs made by those attending.
- Ethnographic work with a Birmingham (UK) based project called Breaking The Cycle/Breathe, Trust, Connect (BTC) in 2022–2023.[4] BTC support parents who have lost their child/ren to adoption. Research involved participant observation; interviews with staff; participatory creative workshops with staff and families using bespoke materials from Art of Attachment. Data comprises observational fieldnotes, transcripts of interviews and workshops, and photographs of outputs from these workshops.
- Analysis of VDT's Art of Attachment film installation, which was co-created with women in recovery from substance misuse who were then accessing support from Brighton Oasis Project for substance misuse. Art of Attachment translates multiple stories, gathered by Vincent over 18 months working with Oasis, and includes personal stories, translated into script by VDT collaborator Wendy Houston, of the four women involved in the making of the work. The work explores themes of attachment, loss, trauma and recovery.

Doing this research I have been able to learn from and alongside practitioners delivering support to families in the most challenging circumstances. I have also encountered many amazing, tough, smart parents, whose strengths and knowledges are at best under-utilised. At worst, they are invalidated or unheard (see also Charlton et al, 1998; Alper, 2019; Deblasio, 2021). Their stories and knowledges inform and infuse the arguments throughout. These parents represent some of the most marginalised voices in contemporary society, navigating and bearing the weight of inherited trauma and its manifestations in the form of addictions, abusive relationships, and poor mental and physical health. They are fighting for themselves and their families in the context of economic precarity, facing up to stigma at every turn. These parents have so much written about them, so much documentation (and judgement) made on their behalf, with so little opportunity to say anything themselves or to re/present themselves in any different light. With the creative resources at my disposal through ongoing collaboration with VDT I have tried to make space for hearing, validating, utilising these stories, knowledges, resources. *Troubling Adoption* leans in to listen, sit with, and understand some of the stories. Some are told in words, fluent and stuttering; others are told in languages of movement and making. These stories became tellable and intelligible through a methodology attentive to difficult and slippery knowledges; a methodology of uncertainty, open to mess and contradiction, attuned to bodies and embodiments, emotions, and senses (Back, 2007; Gunaratnam, 2013; Lambert, 2018).

Bringing existing critique and new empirical analysis together, *Troubling Adoption* makes a case for changing adoption narratives, policies and practices. This case builds throughout the following chapters and is laid out in the book's conclusion in the form of a manifesto, where possibilities for large scale radical transformation as well as more immediate and localised reforms are detailed. For now, this chapter begins with the wider social and political context in which the breaking and making of families through child removal and adoption takes place. Staying with the 'big picture', key themes from the scholarly literature on transnational adoption are highlighted, before turning to the work of Dorothy Roberts (2022) in the US and others who make use of the conceptual framing of 'industrial complex' to explain alliances between social welfare, economic and political interests. The discussion then focuses on adoption in the UK, providing a brief overview of key facts, figures and policies, before turning to consider the range of critical voices troubling adoption in all its temporal and geographical manifestations. Asking how, and how far, this trouble can be taken, questions of abolition and reform are addressed before providing a chapter-by-chapter overview of the rest of the book.

An urgent and contradictory moment

This book troubles adoption at a time of increasing urgency. A series of intersecting emergencies characterise the contemporary world. These include a dangerous rise in neo-fascism, racial injustice, devastating violent conflicts, deepening economic inequalities, damaging culture wars and environmental catastrophe. Vast structural inequalities in wealth have always been key to the geopolitics of adoption, 'saving' children from poverty in what amounts to a transfer of children from impoverished to wealthy countries (Dorow, 2006; Joyce, 2013) and from working to middle class families within nations (Sales, 2018). The extent to which poverty plays a role in creating conditions of child abandonment and removal is often neglected (Gupta, 2017; Bywaters and Skinner, 2022; Webb et al, 2022). As economic disparities deepen and widen, with many nations gripped by a 'cost of living' crisis, more families are pushed into economic precarity and the already profoundly inadequate social services supporting vulnerable people worsen. There is evidence that when families are well supported, for example new mums are given access to mother and baby placements and therapeutic support services, when they can get 'ordinary help' (Featherstone et al, 2014: 96), parents can care for their children (see Morris and Featherstone, 2010; Alper, 2019). As I write, state services are in dramatic and ever deepening crisis. Every day we witness, or if we are unlucky, experience, the effects of brutal cuts to health services, social care, welfare budgets, housing, mental health provision. In the city of Birmingham in England, where some of the fieldwork with parents and social workers was undertaken, a 'bankrupt' council has led to drastic reduction in already inadequate child and social care budgets. A report on poverty in the city (Haynes, 2024) informs that

> More children are in poverty in Birmingham now than at any time since records began. No fewer than 46% of the city's children are impoverished – up from 27% in 2015. It's more than twice the national average, and getting worse. Ten years ago, Birmingham had the eighth-highest child poverty rate in the UK – now it's third.

All these factors create hostile conditions for vulnerable and struggling individuals and families. As we see in later chapters, for the parents involved in this project, economic distress was never far from the surface of their lives and stories.

These conditions contribute to a cultural environment in which discourses and practices of adoption, both reactionary and revolutionary, can be articulated. A key example here is a tangible shift to the right in global politics, which provides a febrile environment for what Derek Kirton (2019) calls 'adoption wars'. 'Family' and the role it plays in national politics, has always been at the heart of right-wing and conservative discourses (Hill-Collins, 1998). Recent political developments around reproductive rights bring these debates to the fore. In June 2022 a landmark decision of the US Supreme Court (Dobbs v. Jackson Women's Health Organization) held that the Constitution of the United States does not confer right to abortion. The court's decision, overruling Roe v. Wade (1973) and Planned Parenthood v. Casey (1992), gave individual states power to regulate any aspect of abortion. The momentous ruling gave a huge boost to the Safe Haven movement in the US and elsewhere. Safe Haven laws promote adoption as an alternative to abortion, leading in some states or countries to decriminalising abandonment of babies left in designated 'safe boxes' or 'drop boxes'. Located at hospitals or other public institutional sites, these provide a place where a baby can be left anonymously in a container, giving the person leaving them time to disappear before the baby is collected. Baby drop-boxes can be found in increasing number across the world (Oaks, 2015; Foster, 2022) and anti-abortionists seek to expand the reach of Safe Haven laws. In the wake of the US Supreme Court ruling, images of smiling white heterosexual couples holding signs saying 'we will adopt your baby' at anti-abortion rallies went viral on social media, attempting to recuperate adoption as the ultimate form of child protection. We see here the complex role of adoption as family-making, together with the incorporation of adoption into moral, religious and far-right ideologies. This example serves to highlight the multiple and paradoxical framings of adoption in circulation at this contemporary juncture. Any troubling of adoption needs to grapple with adoption as a contested, emotional, political arena.

Holding structural and state forces in mind is key to *Troubling Adoption*'s analysis and to the arguments it makes for change and reform. Dominic McSherry, Gina E. Miranda Samuels and David Brodzinsky (2022: 8) suggest that 'As part of an emerging critical adoption science, our field needs research that contextualizes our understandings of adoption and trauma beyond the level of individual and family, to understand adoption within its colonialist, political, economic, and global contexts'.

I map these contexts here so that their significance can be teased out in relation to more localised and individualised experiences in later chapters. Although the empirical focus of this book is domestic adoption within the UK, there are important reasons for beginning with broader understandings of adoption, including transnational adoption (also known as international, inter-country or global adoption). Developments in the field of transnational adoption impact on domestic adoption in material and practical ways. For example, in countries where domestic adoption is minimalised in favour of family preservation and fostering, people wishing to parent through adoption instead look to adopt from a different country (van Wichelen, 2018). This is an important point when considering the case for adoption reform in any national context. While there are some significant differences between transnational and domestic adoption practices, the argument that they are unrelated, or are binary opposites (where transnational adoption is considered problematic and domestic adoption not) can be used for political purposes in careless ways. There is justifiable criticism of perspectives 'defending' UK domestic adoption by highlighting how differently it operates from, for example, the US adoption industry. Similar arguments attempt to draw clear distinctions between modern adoption practices and those of 'the past' (Stanley, 2015; Fitzpatrick et al, 2023). On the contrary, I believe it is important to both understand the specificities of the contemporary UK domestic adoption context while recognising the ways in which it has roots in historical practice and shares problematic presumptions and justifications characteristic of transnational adoption narratives and practices.

Transnational adoption: colonial legacies and the adoption-industrial complex

Critical adoption scholarship around transnational adoption helps us understand how an intimate entwining of politics and kinship frames adoption policies and their implementation. Adoption can be understood alongside other kinship practices through which nation states, as well as non-state actors such as international corporations or non-governmental organisations, regulate and control populations and individuals. The power to determine who does and does not count as kin has been, and remains, integral to practices of slavery, settler colonialism and migration (Patterson, 1982; Dorow, 2006; Blencowe, 2021; Possoco, 2022). Recent literature on transnational adoption industries presents a sense of crisis and imminent change (Smolin, 2023). van Wichelen (2018) notes a decline from the 'heyday' of international adoption in the mid 2000s (see also Selman, 2023). The removal of children from certain (poorer) countries and cultures for placement in different (wealthier) countries and cultures was originally conceived of, and widely accepted as, a humanitarian response to the problem of abandoned or uncared for children. This movement of children, often linked to wars and conflicts in (for example) Korea, Vietnam, Guatemala, led to large numbers of infants being adopted by families in North America and Europe (see Dubinsky, 2010; Briggs, 2012; McKee, 2019; Myong and Bissenbakker, 2021). In the past decade, an increasing globalisation of adoption has occurred, influenced by advances in reproductive technologies, shifting adoption from a benevolent response to children in need, to a kinship choice for would-be parents whose fertility treatments have failed. Alongside this demand from prospective parents there has been a decline in the availability of 'adoptable' (young, healthy) babies from many of the 'supplying' countries, often because these countries are developing their own policies for domestic adoption and/or family preservation (van Wichelen 2018; Davidson, 2024).

At the same time, there is increasing discomfort about the legitimacy of transnational adoption as its imbrication in imperial and colonial legacies is better understood. The rise of a global adoption industry raises concerns about commodification of children's lives and the risks of human welfare being subsumed to market and economic forces (Condit-Shrestha, 2018; McKee, 2019). Popular and social media has facilitated the generation and sharing of critical perspectives, enabled dissenting voices to connect and to reach a wider, international audience. Adult adoptees increasingly speak out about their experiences, telling their own stories and questioning the legitimacy and validity of processes of child removal.[5] A vocal element of this critique defines adoption itself as inherently traumatic, turning the 'adoption as saving children' narrative on its head (McSherry et al, 2022).

Another powerful critique of historical and contemporary adoption emerges from the abolitionist arguments developed by Dorothy Roberts (2022). Her focus is the US's child welfare system and its disproportionate targeting of Black families for intervention, child removal and domestic adoption. Roberts (2022) invokes the critical framework of 'industrial complex' to consider the state removal of children to be fostered or adopted as part of 'family policing systems' enacted by a carceral state with punitive effects for poor, Black populations. 'Industry complex' highlights economic and political interconnections between private funding and state concerns. These interconnections are relevant to all international and national contexts, including the UK. As Roberts (2022: 148–149) documents, the concept originated from a 1961 speech by President Dwight D Eisenhower warning how entanglements between US military and defence contractors created a 'military-industrial complex'. The same entanglements of financial profit and the penal system – a 'prison-industrial complex' – were picked up by Angela Davis (2003) in her influential work on prison abolition. Roberts (2022: 24–25) notes that protests following the racist murder of George Floyd in 2020 by police in the US 'brought new attention to abolition as a political vision and organizing strategy ... the most prominent demand emerging from the protests was to defund the police and reallocate the money to provide health care, education, jobs with living wages, and affordable housing'.

But 'family policing' was absent from these demands, as people saw child protection as benevolent, going so far as to suggest funds be transferred from policing to child protection. Roberts (2022: 25) argues that

> The child welfare system must be seen as part of what I call the foster-industrial complex – and, like the prison-industrial complex, it's a multibillion-dollar government apparatus that regulates millions of vulnerable families through intrusive investigations, monitoring, and forcible removal of children from their homes to be placed in foster care, group homes, and 'therapeutic' detention facilities that resemble prisons.

This led to her plea that 'Rather than divesting one oppressive system to invest in another, we should work towards abolishing all carceral institutions and creating radically different ways of meeting human needs and solving social problems' (Roberts, 2022: 26).

For Roberts, funds need to be diverted from any state apparatus towards community care networks (such as National Coalition for Child Protection Reform in the US). Similar arguments are developed by The Care Collective (2020) raising complex questions for adoption reform, or indeed a programme of social change, around the role of the state. Can the relationship between state and community be re/formed in such a way as to ensure equity? Can a radically different contract between state and society be sufficient to make the radical changes necessary, or does it mean disconnecting from state interference to organise different ways of living? What does it mean to have a system of family welfare so deeply interconnected with economic profit? Locating adoption in these wider social and political frames, while necessary, leads to difficult if not impossible questions. These 'complexes' and alliances are a feature of all neoliberal capitalist states. In their book *Challenging the politics of early intervention*, Val Gillies, Rosalind Edwards and Nicola Horsley (2017) provide detailed analysis of the interlinked interests of business, politicians and professionals in the UK. Many have called repeated attention to the increasing privatisation of children's services for profit (see Barrow, 2021)[6] and Robin Sen and Christian Kerr (2023c: 60) highlight a 'social work complex' 'of close alliances between influential individuals and organisations in the spheres of knowledge production, knowledge utilisation, policy making and practice in children's services'.

Framing adoption as part of a repressive, policing state system fuelled by powerful business and economic interests understandably generates abolitionist responses. The languages of 'industrial complex' and 'abolition' may feel extreme, particularly when working closely in practice-based contexts where daily demands deflect from more abstract debates. However, we see increasing use of abolition in applied contexts, including prisons (Davis, 2003; Martinez and Mukerjee, 2025); policing (McElhone et al, 2022; Kaba and Richie, 2022); universities (Neary and Saunders, 2016); families (Lewis, 2022; Weeks, 2023) and social work (Copeland, 2023). Across these movements, there is greater appreciation of the conceptual as well as political potential of abolition, moving debates beyond abolition as 'destruction' towards a generative movement for material change. I return to these discussions in Chapter 8, where I suggest that both reform and abolition have interconnected roles to play in doing and imagining adoption differently. For now, having established broader political and ethical issues raised by scholarship and debate around transnational adoption and child intervention in the US, the next section considers adoption in the UK context.

Adoption in the UK

In the UK, adoption offers a legal solution for children whose birth families are deemed unable to care adequately for them. The decision to place a child permanently with a family with whom they have no existing kinship is arrived at through a series of complex social and legal interventions and should be a case of last resort 'when nothing else will do' (McFarlane, 2016). Where concerns are raised about a child, an assessment of their parent/s takes place to ascertain levels of risk and necessary action (see Woodcock, 2003). The child/ren may be placed with a temporary foster family while the assessment is undertaken. If immediate family are judged to be unable to safely parent their child/ren, assessments of wider family are undertaken. This might lead to kinship or Special Guardianship Orders with grandparents or other relatives. If neither parent/s nor wider family are considered able to adequately care for the child/ren, and adoption is considered possible and in their best interests, a court will order for them to be adopted. In the interim, they will reside in foster care and may have some direct supervised contact with birth family. Subject to an often-lengthy wait (on average two and a half years; see DfE, 2024) they are placed with an adoptive family, who have been recruited, approved as suitable to be parents, and assessed as an appropriate 'match' for a specific child or sibling group. Following a period where parental responsibility is shared between the adoptive parent/s and Local Authority, full legal responsibility for the child/ren passes to the adoptive parent/s at the point of the Adoption Order, removing all legal ties with their birth family. Unlike 'closed' adoption in the past where the very existence of birth family could be kept from adopted children, contemporary adoption culture promotes 'openness' in sharing a child's family history with them and engaging in facilitated contact between the parent/s and adoptive parent/s and child/ren as they grow up (see Sales, 2012). As considered in more detail in later discussion, this is one of the many aspects of adoption in need of urgent reform (Neil, 2018; AUK, 2024). Emphasising the significance and power of the Adoption Order, Murray Ryburn (in Charlton et al, 1998: 3) observes that

> The adoption of children against the wishes of their birth families represents the most forceful of interventions by the State into family life. This is so because, aside from death, only adoption or freeing for adoption extinguish absolutely and irrevocably all former parental responsibility. The parents of children who are adopted compulsorily become, in law, strangers to their children.

In earlier decades (pre-1970s) a combination of inadequate access to contraception and abortion, and stigma around being a young and/or unmarried mother, led to healthy babies being 'relinquished' for adoption (Sales, 2012). Now that is almost never the case. The UK does not have Safe Haven laws or baby drop-boxes. Almost all babies and children in the care system in the UK have been removed due to concerns about their welfare. Birth parents are asked to consent to the permanent removal of their children from their care. Sometimes that consent may be granted, however most contemporary adoptions are, as Ryburn notes, 'against the wishes of their birth families' in the sense that the Adoption and Children Act 2002 (section 52b) allows courts to dispense with parents' consent in making an Adoption Order if it is deemed that the welfare of the child requires it. Even if parents acknowledge they cannot provide good enough care themselves, most prefer not to lose all their parental rights and quite often all contact with their child/ren.

Most adoptions in the UK are domestic. Although some children are adopted each year from other countries, the number is small. This may be in part due to sensitivities around the UK's shameful historical record of forced emigration of poor children to Australia, New Zealand, Canada and South Africa (see Melville and Bean, 1989; Rundle, 2011; Berry, 2023). It is also because high rates of removal of children from families in the UK means that there are many children available for domestic adoption. In England in March 2023, there were 83,840 children with 'Looked After' status, being cared for by the state in some form or another. This figure equates to around one in 140 children. It is up 2 per cent from the previous year and represents an increasing figure (DfE, 2024). The number of children adopted during the same timeframe was 2,960, down 2 per cent from the previous year and continuing a pattern of decline (DfE, 2024). The numbers of women involved in 'care proceedings'[7] in England has doubled in the last decade to currently around 10,000 per year. A third of these are 'recurrent', with women having a second care proceeding within eight years. Young mothers are over-represented: almost half have their first baby before they are 20, and 80 per cent before they are 25 (Ireland et al, 2024: 8). The risk of being subjected to care proceedings and having a child removed and placed with another family is over-determined by intersecting practical and emotional hardships including poverty, inadequate housing, poor physical and emotional health, domestic abuse and addictions (Gupta and Blumhardt, 2016; Keddell, 2022; Ireland et al, 2024). Parents at risk are often themselves born into families who were unable to provide them with good enough care, and/or they were removed from their families and grew up in state care (Broadhurst et al, 2015). Being 'care experienced' is itself enough to put women at high risk of being subject to care proceedings (Roberts et al, 2017). At the time I completed fieldwork with BTC they were opening their service to pregnant care-experienced people, regardless of whether they had had a previous child adopted. Establishing the need for this service and preparing for a significant increase in referrals, staff visited maternity hospitals. Nothing highlights more clearly the operation of anticipatory risk in the system than BTC's description of the process by which vulnerable mums-to-be are identified:

> When community midwives do the [hospital] booking-in scan for a person … there's a trigger question that comes up that says 'Have you been a looked after young person or child in care, or are you a current care leaver?' … It will trigger that they can make a referral to us. (Laurel, BTC staff interview)

While a referral to BTC is a positive intervention, the fact that such a 'trigger' exists highlights some of the failures embedded in the system: pregnant care leavers are at high risk of losing their child to adoption, reflecting the poor life experiences they have had, including childhood trauma, lack of ongoing support from family and family networks, and harms often caused or exacerbated by the care system itself (Dominelli et al, 2005; Purtell et al, 2021). The UK is one of a few national contexts where a focus on the *prevention* of 'future harm' to children results in high numbers of babies being removed from hospitals (Bilston and Bywaters, 2020; Broadhurst, Mason and Ward, 2022). If parents are assessed as being unlikely to be able to care for their child, the decision to remove the baby is made before it is born. There are no statistics about the number of babies 'born into care' in this way, however pre-birth assessments appear to be increasing, despite a directive that removal should only be for extreme circumstances (Pattinson et al, 2021; Bleasby, 2023). This focus on future harm is significant as it makes parents who have already had their child/ren removed from their care a target for 'early intervention'. Increasingly, assessments of risk may be based on, or informed by algorithmic information generated by databases (see Gillies et al, 2017; Redden et al, 2020; Gorin et al, 2024).

As Karen Broadhurst and her colleague's (2022) research demonstrates, legal sanctioning of emergency action to remove babies at risk can lead to rushed and unjust interventions. Babies are taken from parents when they are in hospital and before they can consider and contest the case against them. Having a baby removed so soon after birth unsurprisingly has devastating and long-lasting effects on the emotional health of parents, particularly mothers (Broadhurst and Mason, 2020). This can reduce the chances of reuniting mother and baby. Using evidence from families and professionals across England and Wales, Broadhurst et al (2022: 28) document how 'When parents are separated from their babies, their relationship with their baby is then circumscribed by formal time-limited contact arrangements, assessment, and scrutiny. This is far removed from the majority of parents' everyday experiences of caring for and bonding with a new baby.'

The only chance for many of these new mums to keep their babies is by going to a mother and baby unit from hospital. As well as the shortage of these placements, (lack of) time is cited as a reason for not being able to offer them: 'Pressure on hospitals to discharge mothers and babies within 48 hours of birth compounds the difficulties that professionals face in trying to work transparently and fairly with parents' (Broadhurst et al, 2022: 30). Increases in pre-birth assessments and the pre-emptive removal of babies at birth is fuelled by a culture of panic around child protection, combined with an increasingly interventionist if not punitive approach to struggling families (Critchley, 2020). The political and economic landscape giving rise to these panicky and punitive approaches has been well documented (Gillies et al, 2017; Sen and Kerr, 2023a). Writing from her perspective as a parents' advocate (parents who have themselves gone through child protection investigations and often removal of their child; see Featherstone and Fraser, 2012), Taliah Drayak (2023: 85) observes that 'Our current child protection system is full of fear and in thrall to risk'. Fear, an emotion whose political effects are considered in Chapter 7, fuels moral panic around the importance of children's early development. This in turn bolsters 'early intervention' in families where there are concerns, and 'early permanence' in the form of 'concurrent planning' or 'foster-to adopt', where adoptive parents might have a new-born baby placed with them with a view to future adoption if that is the legal outcome of care proceedings (Monck et al, 2004). Although such arrangements mean much less disruption for the child and enable early attachments to be made between adoptive parents and baby, they arguably make reunification between birth parent/s and baby less likely (Broadhurst et al, 2022).

Despite the political drive for early intervention, the average age for children in England to be adopted is three years and five months (DfE, 2024). While all adopted children experience the trauma of separation from their parent/s and ongoing feeling of loss in some form, older children coming into the care system can present with different challenges to babies removed at birth. Older children subject to care proceedings have experienced crises within their families and are likely to exhibit demanding behaviours in line with early trauma. The effects of separation from their families, often taking the form of several moves, for which they may be ill-prepared, further compounds this distress. Separation of children from their siblings and wider birth family, while sometimes necessary, can be emotionally devastating for them. Even if the court's recommendation is adoption, such children are often 'hard to place' with adoptive families, who can feel overwhelmed by their needs and worry they will present greater attachment difficulties than babies or toddlers. These children can spend their childhoods living in, and often moving between, foster families, children's homes and their families. Such children are hugely over-represented in Child and Adolescent Mental Health Services (CAMHS), Pupil Referral Units (PRUs), probation services and prison (Brown et al, 2017; Paine et al, 2021; ONS, 2022). As they become adults, care-leaving women are significantly more likely to lose their child/ren to adoption (Roberts et al, 2017). In this way, generational traumas are often passed onto them, with little prospect of the cycle being broken. Adoption is widely regarded and politically endorsed as the preferred means for breaking this cycle. This policy solution lays blame on individual parents (usually mothers) and families for failing in their capacities and responsibilities, necessitating state intervention (Gillies et al, 2017). It does not account for the social and economic contexts in which families can struggle to survive. Briefly considered here, this struggle is revisited in later chapters.

Why families struggle: is adoption a solution or part of the problem?

The context of increasing economic precarity – for some, an emergency – has already been highlighted. Links between poverty and state intervention in families have long been established (Featherstone et al, 2014; Tepe-Belfrage and Wallin, 2016; Gupta, 2017; Morris et al, 2018; Webb et al, 2022; Bywaters and Skinner, 2022). Family poverty is caused by social and political neglect. Such neglect and its effects are intergenerational. The current 'cost of living' crisis, pushing more and more families into economic insecurity and making the circumstances of the already precarious even more dire, is an important causal factor in the removal of more and more children from families into state care (Mckay, 2024). Economic deprivation does not cause parents to mistreat their children. However, the sustained impacts of poverty, including inadequate, insecure housing and physical and emotional ill health, can significantly reduce the capacities of parents and wider family members to care for their children. Key factors leading to the removal of children are domestic abuse, substance misuse and poor parental mental health (Featherstone et al, 2014; Ireland et al, 2024). Many parents who lose their children to the care system themselves experienced trauma as children, including growing up in state care. All these factors are often underpinned by sustained cycles of generational harm for which parents have not received adequate support or treatment.

Where does adoption sit in relation to these complex social problems and state failings? Echoing 'rescue' narratives that circulate globally, in the UK accounts of adoption are constructed by government discourse and secular and religious adoption agencies, including private sector and charitable organisations. These offer a version of adoption which edits out a child's family of birth other than reference or allusion to failed or troubled parenting and presents a happy-ever-after story for a child in their new adoptive family (Featherstone et al, 2018; Gupta and Featherstone, 2020). Justification for the removal of children from their families and 'placement' in other families is framed in terms of saving children and offering them better lives. Recruitment of adoptive parents is closely linked to these positive representations. Adoption campaigns gloss over negative emotions, ethical complexities and the challenges of adoptive parenting. Difficulties attracting adoptive parents, in the context of rising numbers of children entering care, makes adoption recruitment agencies even more 'risk averse'.

Many adoptive families are unable to live up to happy-ever-after expectations and enable their children to 'break the cycles' of deprivation, poor parenting and trauma as they go on to adulthood and may become parents themselves. A significant number of contemporary adoptive families are 'struggling', and some are in crisis (Selwyn et al, 2014; Selwyn and

Meakings, 2016; Stones, 2023; AUK, 2023, 2024). Adopted children deal routinely with complex traumas which may include in-vitro and early life neglect and adversity; separation from birth family; (often multiple) transitions in the care systems; being adopted. These traumatic experiences result in behaviours which in some cases can be extremely difficult if not impossible to manage within a family environment. In the Foreword to the Adoption Barometer (AUK, 2023: 3) Eloise Jones argues that

> Adoption needs to change …. As the last five years of the Adoption Barometer show, many [adoptive] families are reaching crisis in a traumatised state, feeling lost and unsupported. The support is inadequate and ill-informed. Some social workers are still making assumptions, and laying blame, leading to catastrophic outcomes for those families and their children. Services need to provide support before families reach crisis point, and the practitioners providing that support must be experienced, trauma informed and have a true sense of the history of that child. Too often, compassion is missing. As families we are living in fight and flight mode, but we didn't start the fight and neither did our children. There are still too many parents being blamed for the situations they find themselves in.

Coming from a pro-adoption perspective (the annual Adoption Barometer is coordinated by Adoption UK, 'the largest voice representing the adoption community' according to their website), this is an astonishing statement, clearly illustrating that instead of being able to *remedy* early childhood trauma, adoptive families are themselves 'in a traumatised state … in fight and flight mode'. In increasing numbers, some adopted children are returned to the care system from adoptive families. In 2022, 5 per cent of families surveyed reported their child had 'left the family home prematurely', a figure rising to 7 per cent in 2023 (AUK, 2024: 17) when it was reported that 69 per cent of families reported they are struggling, half of whom are facing 'severe challenges or reaching crisis point'. Taken together with a wider body of experiential accounts and research evidence (see Palacios et al, 2019; Coates et al, 2020; Lyttle et al, 2024; Rutter, 2024), adoption is clearly not working for a significant number of adoptive families, putting already vulnerable children at further risk. As we consider in detail in Chapter 7, these experiences close the gap between birth and adoptive families in terms of their support needs. All families dealing with trauma, regardless of the source of that trauma, need support before they reach crisis point, as well as compassion rather than blame. Adoptive families in crisis find themselves, albeit in different ways, subject to the same scrutiny and judgement from the state system that assessed their children's birth family and removed their child. Adoptive parents who entered adoption thinking they were part of breaking the cycle find that they themselves become part of the heartbreaking reproduction of children who re/enter the care system and as adults have *their* children removed from their care. Many other outcomes for adopted young people are bleak (Grotevant et al, 2017; Selwyn, 2023). Our current political and economic model of family as a privatised, self-sufficient unit responsible for the work of social re/production and care with minimal state involvement, offers poor protection to any families in crisis (Weeks, 2023), necessitating a much wider critique not just of adoption but of the constructions of 'family' which underpin it. This argument is taken up in Chapter 7, calling for different conceptualisations and structural organisation of childcare and interdependencies between families and the state.

Rescue and happy-ever-after narratives only have traction if adoption is genuinely a last resort. If not, moving children from certain families into others veers uncomfortably towards social engineering. *Can* adoption be defended as only a case of last resort? As Chapter 7 considers, using empirical evidence from interviews and workshops with social work professionals and parents who have had their child/ren taken from their care and adopted, there are significant gaps in provision of support that might enable parents to care for their children. As the current system stands, inadequate help is provided to enable struggling parents to provide adequate care, and insufficient funding and attention is paid to alternative care arrangements such as kinship and long-term fostering (Shuttleworth, 2023). This means that for many children adoption is the only (and therefore 'best') option available. However, adoption is far from a simple 'solution' to the 'problem'.

As we saw from the facts and figures presented earlier, the rise in children entering care does not translate to rising numbers of adoptions. Across the UK, the number of children being adopted has been in decline (AUK, 2022; ONS, 2023). As well as practical reasons that explain this decline, such as a growth in availability and success of fertility treatments, and the difficulties of finding adoptive families for older children with more complex needs, there is also more critical awareness about adoption. Writing in 2014, Featherstone et al (2014: 2) noted that 'More and more often we encounter some disquiet about contemporary policy and practice, and, in particular, anxiety that the social justice aspect of social work is being lost in a child protection project that is characterised by a muscular authoritarianism towards multiply-deprived families.'

In more recent years, this disquiet has amplified to a distinct noise comprising different voices and perspectives. More cacophonous than harmonic, it demands we listen and attend to the discord. Enhanced critical awareness, also highlighted at the transnational level, indicates present and future possibilities for thinking differently about family intervention and for troubling adoption narratives and practices. In the UK an overtly critical stance towards adoption is most likely to focus on adoption practices located in the *past* and/or *far away*. Adoption wrongs pertaining to historically and geographically remote cases are highlighted through high profile international cases, such as the scandal of Mother and Baby homes in Ireland (Garrett, 2017; Page, 2022) which have brought adoption into mainstream news. As people understand more, anger and criticism intensify. Although these scandals are often packaged and narrated in ways that attempt to distinguish them from local adoption practices, making them about 'bad apple' examples rather than illustrative of a problematic industry, they enable a critical lens that can, and has, been turned towards historical practices of adoption in the UK (Stanley, 2015). This has led, among other things, to calls for apologies or reparation. In 2018 the Irish Prime Minister apologised in parliament to 126 people who were illegally adopted between 1946 and 1969. In 2023, the First Minister of Scotland offered an apology for forced adoptions, acknowledging the state's inhumane treatment of women and the fact that babies were not 'given up by' but rather 'taken away from' young mothers. These apologies offered public recognition that such mothers were not neglectful but were victims of abusive state power. In England in 2022 a Houses of Commons and Lords Joint Committee on Human Rights (JCHR) enquiry reported on the experiences of unmarried women whose children were adopted in the same three decades. The enquiry identified historical injustices with ongoing impact and recommended an apology be issued (JCHR, 2022). Despite lobbying, and precedents set by Ireland and Scotland, the English Government has not (yet) apologised. While there is some truth in the defensive assertion that contemporary adoption practices are different from those in the past, recognition of historical injustices opens a crack in the door for campaigning groups to exert pressure for better understanding and action around legacies of trauma for birth parents and adopted people, and problematic practices in contemporary adoption (Sales, 2012; Broome, 2021).

Enhanced by possibilities of communication and exchange of knowledge shared via social media, young people and adults who have been in care and adopted are increasingly countering dominant narratives with stories of their personal experiences. These stories highlight neglect they have experienced through state 'care' and the unacknowledged loss and trauma of being adopted (Dann et al, 2021; The Dunbar Project, 2024; Merritt, 2024). They often express anger and distress at how adoption has legally severed them from their birth families and cultures. The understandable rage and hurt of many adults who were adopted as babies or young children several decades ago fuels an uncompromising anti-adoption argument which shares an emotional tenor with abolitionist arguments. These critical accounts mingle with, and trouble, dominant rescue and happy-ever-after narratives communicated via mainstream and pro-adoption media.

The voices and stories of families who have lost their children to adoption are less often heard, but here too there is evidence of emerging counter-narratives. Some parents (mostly mothers) who have had children removed have formed activist or therapeutic alliances with other parents who have had similar experiences.[8] Some of these parents, able to reflect on and offer cogent accounts of what happened to them and why, have spoken at industry conferences and contributed to consultations, doing vital work in terms of bringing birth families' perspectives to the debates.[9] Together with critical media attention to transnational and historical practices, the (often) emotional accounts provided by adoptees and birth families contribute to increasing unease being expressed by some adoption agencies and advocates, as well as some adoptive parents.

There is need for careful listening, learning and dialogue between those differently positioned in relation to adoption, and the adoption knowledges they recognise and re/produce. As well as amplifying these voices, social media has provided spaces where differently positioned actors (adopted people, birth family members, adoptive family members, social workers, policy makers) can engage directly: this can enable sharing of ideas and perspectives, and learning from each other, but also conflict. What chance is there of these interconnected articulations of discontent bringing about real reform of policy and practice? In early 2021, an independent review of social care in England was commissioned, promising a wide-ranging review and calling for a 'radical reset of our children's social care system' (MacAlister, 2022: 4). The evidence available in the Review's Final Report provides a damning indictment of children's services and their failure to support families and children. The Review offers insight into serious problems with child protection and family intervention processes. It acknowledges – as research has already demonstrated – that chronic lack of appropriate support for families in crisis leads to high, and rising, numbers of babies and children being taken into care rather than being cared for by their immediate birth families or other birth relatives. The Review suggests, again echoing existing research findings, that 'Evidence is strong and growing that well targeted spending on help can enable children to stay safely at home' (MacAlister, 2022: 47). Instead, there have been *reductions* in spending (MacAlister, 2022: 19). The Review also echoes evidence from the research literature that adoption in the UK re/produces social and economic inequalities of social class, race and ethnicity (Sales, 2018; Bywaters et al, 2019; Webb et al, 2020; Ahmed et al, 2022). What the Review's political statements mean for actual change is less clear. Responses to the Review have been critical of its scope, methodologies, and findings. Robin Sen and Christian Kerr (2023c: 76) note that

> While the MacAlister Review did identify the lack of support for families in the current child welfare system in England, and make some useful recommendations to address these, it failed to cite the

government policies which have been a contributory cause of it. The unwillingness to call out the brutal impacts of austerity policies since 2010 is a hole within the Review.

In November 2024, an interim report was published by the adoption subgroup of the Public Law Working Group (2024), making far reaching legal recommendations for legal reform to adoption in England and Wales. These important insights and recommendations highlight familiar concerns about how children and families are failed by child protection services. The case for reform of adoption is uncontested. However the form, scale, tenor and detail of what such change should and could look like are harder to articulate and turn into reality.

How (far) to trouble? Abolition, re/form and radical re-imagining

I use *trouble* to unsettle existing knowledges, understandings, policies and practices, and to develop ideas and evidence for reforming how adoption is thought about, talked about, and done. Discussion so far in this chapter makes clear that however you look at it, adoption troubles: it troubles people, in different ways, and it troubles assumptions about family, identity and belonging. It is also *in* trouble, subject to suspicion and critique, with calls ranging from modest policy reforms to total abolition. Trouble cuts through the binarised framing of abolition versus reform. At a simple level, abolition and reform can be seen as operating at different scales of analysis. Abolition reaches for abstraction or what Kathi Weeks (2023: 434) calls an 'upscaled' mode of knowledge production, focusing on changing systems, institutions and discourses. Reform sits more conservatively and pragmatically in the realm of the currently thinkable, working with what we have, to change it for the better. Moving beyond either/or binaries that can fix us in unhelpful ways, we need *both* reform *and* abolition. Adoption operates as a global social and commercial institution, rendered in its application through international and national political and economic systems. It is also a localised practice, impacting on communities, families and individuals. The systems-level framing of adoption shapes the localised and experiential effects. Possibilities for meaningful change need to be thought out at the macro level but they also occur in the micro-political interactions of every-day experiences, within families and between families and social work practitioners. How to examine these multiple layers of adoption without collapsing different levels of meaning and knowledge production? *Troubling Adoption* is an attempt to achieve this. After examining empirical evidence relating to the manifestations of diverse adoption knowledges and the potential for learning from them how we might do adoption differently,

I return to this relationship between abolition and reform in Chapter 8, making recommendations for change.

Throughout the book, a range of conceptual resources that trouble is utilised to analyse empirical findings. What these conceptual resources have in common is that they are all theories that keep things *moving* and *shifting*, both verbs which take effect in physical and emotional ways. Trouble also serves as a methodological approach, a way of generating knowledge. Key features of a troubling methodology are that it engages time and space in less linear and fixed ways. This enables movement between and different scales of analysis (such as macro, meso and micro) and challenges temporal narratives based on 'progress' (the past was bad, but the future will be better). The empirical focus is on the present, but I understand the present as incorporating the weight of past emotions, harms and stories. Thinking about the future is vital to social change, but not necessarily in a progressive, problem-solving way which can re/produce damaging knowledges and practices (Caswell, 2020). In practice, this aspect of troubling means paying close critical attention to how time and space shape, and are made use of, in people's experiences and stories.

Another key feature of trouble as methodology is that narratives are not just told in words, but in the moving languages of bodies and emotions. As we see in later chapters, words alone cannot do justice to all adoption knowledges, acquired through experiential and embodied forms. Experienced as grief and heartbreak, some stories are barely tellable and need different kinds of listening and narrating to become intelligible, demanding a willingness to be with and attend to uncomfortable emotions. Working with Gargi Bhattacharya's compelling arguments in her 2023 book *We the Heartbroken*, I suggest heartbreak in adoption reform as a necessary part of political change rather than something which must be overcome or side-lined. Bhattacharyya (2023: 4) argues that any transformative politics needs to acknowledge the role of grief, sorrow and rage: 'We are the broken-hearted not only because of loss, but also because of knowledge. ... grief is a necessary component of a revolutionary imagination.' This argument that feelings have revolutionary potential has been made in the context of Black women's lives (Lorde, 1984) including in social work (see Nayak, 2020). The cost of knowledge can be grief. It would be easier to accept dominant, more palatable accounts of adoption and continue to silence or ignore the difficult marginal ones, however as Bhattacharyya (2023: 27) notes this 'takes its own toll': 'Silencing heartbreak only returns us to the crassest celebrations of strength. Or the most dubious displays of empathy. Sadness appears as something to fight off or to transform into charity'. Dominant narratives perpetuated by the adoption industry could at times be described as crass celebrations of strength and dubious displays of empathy, transforming sadness into charity rather than acknowledging the fragility of families and the enduring sorrow which adoption entails for many of the people affected by it. In a study on children's Sure Start Centres in the UK as 'a site of emotional politics', Eleanor Jupp (2022: 21) argues the contemporary state 'was founded on an erasure of personal experience from the public sphere and policy making, but that political and cultural shifts have enabled as eruption of subjective, emotional and affective experience into public spheres at various levels'. Understanding emotion in relation to social policy has created possibilities for the 'collective power of emotions and feelings': 'If researchers wish to intervene in contemporary social policy debates they need to consider these emotional dynamics, and work with these rather than seeking a 'return' to social policy as a technical, rational and non-emotional sphere' (Jupp, 2022: 20). Certainly, the terrain of child removal by the state constitutes a 'site of emotional politics'. Working with emotional dynamics, which include the workings of trauma, needs to be at the heart of practices of troubling adoption. Such a site of emotional politics is not merely a response to social and political systems and their effects but is where (counter) political possibilities and resistances reside. Jupp (2022: 23, original emphasis) suggests that

> approaches to affect ... as well as politics and public debate infused by emotions, have created a context in which emotions may be thought of as providing *challenges* to social policy regimes; generating alternative attachments and feelings that might speak to the overall designs, values and ethics framing social policy. In this sense, the micro-emotions of social policy interactions can become linked to larger scale dynamics of political and economic change.

These challenges and possibilities are addressed in the following chapters where empirical analysis provides further evidence for the role emotion must play in social reform.

Conclusion and outline of the rest of the book

This introductory chapter has reviewed the contemporary state of adoption discourse and practice. Although popular understandings of and justifications for adoption invoke the rescue of children and the construction of happy families, locating the arguments in relation to a global adoption industry enables us to see adoption historically and in the present as interwoven with state and economic power. There is consensus from academic, activist and mainstream political sources that we must expand our knowledges and understandings about adoption to re/form current policies and practices. Arguments against adoption or calling for reform in child intervention and adoption policy and practice are not new. They are as old as adoption itself, and in that sense the time for troubling adoption has been always. However, we are at an historical juncture, beset by multiple crises of political and social failure, with new languages, new knowledges and new levels of emotional intensity at our disposal. Although the conversations are fraught and difficult, they are happening. The research on which this book is based harnesses these knowledges and emotions, enters the difficult conversations and adds its evidence and arguments to urgent calls for adoption reform. A key argument threading through *Troubling Adoption* is that it is not just about knowing *more*, but also about knowing differently. Relations of power are embedded in dominant narratives and policies. *Troubling Adoption* draws attention to these narratives, as well as exploring alternative knowledges and ways of knowing by working in embodied, sensory and emotionally attuned ways with people whose stories and experiences so often go unheard and unrecognised.

The rest of the book proceeds as follows. The next chapter attends to dominant narratives and knowledges around adoption and their creation and maintenance through archives and archival practices. Whose knowledge is heard, authorised and circulated, and whose is unheard, silenced, or invalidated? If a wider range of stories can be heard and validated, what sorts of new understandings about adoption might emerge and with what consequences? What sort of archives and archival practice might enable this to happen? Thinking with archives in this way, the chapter begins with a focus on adoption archives, addressing questions of identity, access and memory. 'Live' archives in the form of life story work connecting a child's birth and adoptive families are considered, exploring potential for counter-knowledges around un/making family. Recognising that possibilities for different and more open relationships between birth and adoptive families are limited in practice by structural constraints, lack of support for all parties and a pervasive fear of risk, the chapter concludes by exploring more radical archival interventions. These offer potential to re/fuse and re/form adoption stories and archives in the interests of changing current and future understandings and practices.

Questions of knowledge production are carried into Chapter 3. Some adoption knowledges are barely speakable, either because they are too heartbreaking, or too challenging to dominant ways of knowing and doing. Different methods are needed to enable alternative stories to be told. These include knowledges and experiences expressed in emotional and embodied forms. After mapping the feminist and queer approaches to knowledge production underpinning the research and analysis, I describe my collaboration with artist-led organisation Vincent Dance Theatre (VDT) and the first stage of empirical research in the form of Art of Attachment workshops. These creative workshops with social work practitioners, as well as artists and students, took place within a film installation space where VDT's Art of Attachment on film was shared and we used this creative resource to encourage facilitated discussions. At one such workshop I met the social work team Breathe, Trust, Connect (BTC), a local authority service in England supporting parents who have had at least one child removed from them by the state and placed for adoption. The next sequential stage of research involved ethnographic work with BTC. I introduce the service and describe the varied methods utilised as part of ethnography. The film materials from Art of Attachment had significant impact on BTC when they first encountered them. We continued to work with VDT to develop these materials for use in BTC's service. In this way Art of Attachment threaded through the different phases of the research, providing us with a vital resource of stories we could all relate to and insights into attachment and recovery. For these reasons, elaborated in Chapter 3, I undertook analysis of Art of Attachment film installation as a piece of work itself.

Analysis of VDT's Art of Attachment film installation informs discussion in Chapter 4, which considers how influential theories of attachment, developed in child psychology and brought together with neuroscientific discourse, influence contemporary adoption policy. In doing so attachment becomes a tool for blaming and punishing families and parents (usually mothers), ignoring the role played by structural violence and social and political failings. Recognising critical debates that problematise this use of attachment, I turn to other resources in the form of social theories of attachment, offered by Judith Butler and Lauren Berlant, and close analysis of Art of Attachment, in which four women (Annette, Leah, Louise, Vikki) accessing support for substance misuse use scripted words, movement and visual metaphor to share their stories of loss, intergeneration trauma, and hope. The chapter explores if, rather than avoiding attachment completely, other conceptualisations and application of attachment can do different political work that is vital for better understanding people's complex behaviours and bringing about social change.

Annette, Leah, Louise and Vikki's input to making Art of Attachment and the way their narratives have been performatively translated within the work, are picked up in Chapter 5 which focuses on stories and storytelling. Put together with data and analysis from Art of Attachment, and creative workshops undertaken with parents and social workers at BTC, we see how words are powerful in different ways, doing harm as well as offering hope. Different ways to tell stories, using creative resources that enable embodied and emotional knowledges and find metaphors to be communicated, offer insight into stories or fragments of stories which are rarely told or heard. Like the theories of attachment explored in Chapter 4, storytelling has momentum, functioning as a force to keep things moving and thereby keep hope alive, even when the stories themselves are full of heartbreak.

Emotion becomes centre of attention in Chapter 6, staying with empirical material and analysis from parents and social workers at BTC. Drawing on Bhattacharyya's (2023) argument that heartbreak is key to social and political change, attention is paid to support offered to parents experiencing the trauma of losing their child/ren to adoption. Creating opportunities for emotional safety and regulation is demonstrated as a central aspect of social work. The resources needed to sustain this are not just increased financing, reduced caseloads and so on; therapeutic training and supervision, and (more) time is often necessary to do this difficult work. BTC workers need to 'sit with' and 'walk alongside' those accessing their service, being with their heartbreak rather than rushing to solve problems, requiring different skills and timeframes than those demanded of 'front-line' social workers under pressure to safeguard children and families. The chapter considers how these different types of labour practice might interconnect and how, if social workers with different roles can support each other, outcomes for parents and families would be enhanced.

Families are considered in Chapter 7 through a focus on interdependencies. The political organisation of families as independent units, responsible for re/producing life and providing care with minimal state support, is held to account. This neoliberal model creates difficulties for many families, but those experiencing intersectional structural injustices such as poverty, racism and poor health, are set up to fail. Greater provision of state support for all families based on need is argued for, supported closely by evidence from BTC. The discussion also calls for greater accountability from the state, both in recognising its failure to offer adequate support, and for providing inadequate parenting itself when children are removed from their families. Interdependencies between birth and adoptive families are also considered in this chapter, revisiting the technologies of life story work established in Chapter 2 to make a case for more open communication and sharing of lives between all the family members with attachments to an adopted person, not only when they are a child but as they grow into adulthood.

The concluding Chapter 8 is written in the form of a manifesto for troubling adoption, moving between the scalar ambitions of small-scale reforms and re/imagined futures. Arguing that both reforming programmes and abolitionist imaginaries are required, the discussion makes eight 'demands'. These are that we: safeguard everybody; take emotion seriously; challenge and change the stories; support all based on need; re-imagine families; make adoption as open as possible; enable social justice work; generate space and time for reflection, dialogues, alliances. Although the detailed and complex arguments underpinning these demands are made in the preceding chapters, supported by existing research and new empirical materials, this concluding chapter is intended to stand alone as a summary of concerns and a call for action. If you don't have time right now to read the whole book, or you are an impatient and non-linear kind of reader, feel free to turn to Chapter 8 first. For those proceeding in a more orderly fashion, the next chapter uses an expansive notion of archive to examine issues of power, identity and understanding in dominant and hidden adoption stories.

2

The role of archives in adoption narratives

Introduction

How do certain narratives and accounts of adoption become and remain established and seemingly intractable while others struggle to be told and heard? Powerful stories framing adoption as the rescue of children and creation of happy families may silence stories which are ambivalent, critical and/or traumatic. How might this power be challenged in the interests of enabling different stories to be told? The previous chapter examined the political, economic and cultural imperatives which underpin dominant adoption narratives. To understand the construction and power of knowledges in and around adoption, the discussion here uses theories and practices of archive. Specifically, it considers the work of the archive and archival politics and practices in the generation of adoption narratives. Physical archives and the archiving of historical records around family intervention and adoption are central to the entrenchment of some stories and neglect or refusal of others. Archives as physical locations housing records of state represent materially and metaphorically the authority and power of adoption knowledge/s. Through stories and accounts documented and stored in government filing cabinets, adoption archives establish and sustain relations of power between people, their lives and experiences. As well as this spatial containment, archives and archival practices construct knowledges over time, holding and preserving the past and shaping what can be known about the present and future. People's (lack of) access to records and redaction of information highlight injustices around adoption knowledges.

At the same time as this material influence over adoption knowledges, theories of archive help us understand how power over narrative operates. Explanations of archival power offered by Michel Foucault and Jacques Derrida offer insight into the symbolism of the (adoption) archive as *the* official source of knowledge and evidence. Understanding this is key to shifting power dynamics through alternative forms of archival content and practice. Despite the undisputed 'top down' power of official archives, there is also scope for creativity and disruption. Both the authority of the archive as a site and source of official knowledge and history, as well as the creative and generative possibilities of archive, are important for the work of troubling adoption. As Derrida (1995: 57) notes 'Nothing is less reliable, nothing is less clear today than the word 'archive' … Nothing is more troubled and more troubling.' Following what anthropologist Ann Stoler (2002: 93) calls the 'archival turn', archives have increasingly been regarded not only as a site of research and source of knowledge, but have become themselves subject to critical investigation, moving 'from archive-as-source to archive-as-subject'. This has enabled more critical and creative conceptualisations of archive, drawing on queer, feminist, critical race and decolonial thinking. Work in these intersecting fields highlights the inadequacies and violences of official archives, where lives and stories of the oppressed and marginalised are mis/represented and/or excluded. It also means working differently *with* archives, for example by using creative interventions to address ambiguous or missing knowledges and stories. Any reform of adoption requires a re/forming of adoption archives. Attending to archival practices of the past and the present allows us to ask, if we are to reform adoption, what kinds of archival practices need to be part of that process? How do we archive differently, more critically, more ethically, in the present and for the future? Michelle Caswell (2020: 162) names such a project as building a 'liberatory memory work'. In keeping with the troubling ambitions of this book, such work

> Is not seduced by a false sense of hope or an easy sense of solidarity but that instead unsettles us. That takes feelings – our feelings and those of others – seriously, that investigates and leverages those feelings for deep structural changes, that takes great, messy pleasure in mobilising records to cultivate disruption in our current political moment.

These investigations and disruptions explored here lay important groundwork for empirical analyses and suggestions for reforming adoption practices that come later in the book.

The remainder of this chapter addresses these questions by first providing an overview of theories of archive which establish its claims to 'original' knowledge. The significance of this for adoption is drawn out, considering the 'adoption archive' and how lives and stories are created and maintained through documenting and controlling access to the past. Different kinds of adoption knowledges generated through post-adoption documents (life story books and later life letters) and communications between birth and adoptive families, usually taking the form of exchange of letters (known as letter box) are explored. These practices are revisited in later chapters in relation to analysis of workshop and interview data generated with parents and staff at Breathe, Trust, Connect (BTC). The kinds of knowledge-work made possible by different kinds of adoption documentation and archiving inform arguments in Chapter 8 in favour of radical reform of post adoption contact. They also challenge the powerful presumptions of 'origin stories' with potential to displace the conceptual stranglehold that official (state) archives have over definitive accounts of history, whether pertaining to nations, communities, families or individuals. The final section of this chapter attends to crucial and creative interventions in archival practice which have been developed within feminist, queer, critical race and decolonial studies as ways to redress absent, partial and pathologising histories. These archival interventions dis/locate the spatial power of knowledge from the secure state building under lock and key, and trouble temporalities of knowledge made possible through different archival approaches. A focus on the role of emotions and embodiments around archives brings new knowledges and ways of knowing to the fore, which are then further developed in Chapter 3.

Thinking with archives

Archives are a locus of political power. The word archive derives from the Greek 'archaeon' referring to 'the house' and 'archons' to 'those who commanded'; those with power to deposit, to guard, to interpret the archives. Archaeon is also the root of 'archaeology', evoking material structures that organise, structure, contain (Foucault, 1969). For Foucault, archive is part of the production and authorisation of discourse. Derrida (1995: 9) notes that 'Arkhe ... names at once the *commencement* and the *commandment*'. Emphasised in the original text, these words convey the sense of primal knowledge and power such knowledge holds. In fact, Derrida goes so far as to state that 'there is no political power without control of the archive, if not memory' (Derrida, 1995: 4). By controlling 'memory', distilling and securely guarding what can be known about the past and who can know it, the dominance of certain versions of history can be maintained. That such archives stand in for the 'commencement' and 'commandment' is key to their authority, operating not just at discursive but psychic levels where people's investment in the idea of 'origin' runs deep. We confer authority on 'the archive', or certain official state archives, because we believe they hold the key to understanding things from the beginning, the key to the 'truth' perhaps. Derrida (1995) suggests that people's *desire* for this foundational 'original' knowledge shores up the archive's power: his much-cited 'Mal d'archive' (1995: 571) was translated into English as 'archive fever', capturing the intensity of this desire. To have archive fever is

> to burn with a passion. It is never to rest, interminably, from searching for the archive right where something in it unarchives itself. It is to have a compulsive, repetitive, and nostalgic desire for the archive, an irrepressible desire to return to the origin, a homesickness, a nostalgia for the return to the most archaic place of absolute commencement.

The emotional register of Derrida's theory of archive resonates with the affective politics of adoption archives. Notions of 'compulsion', nostalgia', 'homesickness' align with psychoanalytical accounts of people's search to locate and understand their origins, to return to a place of 'commencement' – the 'primal wound' (Verrier, 2009; Dann et al, 2021). While the emotional appeal to our desire to know, to 'unarchive' original truth, is compelling, it can be problematic in its conviction and abstraction. Carolyn Steedman's (2001) careful and pragmatic reading of 'archive fever' offers a more measured account. Steedman (2001: 1175) challenges Derrida on the metaphorical nature of archive and brings in the materiality of archive as a more down-to-earth place of (dusty) storage and (boring) labour. She is critical of what she notes as a 'western obsession' with beginnings and origins, offering the following rebuttal:

> Archives hold no origins, and origins are not what historians search for in them. Rather, they hold everything *in media res*, the account caught halfway through, most of it missing, with no end ever in sight. Nothing starts in 'The Archive', nothing, ever at all, although things certainly end up there.

While archive fever might capture the urgent and hopeful drive people bring to their archival searches, imagining clear and complete answers to their questions contained in the files, the reality is more likely to be missing documents, redacted paperwork and trails of evidence which fade away. Countering the mythical status assigned to archive in accounts like Derrida's, Steedman (2001) highlights the 'ordinariness' of the archive (see also Osborne, 1999). Requesting information, going through the administrative processes to gain access, waiting, waiting, waiting, before receiving limited, partial, heavily redacted paperwork, can quickly quench any desire driving their search and instead people experience disappointment, anxiety, frustration and reminders of absence and loss (Sissay, 2019; Rees, 2024).

Adoption archives: paper/work and people

We have seen that the etymological root of archive is structure, the secure site of knowledge with material and symbolic authority. This structure manifests in buildings, systems and paperwork. It is barely possible to think about archive, particularly official archives of state, without conjuring 'paper/work' – the paper itself and the labour involved in generating it. Paper/work has powerful symbolic and emotional resonances. Paper, and increasingly, digital forms of documentation, are central to state processes of family intervention. As later chapters show, paperwork is a powerful symbol of much that is felt to be 'wrong' in social care. The labour of paperwork constitutes a significant burden on social workers with excessive caseloads. While such administrative work can be seen as secondary to and distracting from the 'direct' work (see Humphreys and Kertesz, 2012), paperwork is where official versions of people and families are produced. Production and maintenance of reports and files are key to processes of assessment and decision making that document and *authorise* acts of removing a child from one family, holding them in foster care, and placing them with another family for adoption. Many of the reports and records produced through processes of removing and processing a child for adoption contain evidence which informs legal decisions and court orders. These records can thus be simultaneously banal and vital for the protection of life. When they complete a Pre-Birth Assessment or Child Permanency Report within a tight timeframe, social workers may well be thinking only of the immediate function of their report. They may not be thinking of the child/ren or parents at the heart of the report reading it in the future, trying to make sense of what decisions were made, when and why, trying to find themselves and their family in the words and stories. The authors' focus is likely to be the clarity of the evidence and documentation and how it makes the case for keeping a child with their birth parent/s or removing them and placing a child for adoption. After the reports have done their work and their purpose has been served, they are archived. In the UK, Local Authorities store documentation relating to adoptions carried out in their jurisdiction.

Paperwork can generate powerful versions of people, who can often be reduced to the stories told about them on paper. Social workers attending Art of Attachment workshops talked about how, in their professional experiences, words written in documents are sometimes digitally 'cut and pasted' from one text to another, transferring stories written about a person from, for example, a parenting assessment to a court document. This means that one incident in life, such as a crime, can 'follow a person around' as it is repeated in documentation about them. The incident and the words used to describe it become 'stuck' to people who are subject to care proceedings in a way that is not true for individuals who can 'unstick' from past events which they no longer feel define them. Not being able to 'speak back' to reports written about them makes it hard for people to escape this version or choose what others know about them. People change, but sometimes the ways in which they are described in documents, does not (Kim, 2019). In the words of the Howard League for Penal Reform (2015: 8):

> What is written about us can feel like it takes over our identity and becomes all people see about us. It can seem that professionals are more interested in what happened in our past and what is written about us on paper than who we are in the present. We can struggle to show that we are more than just what is written about us, but this 'paper self' can take over our identity and feel like it is stapled to us.

Thalia Drayak (2023: 87) articulates the emotional impact of this: 'During an assessment your entire life, warts and all, is on display and it often feels that your entire life is reduced down to only warts, that your mistakes are the total of your person.' As assessments and the documentation of them become increasingly digitised, perhaps the paper self is becoming a 'digital self'. In Sarah Gorin and colleagues' (2024: 241) research on birth mothers' applications to access their data via Freedom of Information requests, 'the mothers and children were read as data and their data was seen as them':

> parents felt they were 'seen' or datafied through records and the written word, affecting the way they were subsequently treated and understood … information written by professionals in records was taken as a truth, with life changing consequences. Reports of inaccuracies and errors in records were common … Given the importance records are assigned, and with the increasing linking and use of data for predictive analytics purposes, this is a significant and concerning finding, that requires further investigation. (Gorin et al, 2024: 239)

'Datafication' entails turning people into data that can be then used to make crucial decisions about individuals' eligibility for, allocation of, or exclusion from, resources. Parents in Gorin et al's (2024) study reported errors, extensive redactions, partial accounts, and use of inappropriate language. The 'predictive analytics purposes' that Gorin et al (2024) observe indicates use of data to flag individuals as a child protection risk, which together with other predictive risk-based approaches, as noted in the previous chapter, can lead to potentially unnecessary and unjust surveillance of families and interventions including child removal (Edwards et al, 2021a, 2021b; Broadhurst et al, 2022). In Chapter 5 we hear from parents currently accessing support following removal of their child/ren for adoption, and they are critical of how assessments, and what is written and documented, construct them in negative and partial ways.

Once deposited for (physical or digital) storage, most documents and reports remain untouched. However, some will be pulled from their files or downloaded and re-read at a different point in time, by new eyes, for new purposes. Deeply bureaucratic as these forms and reports often are, they not only have the power to change dramatically the course of individuals' and families' outcomes, but they also contain information which years, decades and often centuries down the line, is the only source of knowledge about people's identities and stories. We are all familiar with the story of the person separated from their family as a baby or young child, with few or no memories to draw upon, seeking information about their origins. This trope informs fictional narratives and is also the basis of memoirs such as Lemn Sissay's (2019) moving story of his childhood in institutional care, or

Jackie Kay's (2011) poetic account of finding out about and contacting her birth parents from whom she was removed and placed for adoption as a baby in Scotland. The search for family origins is popularised in the successful television show Long Lost Family which has aired in the UK on ITV since 2011. There are versions of this show in Denmark, Finland, Australia and the United States. The very existence of these programmes, documenting the struggles of people separated from family members, desperate to find information and make contact, has a powerful effect. It opens the possibility of successful 'reunions' and arguably helps generate a sense of responsibility, if not compulsion, to seek knowledge and connection about 'lost' family members. In 1995 a television documentary called Barnardo's Children: The Largest Family in the World was broadcast, leading to thousands of people realising they could access their care records. Gill Pugh and Gillian Schofield (1999: 7) carried out a study of the experiences of 12 such people, noting that 'for many, the programmes stirred up long-buried, or half-forgotten memories and emotions, and aroused or revived a hunger for information about themselves'.

They also documented the long wait people had to access files, which provided 'ample time in which to construct fantasies, hopes and fears about what the records may contain' (Pugh and Schofield, 1999: 16). Their respondents used metaphors of keys and un/locking doors to describe their experiences of accessing their information, highlighting an aura of secrecy and gatekeeping. Since then, the desire to know about blood kin, family history and one's own origins is increasingly recognised and validated. Alongside Long Lost Family and Who Do You Think You Are? – a BBC series in which celebrities trace their family trees – there has been an expansion of genealogical services enabling anyone to search via online databases for information contained in census or other records (Kramer, 2011a, 2011b).

Despite this, there is uneven provision around access to care records and support for people (Goddard et al, 2008; Horrocks and Goddard, 2010). For adult adoptees, particularly those who have experienced a 'closed' adoption and so may have little information to begin with, gaining access to files can be challenging and emotional. Legal rights for people to access information produced about them and their family by social services are limited. In Scotland, the right of people who have been adopted to access their files when they reach adulthood has been in place since the legal inception of adoption in 1929. In England and Wales, this right was not granted until 1976 (Section 51 of the 1976 Adoption Act) (see Triseliotis, 1973; Sales, 2012). Enacting these rights can be a lengthy and fraught process (Kirton et al, 2001). Contemporary social media is awash with adult adoptees desperate for information about their families and the circumstances of their separation. The extreme and often unnecessary challenges they can face finding and accessing this information has been well publicised through high profile cases such as mother and baby homes (Houliham and Kinder, 2024). Greater public awareness of historic injustices across the globe fuels archive fever to delve into records and uncover family secrets, discover new relations and identities and perhaps seek redress for historical wrongs. Lauren Berlant's (2011) concept of 'cruel optimism' comes to mind. Developed and applied in Chapter 4, cruel optimism describes a situation when something we desire becomes damaging to us, yet the promise it offers keeps us attached and hopeful, so we continue to pursue it despite its negative effects. People who have grown up with missing information about their families and their own early lives cannot help but anticipate finding out this information, but when they gain access to the files, they can be devastatingly disappointing, perhaps raising more questions than they can answer. There are practical and ethical questions over who can access what information, how the past can and should be communicated with appropriate levels of emotional support, and what the impact of knowledge gained can be.

As research in the field of transnational adoption demonstrates, the construction, maintenance and politics of access to adoption archives tell us a great deal about power and authority in adoption practices. Kelly Condit Shrestha (2021: 157) documents the difficulties Korean adoptees have accessing their own files. She draws attention to the unethical gatekeeping behaviours of record keepers, noting how much easier it is for adoption agencies, or researchers, to access files, while the people who are themselves the subjects of the files are denied the right to know: 'The historic and contemporary construction of adoption record archives – their documentation of alleged truths and politics surrounding rights to access – have created an unethical discourse of power and ownership that benefits adoption institutions and adoptive parents, and disempowers adopted persons and birth/first parents.'

This denial of access to their own lives and stories withholds knowledge and in doing so maintains authority of one type of family connection (adoptive) over another (birth) with significant impact on individuals and communities. Condit Shrestha (2021: 166–167) notes the lack of agency adoptees have over 'their own stories' and she asks a question that resonates across multiple geopolitical manifestations of adoption: 'What are the ethics of a regime of childhood that would deny its children the knowledge to make claims to their own heritage?'

Families who have had their child/ren removed and adopted also face significant challenges accessing records relating to themselves and their families. This is the case across national contexts. We have seen the challenges faced by respondents in Gorin et al's (2024) UK based research. Writing in the US, E Wayne Carp (1998: 23) tells us that: 'Due to increased stigmatization, by the close of the 1950s, birth mothers were no longer granted access to adoption court records. Adoption agencies soon followed suit and case files were withheld.'

The punitive effects of stigma are noted here. Access was denied with implications of blame and lack of entitlement to knowledge about one's own children once they have been removed by the state. There is a lack of research in this area, no doubt in part reflecting this stigma and the impact it has had on parents who do seek information from the archives: if they do, it is without the public good-will and encouragement offered to adopted adults. There is a clear case to be made for better care of records, and better care for people accessing records (Humphreys and Kertesz, 2012; Shepherd et al, 2020; Williams et al, 2024). Later empirical discussion shows that social workers have increasing awareness of how stories about people are told and documented, acknowledging the power of these records to shape lives not just at the time of production, but many years, decades and centuries into the future. However, what this means for practices and processes of documentation, access to files and support to make sense of the past, needs further attention.

Alongside these fundamental improvements relating to current archival practice, a critical account of 'origin narratives' is called for, and in turn attention to new archival practices that enable stories to be told (and heard) differently. While understanding family history is important and access should be provided to documentation produced about people and their families, there is rarely a singular or linear narrative to be told, particularly when trauma is involved (Edkins, 2003; Myers, 2014). In dominant adoption narratives, a linear and teleological account of family fulfils the immediate function of appearing to stabilise the adoptive family, upholding wider ideologies of nuclear families. This has powerful effects, as Kit Myers (2014: 186) notes:

> The undoubtedly 'real' relationship formed in adoption through stability and reciprocated love is undergirded by a fear that if adoptees talk or ask too much then they could lose everything. Thus, the symbolic structure of violence in adoption practice and discourse informs adoptees' convoluted negotiations of identity that explicitly negates and rejects their past and birth parents or implicitly foreclosures them by never inquiring about these issues.

Archives are holders of the past, keepers of memories and ghosts. Archival systems are designed around dating and organising events and information, attempting to fit the disarray of lives into the order of linear and teleological progress. Linear narratives and the attendant fixed binaries (past/present; real/unreal) are also constructed and upheld in traditional archives: chronologies of events and documentation can impose a sense of coherence which tells only a partial and preferred account of family and identity. Legal documents in adoption also contribute to this. Condit-Shrestha (2021: 157) observes how 'The birth certificate legally sanctions the erasure of the adopted child's birth name and birth parents – her birth story – so that her life narrative begins at the point of adoption'. Restricted access and omissions and redactions in adoption archives reinforce this idea of a child's life beginning when they were adopted. The fear noted in the previous chapter fuelling early intervention in families and 'closed' approaches to adoption also influences control over archival access. There is concern that adopted children and adults will reach 'back' to the past (their family of origin) rather than focusing on the 'present' of their adoptive family and in so doing disrupt the material and symbolic unity of the adoptive family unit. Condit-Shrestha (2021: 162) makes important links between the kinds of constraints and limits put on different people seeking access to records and wider ideological investments in particular, narrow forms of family, which 'solidifies a knowledge-regime that obstructs adoptees under the misguided notion that these constraints better uphold the adoptive family unit'. Attention is paid to how this 'misguided notion' manifests in contemporary UK based practice, and the consequences of it for all involved, in Chapter 7.

Drawing attention to the temporalities of archives in the ordering of knowledge (and lives) brings *time* to the forefront and invites us to think about what a different approach to time might reveal or enable. Avery Gordon (2011: 2) invokes 'haunting' as a way of knowing, being attuned to echoes from the past, suggesting that it

> alters the experience of being in linear time, alters the way we normally separate and sequence the past, the present and the future ... haunting is one way in which abusive systems of power make themselves known and their impacts felt in everyday life, especially when they are supposedly over and done with.

Here haunting appears to do similar work to *troubling*: 'Haunting refers to this socio-political-psychological state when something else, or something different from before, feels like it must be done, and prompts a something-to-be-done.' (Gordon, 2011: 2–3) Haunting recognises the lost, missing, grieved for, in such a way that it is brought into view, and something must be done about it. Perhaps nowhere can the power of knowledges that haunt be felt more keenly than in the archive. The invocation of ghosts and haunting as ways to think about and articulate the complex griefs and temporalities of adoption reoccur in the research literature (Hipchen and Deans, 2003;

Lifton, 2009; Buckwalter et al, 2017; Gunsberg, 2017; Morriss, 2018; Lambert, 2020; Clapton, 2024). These ghosts may be abusive systems, or they may be partial and missing stories, people, events, images. Bringing the past into the present, haunting reaches into the future. Julietta Singh (2018a: 96) invokes 'the ghost archive' to capture our desire for ghostly knowledge in spatial terms:

> The stories that comprise us have left us wanting more, wishing we had access to a fuller narrative frame. I call this wishing-wanting desire 'the ghost archive'. Everything we need to know but cannot know as we keep circling and sniffing around the edges. Everything that keeps affecting us and affecting others through us. Everything that remains right there, but just out of reach.

The next chapter attends to how we might 'reach' those knowledges that we can sense and that affect us, but we cannot fully grasp. To refuse expectations that the adoption archive will offer up a coherent origin story, and instead recognise possibilities that follow from different forms of engagement with archival materials, is to trouble binaries (of past/present; un/real; natural/social; un/known) and the limited models of identity and family they uphold. The next section turns to consider the paradoxical effects of contemporary 'open' adoption practices before concluding with an exploration into alternative, creative archival approaches.

'Live' archives: life story and letterbox

In the UK adoption has changed in recent years, in theory at least, from being a 'closed' to 'open' practice (Howe and Feast, 2000; Sales, 2012; MacDonald, 2023). Sally Sales (2012: 160) notes that 'Whilst an adoption order severed the child's legal ties to its family of origin, the notions of both partnership and contact installed by the [1989] Children's Act worked to reintroduce the presence of that family through open practices'. As argued in Chapter 1, and Sales' research demonstrates, change may be evident, but enduring legacies create what she describes as the 'paradoxical' nature of contemporary adoption. Sales (2012: 7) is critical of 'a reductive opposition – from closed and secretive to open or its reverse'. She suggests:

> This opposition is an inadequate description to characterise the myriad and contradictory practices that addressed the adopted child's relationship to its birth history. Traditional adoption commentaries cannot account for the simultaneous emergence and deployment of both inclusionary and exclusionary forms of practice around the place of the birth family in adoption work. Most importantly, these accounts

do not locate adoption within the wider field of western kinship where the blood tie occupies a foundational place.

These are adoption's contradictions: removing a child from the family of origin, while attempting to maintain a child's connections with their origins and striving for normalities of 'natural' (biological) family, while minimising if not disavowing the significance of blood kin. Such paradoxical impulses play out in the documentary and archival practices of contemporary adoption. Sales (2012) studied adoption archives in one English Local Authority, tracing the emergence and deployment of practices of open adoption between 1989 and 2000. From the outset, she noted that paperwork relating to 'dead history, where events described are past' was geographically inaccessible 'at the back of a locked basement': in contrast, the record of 'living history' in the form of documentation of correspondence between birth and adoptive families was more accessibly storied in social work offices (Sales, 2012: 141). I pay attention here to the idea of a 'living' archive and the possibilities for contestation and new stories offered by ongoing communications and their documentation. Sales' (2012) analysis, and empirical evidence presented in later chapters, demonstrate significant failures in how 'openness' in adoption is practised. However, I suggest that troubling dominant versions of adoption stories and re/narrating not just individual lives but also what adoption means involves interrogating and intervening in these practices and their archival processes.

The technologies of 'open' adoption practice are primarily the life story book, later life letter and exchange of letters via so-called letterbox schemes. The provision of life story materials in these formats is a statutory requirement, although this does not mean that it always actually happens. Sales (2012: 102) describes life story books as 'predicated on the importance of the recovery and reconstruction of lost histories as an important regime of truth about the adopted person'. Life story books are usually produced by a child's social worker, or dedicated life story worker, who construct a document from material contained in a child's files to record significant events from before their birth until the point of adoption. Life story books are intended, in age-appropriate ways, to help children understand where (and who) they came from, why birth family members were unable to care for them and what their 'journey' to their 'forever family' was. Using photographs and often stock images such as cartoons, they offer a fixed narrative recorded at a point in time. They rely on adoptive parents making use of the books with their child/ren, reading, interpreting and filling any gaps over time: it is an expectation that contemporary adoptive parents will therapeutically interpret this information for their child/ren as they grow older. In this way the stories represented in them remain the responsibility of adoptive families until young people reach adulthood. Good practice also requires a 'later life letter' be written, usually by a child's social worker, which explains why they came into state care and were adopted, offering a more detailed account appropriate for a young adult. As both life story books and later life letters are written from information on file, they are likely to reproduce narratives from assessment documentation where the focus is on birth family as a risk and concern (for a scoping review of literature on life story work, see Hammond et al, 2020). Lisamarie Deblasio (2021: 143) highlights the 'institutional control' involved in producing these stories, which in effect are a story of birth parents' lives. They are often inaccurate and inadequate.

Compared to the life story book and later life letter, letter box has the potential to be more dynamic and open in terms of content. At the point of 'matching' a child or children with prospective adopters, discussions take place as to what form of 'contact' with birth family members the adoptive parents will be asked to commit to. At the point of 'placement' in the adoptive family, a contract should be drawn up which stipulates a contact agreement. This may be 'direct', such as face to face meet ups and/or phone calls or 'indirect' such as exchange of letters, photographs and cards. Contact may be with either or both birth parent/s as well as grandparents and siblings. Each case is different and factors such as age of child, existing relationships with family members, whether siblings remain with birth family, are adopted or are in foster care elsewhere, perceived risk from birth family and so on, all impact on what is established. In Chapter 1, Thalia Drayak (2023: 85) commented on a child protection system 'full of fear and in thrall to risk'. We can see this fear influencing contact agreements. In Chapter 7, we hear from birth parents, and staff who work closely with them, who believe the threat birth parents pose to their children or to the stability of the adoptive family can be exaggerated by fear rather than evidence. Drawing up a contract which rarely if ever gets reviewed also means there is little consideration that circumstances do not stay the same. As children grow older their needs and capacities develop, and over time parents can also experience significant changes which can make them more able to maintain good relationships with their child/ren. We see evidence of this in subsequent chapters. It is well documented that letter box arrangements favour adopters, both in terms of what they are prepared to offer (how often to write, what to include in the letters, whether to include photographs and cards) and also the 'contract' is not legally binding and can be stopped or only sporadically engaged with by adopters (see Deblasio, 2021).

There is substantial research literature relating to post adoption contact and increasing and urgent evidence-based demands to support better links between adoptive and birth families (see Neil et al, 2015; MacDonald, 2023; Neil et al, 2024; Public Law Working Group, 2024). The main driver for change is the improvements this would make to adopted children and adults' emotional lives. Thinking archivally about these practices and the potential for expanding and updating them via reform of policy and practice offers opportunities for engaging in very different conceptualisations of un/doing family through adoption. Perhaps communications between birth and adoptive families might not just preserve and revisit established stories from the past but also create new inter/connecting narratives and understandings. As an archive of letters and correspondence is established, different versions of (birth) family can be written and stored, enabling different futures to be imagined and/or realised. These new understandings might have profound implications for constructions of self, family and adoption, for all individuals involved. As I noted in previous research using blogs written by adoptive parents, birth family are an active presence in adoptive family life. This presence, felt in multiple complex ways, troubles any attempt to construct and maintain bounded, coherent or linear models of traditional family (Lambert, 2020). Commenting on the content of files in her 'live' archive sample, Sales (2012: 162) observes that

> The impression ... is of a dynamic and interrelated set of people in an active relationship with each other. The conventional self-enclosed family of the wider culture is here challenged: those boundaries have now become porous and the adopted child, far from being rooted in one singular place, lives between two different places. The adopted child's sense of self comes into being though an involvement in the exchanges between its different families ... one could say that the adopted subject is formed through activity, and not a historical origin or essence.

Sales (2012: 162) goes so far as to suggest that awareness of and perhaps minimal knowledge gleaned through letters about their birth family's contemporary and ongoing lives constructs new 'truths', 'unsettling a regime of truth governed by knowledge by installing a regime of truth governed by the transformative potential of relationships in present time'. However, as Sales' (2012) archival research shows, these possibilities can be severely limited by the restrictions and rules around letter writing. Norms around post adoption correspondence are motivated by conflicting ambitions. On one hand, they seek to ensure that children have access to information about, and maintain links with, their families of origin. At the same time, they strive to maintain the stability of their adoptive family. For birth families, the letters they write should be positive and light-hearted in content; they should not express grief, sorrow, loss or love; family members should be only mentioned by name rather than 'mum' or 'grandma'. As Sales (2012: 167) puts it, 'these must be sanitised letters, with any taint of history removed. The birth parent must recreate themselves as someone different from the mother or father they once were to the child'. For adoptive families, the letters they write should be reassuring and include positive everyday achievements and milestones, minimising or erasing difficulties. For both parties, identifying details are not allowed, and although some agreements include exchange of photographs, the advent of social media has meant concerns about sharing digital images often prevent pictures being sent. Letters from both parties are administered through post adoption services, who receive and assess the suitability of letters before they are forwarded. Those with content or form considered problematic may be returned for amendment, or redacted, or adoptive parents be alerted and asked if they still wish to receive correspondence or to have it retained on file.

All these protective/policing strategies can make correspondence formulaic and restrict its potential for establishing new understandings. Nonetheless, there is possibility in life-story work for generating counter-knowledges and shifting understandings of un/making family through adoption. The next chapter pays close attention to attending to the *live(li)ness* of relationships rather than what is 'known' in static ('dead') terms. In subsequent chapters, using materials generated with professionals and parents, this different archival practice of correspondence and contact between families will be revisited. We have considered here latent potential for live relationships and exchange of new stories about family members, no matter how banal, to simultaneously trouble 'origins' accounts by reconfiguring birth parents not as merely playing an historical role but having contemporary presence. At the same time, notions of family as fixed and bounded are unsettled by open practices, making way for what I suggest in Chapter 7 is a necessary reconfiguration of what families should be in a politically and economically functional, and socially fair and kind, society. In the following section possibilities for radically different archives and archives practices are explored.

Re/creating archives: feelings, fabulations and embodiments

What would it take to reform the adoption archive in the interests of political change? While the 'open' adoption practices described offer cautious possibilities for different archival content and form, with potential to change present and future understandings, there is much to learn from the work of scholars, artists and activists whose archival experiments constitute more radical interventions. In Gil Hochberg's (2021) work on Palestinian art and activism, archives are reoriented from the past to the present and future. As well as being 'guardian of the present as we know it' (Hochberg, 2021: x) archives offer opportunities to break with history and create anew. Central to this re/creation is a 'refusal of narrative' (following Edward Said's 1984 call for 'permission to narrate'):

a new mode of artistic expression and political intervention that can be described as a permission to refuse narrative. This refusal of narrative is largely a refusal of familiar discursive frames (for example 'the nation', 'the people') and genealogical narratives of origins, loss and recovery, in which the future is tautologically predestined.

What might it mean for adoption archives to similarly refuse narratives of origins and family, as discursively constructed, and resist the temporal logics embedded within them which close off possibilities of different stories and accounts in the present and future?

As we saw earlier in this chapter, many people seeking answers in care and adoption archives are left disappointed by the absence of information about their own or their families' stories. Particularly useful critiques have emerged from critical race, postcolonial and queer scholars, highlighting the partiality and bias of archives presenting as neutral, and the absences, exclusions and erasures of people, lives, stories and accounts (Carby, 2019, 2020; Hartman, 2019; Charania, 2023). Tammy Rae Carland and Ann Cvetkovich (2013: 76) alert us to the 'epistemological and political challenges of the absent archive', asking 'What happens if the histories you want to know have left no records?' One response to this question is offered by artists/scholars whose practices seek to compensate for, and make meaning from, absences and erasures in official archives. This diverse and interdisciplinary work expands ideas of archive beyond that of repository, using a range of materials and forms of knowledge operating between categories of 'fact' and 'fiction'. Unlike the bureaucratic formality of traditional archives laying claim to objective truths, these archival interventions recognise sensory and emotional knowledges generated and encountered (Lambert, 2018; Caswell, 2020). For those working in historical and contemporary contexts infused with trauma such as slavery; colonialism; war and state violence; AIDS; racist, homophobic and class-based oppression, emotion is unavoidable (Hartman, 2019; Cvetkovich, 2003; Carby, 2020; Charania, 2023). Like adoption archives, historical materials from such archives invite an 'affective' relationship, not merely a causal or teleological one, as histories 'touch' each other (Dinshaw et al, 1999; Koch, 2024). Cvetkovich (2003: 49) suggests that 'the affective charge of investment, of being "touched", brings the past forward into the present' as trauma 'serves as a point of entry into a vast archive of feelings'. Trauma, Cvetkovich (2003: 7–8) notes,

> challenges common understandings of what constitutes an archive. Because trauma can be unspeakable and unrepresentable and because it is marked by forgetting and dissociation, it often seems to leave behind no records at all. Trauma puts pressure on conventional forms of documentation, representation, and commemoration, giving

rise to new genres of expression, such as testimony, and new forms of monuments, rituals, and performances that can call into being collective witnesses and publics. It thus demands an unusual archive, whose materials, in pointing to trauma's ephemerality, are themselves frequently ephemeral. Trauma's archive incorporates personal memories, which can be recorded in oral and video testimonies, memoirs, letters, and journals. The memory of trauma is embedded not just in narrative but in material artifacts, which can range from photographs to objects whose relation to trauma might seem arbitrary but for the fact that they are invested with emotional, and even sentimental, value.

I have cited this at length because it raises issues relevant for understanding and generating different emotions, stories and knowledges around adoption, some of which are developed in the next chapter where I explore how heartbreaking knowledges can appear *barely knowable*, making different demands on archives and archival practices as well as on research. Of course, it is not just traumatic but also everyday aspects of life that evade being 'known' through official means of representation (Gunaratnam, 2013; Lambert, 2018; Mason, 2018; Quinn, 2023). We see here the urgency of expanding notions of archive to include more 'ephemeral' materials, re/forming archives to hold not just words but also sensory knowledges attached to objects, sounds and other forms. Letting go of attachments to truth and certainty makes way for opportunities provided by 'imagination, future vision, playfulness, creativity, speculation, and fabulation' (Hochberg, 2021: ix). An example of such fabulation is Saidiya Hartman's (2019) book *Wayward Lives: Beautiful Experiments*, in which she tells the stories of young Black women who survived and sometimes thrived against the odds in New York in the late 1800s and early 1900s. Hartman (2019: xiii) begins with official archives and libraries from where her characters and the events of their lives are drawn. She tells us: 'Every historian of the multitude, the dispossessed, the subaltern, and the enslaved is forced to grapple with the power and authority of the archive and the limits it sets on what can be known, whose perspective matters, and who is endowed with the gravity and authority of historical actor.'

In these archives, the official documents – 'reports of vice investigators, social workers, and parole officers; interviews with psychiatrists and psychologists; and prison case files', all present the young Black women 'as a problem'. The text she creates in *Wayward Lives* presses at the limits of these materials using speculation and imagination to create a 'counter-narrative'. This counter-narrative asserts that instead of being problems, 'credited with nothing', these (and other) young Black women were 'radical thinkers who tirelessly imagined other ways to live and never failed to consider how the world might be otherwise' (Hartman, 2019: xv). Although her focus, time and place are different from reform of contemporary adoption in the UK, the idea and practical application of 'imagination, future vision, playfulness, creativity, speculation, and fabulation' is valuable. In subsequent chapters we see how different possibilities for knowledge generation and exchange emerge through creative processes. We see how very different forms of knowledge about trauma and its generational effects, such as Vincent Dance Theatre's Art of Attachment film installation, bring urgent new materials to contemporary adoption archives. Working with, rather than seeking to repress or silence, emotional ways of knowing, such archives recognise that bodies and what bodies do (expression, movement, touch) are central to telling and hearing some experiences and knowledges. Such epistemologies of embodied feelings have been explored in the work of, among others, Sara Ahmed (2012) and Julietta Singh (2018a) providing conceptual resources which not only inform the generation and analysis of archives but also underpin the political argument that such archives and archival approaches are a vital part of adoption reform.

Ahmed's generation of 'unhappy' or 'wilful archives' relocates responsibility and authority for creation and curation of archives from the state and official holders of knowledge. She tells us that

> What I offer is a model of the archive ... as a 'contact zone'. An archive is an effect of multiple forms of contact, including institutional forms of contact (with libraries, books, web sites) as well as everyday forms of contact (with friends, families, others). Some forms of contact are presented and authorised through writing (and listed in the references), whilst other forms of contact will be missing, will be erased, even though they may leave their trace. (Ahmed, 2004: 14)

Conceptualised thus, we can take responsibility for the generation of new adoption archives as we create new zones of contact through our research, creativity, activism and writing. Recognising what Ann Stoler (2002: 101) calls the 'emotional economy' of archives reveals and generates different stories and knowledges. Such an economy brings about different temporalities of experience and knowledge, troubling tidy linearity of progressive narratives. It also offers significant challenges to the 'disciplinary' operations of traditional archives. Osborne (1999: 52) describes state archives as an 'obligatory passage point' for other 'centres of interpretation' which include 'courts of law, psychotherapeutic encounters, departments of the humanities and so forth'. Operating in this way archives provide 'credibility'. Such credibility is 'epistemological' in that its content provides certain types of knowledge and reasoning, but also 'ethical' in that it has status and authority: 'a certain right to speak, a certain kind of author-function' (Osborne, 1999: 53–54). This epistemological and ethical question of who can (and cannot) author stories is important. Affective and embodied engagements with archives generate interdisciplinary frames through which we see, hear, sense and feel things differently. Singh (2018b: 17) observes that 'Disciplinary thinking is practical, it enables us to frame ourselves as master of particular discourses, histories, and bodies of knowledge. It safeguards us against the incursions of oppositional frames, or methods of understanding that might unhinge us from our own masterful frame.' Singh (2018b) calls for us to exile ourselves from the comfort of disciplinary framing to allow ourselves to understand differently. As the next chapter explores, the collaboration underpinning the research undertaken for *Troubling Adoption* generates such a re/framing.

Conclusion

Seeking to understand the dominance of certain adoption narratives and the potential to trouble their authority while enabling new stories to be told and heard, this chapter has addressed adoption through different archival practices. Working with archives and archival practices is key to the re/production and exchange of a diverse range of adoption knowledges. In their most recognised form as a purposeful collection, archives occupy multiple spaces and formats: national and state depositories; organisational records; cultural practices; academic libraries; personal collections. They take physical and digital forms. They can be public, private or hybrid. In *Troubling Adoption*, enquiry manifests within and across these different sites and forms, connecting local and experiential knowledges and stories with inter/national politics and practices. Drawing on scholarship around the concept of archive makes it possible to understand the power of archives residing in their status as sources of truth, providing access to foundational, original knowledges. Adoption stories are often narratives of (hidden, unknown, difficult) origins and the momentum, the 'archive fever', for discovering and telling adoption stories can be a quest to uncover and know what happened 'in the beginning'. Such quests are bound up with not just knowing what happened but also seek answers to the searcher's question 'who am I?': as such, delving into adoption archives can have emotional implications for people's identities and belongings. These psychic as well as social attachments to discovering the truth, whether about oneself or others, is powerful and in turn sustains the authority of official archives. However, desire is rarely fulfilled as histories reveal themselves as partial, patchy and subjective, if they reveal themselves at all. In these 'dead' archives, many lives and stories are absent or can only be glimpsed. Legal and archival processes involved in searching for and gaining access to family history reveal inequities in whose stories matter. Legally, birth parents lose any rights to their children's records following adoption, when the story becomes one of hope for the child in their adoptive family. The child's family of birth becomes part of history, and access to their stories and the generation of new ones lies with adoptive parents. This is developed in Chapter 5 when we consider in more detail which and whose stories are given value and intelligibility and how this might change.

The pursuit of absent or partial stories and the knowledge and understanding they provide is crucial to the project of reforming contemporary adoption and as such calls upon new archival practices. This chapter has considered other possibilities in the form of 'living' adoption archives generated by documentation of the ongoing lives and communications of birth and adoptive families. This takes the form of life story materials and letters exchanged over an adopted person's childhood. Following the work of Sales (2012) the potential disruption these archives pose to the power of 'origins' stories and forms of identity and kinship that follow have been considered. There are significant limitations to how far these archives can trouble the dominant narratives they are located within. Using empirical insights from parents who have lost their child/ren to adoption and social workers supporting them, these potentialities and limitations are revisited in Chapter 7. A more radical approach to the conceptualisation, material content and practice of archive has been briefly considered here, offering insight into an exciting emerging arena of archival study, borne out of necessity as 'official' archives have enacted (and continue to enact) violent exclusions, redactions and untruths. As with other situations in which state oppression plays a part, there can be no reform without reform of the archive itself. Alongside better care of state records and fair access to records, which are all important aspects of policy change (Public Law Reform Group, 2024), we need to expand archives of the present and future to include cultural resources expressing emotional and embodied knowledges. The next chapter stays with the importance of emotional and embodied knowledges, looking at how these can be generated by research approaches and methods.

3

Developing alternative knowledges and ways of knowing

Introduction

The previous chapter argued for more diverse archives and archival practices able to accommodate a wider range of adoption knowledges, expressed in different ways. In turn, adoption scholarship needs to incorporate troubled and troubling stories in whatever form they take and participate in the generation of new stories and knowledges which may run counter to dominant forms in content and mode of expression. To listen, to attend to these troubling knowledges, requires careful, inventive, unhurried methods able to sit with uncertainty, ambivalence, discomfort and sometimes heartbreak. The development and implementation of such methods is key to this book. Arguments made throughout *Troubling Adoption* are underpinned by empirical research using 'live', sensory and creative research methods. These methods have been developed in the context of a long-term collaborative, interdisciplinary project involving a sociologist, creative practitioners and social work professionals. As well as setting out the *thinking about* knowledge production which informs the production of methods, this chapter provides more detail about different practical iterations of this project, paying attention to the generation and analysis of data. At the same time, a case is made for the wider use of such methodological approaches when working closely with troubling and traumatic knowledges.

This chapter begins by considering forms of knowledge which may be partial, uncertain and messy; knowledge which may resist being fully known and require different conceptual and practical approaches and methods. Consideration is given to the kinds of knowledge-work involved in designing and implementing such approaches. Resources offered by 'live' sociology including feminist and queer conceptual frames enable uncertainty and can attend to the embodied and affective forms that marginalised knowledges may take. Recognising the emotional nature of working with knowledge around adoption, heartbreak threads back through the discussion, in particular addressing what a political commitment to heartbreak, as established in Chapter 1, means in terms of knowledge production. The role of creative approaches to knowledge production in enabling knowledge of this kind to be articulated and made sense of is considered. The chapter then provides detailed description of methods used to generate empirical evidence, the analysis of which underpins arguments made in *Troubling Adoption*. I present the different chronological stages of the research, beginning by introducing my collaboration with Artistic Director Dr Charlotte Vincent and Vincent Dance Theatre (VDT) and describing Art of Attachment workshops which formed the first stage of this research process. These workshops led to a year-long ethnography with Breathe, Trust, Connect (BTC), a Local Authority Children's Services team working directly with parents who have had their child/ren removed from them by the state for adoption. I provide an overview of key elements of BTC as a service before describing the different methods which comprise the ethnographic research. The ethical implications of the research process are addressed before turning to how creative methods such as those used in the Art of Attachment workshops and with BTC can enable the generation and analysis of affective and embodied experiences and knowledges. The final stage of research, analysis of VDT's Art of Attachment film installation, is described before concluding the chapter. To begin, some considerations on methodology.

Knowing and not-knowing: live, feminist and queer methodologies

Troubling Adoption makes visible invisible experiences and knowledges, and as such it develops a conceptual and methodological framework for 'seeing' and 'knowing' that which may be 'unseen' and 'unknown'. This is not just a means to an end; the process of knowledge production is central to the book's argument. This methodological approach draws on my previous work using live sociological methods (Lambert, 2018; see also Back and Puwar, 2012; Paton and Jackson, 2025). In *The Live Art of Sociology* (2018) I argue for sociology which does not just engage with the social world but also creates it. As the book title suggests, the theory and practice of 'liveness' was developed from live art theory and practices, worked through in relation to sociological investigations. Many of the examples on which *The Live Art of Sociology* draws involved collaborations with artists or experiments in creative practice in the form of art installation, performance and poetry. My aim was to develop and implement live methods able to research that *which is barely able to be represented*: 'the fleeting, partial whispering of social affective, embodied life that slips out of our representational grasp and yet signals to us that it exists and needs our attention' (Lambert, 2018: 59).

Such methods are committed to social change, to making the world a better and fairer place. These two factors – attending to knowledges which slip from our grasp and working towards social change – must be held together, even when they appear to be in conflict. The political will to enact social change often leads to an understandable desire for clear-cut, graspable evidence. Undisputable truths are the preferred currency of social policy reform, if not of sociological enquiry (see Poulis, 2025). In social work and social policy, as across many areas of social science, there is a privileging of observable and measurable phenomena. Yasmin Gunaratnam (in Gunaratnam and Eisa, 2024: 211) observes how 'our care services, as much as universities, are increasingly driven by market imperatives and a fetishisation of measurement and targets that promise clarity, control and of course replication'. Val Gillies, Ros Edwards and Nicola Horsley's (2017) critical account of early intervention in families demonstrates policy makers' dependence on neuroscientific 'evidence' provided by Random Controlled Trials (RCTs) and evaluations and provides thorough assessment of the problems of privileging and relying on such methods, data and analysis. Their concern is echoed by Robin Sen and Christian Kerr (2023c: 63) who in their critical account of the political and economic networks and alliances characterising the UK's social care provision note an 'undue narrowing of the social work knowledge base, the misplaced reification of experimental methods, the potential for greater centralised control over practice and the marginalisation of the voices of those using services and practitioners within decisions about practice methods'.

While of course certainties and truths are always welcomed, social life is rarely that simple and as we have already established, the 'truths' of adoption are multiple, complex, geographically and historical contextual, and do not always yield to traditional methods of investigation. Instead, this research works with the uncertainties of partial knowledges. However, focusing on political reform, as *Troubling Adoption* does, sits uncomfortably with methodologies of uncertainty. Imagining and hoping for change requires projecting outcomes into the future, what queer scholar Elizabeth Freeman (2010: xiii) critically suggests is about 'having the problem solved ahead of time, about feeling more evolved than one's context'. I return to these challenges in Chapter 8, but for now note that just as the difficulties of researching partial and uncertain knowledges does not mean we should cede empirical research to not-knowing, we must commit to social and political reform even though the ground on which demands are made is shifting and precarious.

What Cathy Caruth (1996: 3) calls 'the complex relation between knowing and not knowing' comes even more to the fore through the lens of trauma. The etymological root of trauma is *wound*. Unlike a physical wound we can see and 'know', psychic or emotional injuries can remain 'unknown', perhaps not even consciously present to us, while nonetheless hurting and haunting in their attempts to make themselves known and understood. Such pain 'simultaneously defies and demands our witness' (Caruth, 1996: 5). This chapter contends with the methodological aspects of researching in a context saturated in complex, often extreme emotions. Live sociology offers resources for accessing and generating emotional expression and exchange. These resources include those offered by feminist and queer theory, conceptual tools that have emerged from politically engaged and emotionally charged contexts (Cvetkovich, 2003; Love, 2007; Amin, 2016). Feminist methodologies have always emphasised emotional and embodied forms of knowledge production (Letherby, 2003) and as Mel Chen (2012: 12) notes, queer theory has 'rewritten how we understand affect, especially with regard to trauma, death, mourning, shame, loss, impossibility, and intimacy'. The power to 'trouble' offered by feminist and queer resources extends to methods of knowledge production, harnessing affective politics in the generation of methods which challenge normative, often binary ways of knowing and being in the world (Browne and Nash, 2010; Brim and Ghaziani, 2016; Love, 2016).

Being attentive to what is being communicated by expressions of emotion opens possibilities for encountering embodied knowledges (Bondi, 2014). As Sara Ahmed (2004) and others note, skin is a border that feels. Sensory methods can tap into knowledge expressed in embodied and emotional ways. In their research with teenaged girls, Gabrielle Ivinson and EJ Reynold (2021) explore 'what bodies know', noting that embodied knowledge cannot always be verbally expressed. They used choreography to 'move' the girls who had become physically and psychically 'stuck'. In the following chapter, analysis of Art of Attachment film installation enables closer attention to being 'moved' as a mechanism for feeling and understanding more, and differently. It is not just the moving body that communicates but also embodied responses. Analysis of workshop data revealed expressions (a smile, a grimace or barely perceptible raised eyebrow); reactions on skin (a blush); gestures large and small (a fist on the table, an eyeroll) and so on. Just as absences in the archive are not devoid of meaning but may tell us something else, so absent bodies and silent voices might, if we listen with care, offer different stories and meanings.

In the context of adoption, many of the emotional encounters involve grief, loss and ongoing trauma. Chapter 1 established the argument that heartbreak is a necessary part of any radical or reforming agenda (Bhattacharyya, 2023). In line with this, it has been necessary to develop a way of knowing 'that breaks your heart' (Behar, 2022). Without doubt, this research has at times been heartbreaking. What does it mean to research (with) heartbreak at an everyday, practical level in terms of empirical enquiry? Researching (with) heartbreak involves attending to the emotions of all participants and recognising that people's affective expressions need to be handled with care. Gargi Bhattacharyya (2023: 71) highlights different manifestations of grief, noting that unlike demonstrative and therefore more accessible forms of distress, 'Depressed heartbreak is rarely disruptive or demanding or loudly eccentric ... Learning to go through the motions and not hope too much'. Thinking about people who have 'learned to keep moving through the world while carrying their wounds', Bhattacharyya (2023: 105) invokes an embodied metaphor as people 'Twist themselves around to protect their weakest spot. Maybe build up something else, some extreme bodily endeavour or ritual of service or quest for pleasure that can disguise the carefully tended wound. This is heartbreak held with care, accommodated from life from then onwards'. Research methods able to see and work with this 'disguised', accommodated kind of heartbreak need to be similarly attuned to embodied, deflected expressions and to respect the inaccessibility of some knowledges and experiences. Conversely, but with the same endpoint that some knowledges remain inaccessible, there were times throughout the research when just *being* in the heartbreak and not seeking to extract from it or make sense of it was the most ethical response (Butler, 2004).

Researching (with) heartbreak also entails critical attention to the porous boundaries between research, creative practice and therapeutic input. Research methods I utilised such as workshops and participant observation were often embedded in multi-layered events where the nature of the activities (cultural event/therapeutic intervention/research activity) and the roles of participants could easily become blurred. There were epistemological and ethical gains to developing a research approach which was 'trauma-informed', about which more in Chapter 6. Researching (with) heartbreak also demanded that I identified emotions not just in the data itself but also in my own contributions and responses. Although rarely acknowledged as such, researchers' emotional responses are themselves ethical stances and judgements (Solomon, 1997; Henry, 2012). They are therefore key to analytical claims and knowledge production (see Evans et al, 2017). Bringing emotions to centre stage in the research process demands reflexivity around the embodied experience of research (Evans et al, 2017; Jupp, 2022). Critically, being reflexive about (my) heartbreak is not *about* me or any other individual researcher but is in service of the broader argument that emotion plays a generative role in all research contexts and that any picture of adoption (or anything else) is partial if heartbreaking knowledges are inadmissible.

My approach follows feminist scholars such as Audre Lorde (2017) who embrace what Rachel Chadwick (2023: 2) calls 'epistemic generosity'. A *generous* orientation to knowledge, in line with principles of live sociology (Back and Puwar, 2012; Lambert, 2018) is characterised by openness and has a temporality conducive to 'waiting, slowness and listening' (Chadwick, 2023: 2). Slow and patient work, while challenging for the impatient demands of short-term and solution-focused systems, is of utmost importance in enabling different adoption knowledges to be accessed, heard and validated. The 'sociological art' of listening (Back, 2007) needs to be understood as a relational and embodied activity. Julietta Singh (2018b: 27) writes of listening

> as a critical mode of becoming vulnerable to the voices - human and non-human, audible and muted – that are always sounding even when we have not been trained or allowed ourselves to listen. Listening, as opposed to voicing that which we 'know'. Listening, as an act that might let each other in – psychically, physically – to another's way of inhabiting the world; to being entities that are always touching and being touched by others.

Bringing listening and touching together in this way has been important for developing a collaborative methodology with creative and social work practitioners. The simultaneously emotional and material possibilities of being 'touched' or 'moved' require methods attentive to different languages. Singh (2018a: 58) notes that 'In trying to measure the distance between the pain belonging to me and the pain of others, I came face to face with the limited vocabulary and insufficient metaphors we rely on to articulate something that, in the end, does not really have a place in language'. That 'something' might not have a place in language but nonetheless is a form of knowledge demanding and deserving to be acknowledged. Where possible, that acknowledgement needs to be at the levels of social practice, political discourse and policy making. As others have highlighted, 'emotions and relationships in circulation … often "exceed" policy rationalities' (Jupp, 2022: 25). However, if difficult, painful and marginal knowledges are not represented in these arenas, meaningful reform of narratives and practices around adoption is not possible.

In recent decades there has been significant expansion in the field of visual, creative, sensory and art-based methods across disciplinary arenas (Pink, 2015; Holmes and Hall, 2020). As already highlighted, my own work in this area has been made possible through collaborations with creative practitioners who share political and scholarly interests and ambitions but have expertise in different ways of working. For *Troubling Adoption*, photography, making and crafting, film installation and movement-based practice have all had a part to play, alongside spoken and written forms of sharing stories, experiences, ideas and feelings.

Artistic collaboration with Vincent Dance Theatre

The research activities informing *Troubling Adoption* developed from a long-standing relationship between me as a social researcher and VDT as creative collaborators. VDT was founded in 1994 and produces the work of choreographer and Artistic Director Dr Charlotte Vincent. I have worked with VDT for over a decade, on several different projects (Lambert, 2018; Lambert, Williams and Douglas, 2023). We share hopes, rooted in feminist politics, that our endeavours will affect social change. We share an interest in, and commitment to, participatory ways of working which align with the approach to knowledge already outlined. We are interested in what becomes possible when creative practices such as dance, movement, film production, making and crafting, combine with ethnographic social research to generate different ways of communicating with people and understanding their stories. Charlotte Vincent's most recent work focuses on attachments, particularly between mothers and children, and cycles of trauma that can lead to ruptures in attachment. Attention has been paid to 'care-experienced' children and adults, and in common with all VDT's work, possibilities for developing creative agency, connection and healing through movement are explored (see Vincent, 2023). In 2018, VDT produced Art of Attachment, commissioned by the Brighton Oasis Project, a substance misuse treatment service in the south of England.[1] Six months' intensive work with a constantly changing group of women from the Oasis recovery programme resulted in four women (Annette, Leah, Louise and Vikki) self-selecting to take part in a devising process over four months. This culminated in a one-off live stage performance at the Attenborough Centre for Creative Arts, Brighton, UK. The live performance was captured on film and then reshot and re-imagined as a film installation three years later. In both live and film installation versions of Art of Attachment, testimonies from the four women, delivered by the women themselves, are combined with visual metaphor and movement to reveal the physical and emotional impacts of generational trauma.

The ideas and politics of Art of Attachment resonated with my emerging sociological thinking around adoption, child protection and families. I had done some work on the ambivalence of adoption, using adopters' experiences as expressed through blogs to recognise the troubling aspects of adoption for adoptive families. This highlighted the significance of birth families as an often 'absent presence' in adoptive family life and called for attention to the complexities and contradictions integral to adoption policies and practices at this moment of critical reflection, if not crisis in adoption at national and international levels (Lambert, 2020). The urgency of adoption reform began to occupy my brain and heart as I dwelled in difficult debates about attachment, family, belonging and trauma. Charlotte Vincent and I talked about how to bring our overlapping curiosities, politics and different disciplinary resources together again in the staging of this new work to make it useful for researching the themes outlined above and the issues the work itself raised. Devised and directed by Vincent, working with three of the four women from Oasis who had devised the live performance, and filmed by long term collaborator Bosie Vincent, VDT's Art of Attachment film installation and engagement space screens the film work over two large TVs, with accompanying contextualising interviews on five smaller TV screens. The space also hosts a programme of workshops that enable embodied and affective understandings of the impact of childhood trauma in adult life. As well as Art of Attachment film installation, the space also holds film materials relating to another VDT production, In Loco Parentis[2] which focuses on experiences of adoptive parents and young people growing up in care. There was potential to show film resources from In Loco Parentis, but for our research workshops, with limited time available, we focused on Art of Attachment.

Vincent and I worked together to design research and arts-based workshops that would enable Art of Attachment to be shared with practitioners and other visitors interested in attachment and family intervention. The questions driving the research aspect of Art of Attachment were twofold. Firstly, I wanted to better understand the policies, processes and politics of family intervention. What did these policies, processes and politics look and feel like for those working closely in family intervention and support? Where and how did adoption fit into this broader framework? What ideas and hopes did those working day to day in child protection and adoption have about adoption reform? Secondly, I wanted to explore how arts-based, live methods can make sense of complex and sometimes unspeakable experiences and knowledges. In Art of Attachment workshops, we were able to generate evidence for the role of arts-based resources and methods for enabling such stories to be told and heard.

Art of Attachment workshops

Art of Attachment workshops were delivered in Autumn 2021, four at VDT's premises in Brighton, and seven at Arcadia Gallery in Coventry. Workshops ranged from between two and ten participants, with the average number being six. Participants in the Brighton workshops were in mixed groups including people already familiar with the work of VDT and/or Brighton Oasis Project. Participating alongside creative practitioners and students were professionals working in social work and social care, midwives and teachers. At Coventry, we recruited family practitioners working in Local Authorities across the Midlands region as well as students on relevant programmes within local universities. Groups of participants at Coventry mostly consisted of an established team working together: social workers in Fostering, trainees from a Social Work Academy, university students studying Early Childhood, members of a Family Drug and Alcohol Court team, and staff from BTC from the Birmingham Children's Trust. There were also mixed sessions where participants included personnel from a sexual violence project, dance and sociology students. All participants were over the age of 18, and were diverse in terms of gender, race and age. A few had experiences of growing up in care. Demographic data was not collected but many participants shared relevant personal information and intersectional experiences and reflections were integral to the conversations.

Workshops took place within the Art of Attachment film installation and staged engagement space. VDT's studio space in Brighton (see Figure 3.1) was larger than the Arcadia shop front gallery space used in Coventry, but the design was broadly the same, evoking the theatre and film productions of Art of Attachment to create a stimulating and immersive staged space of engagement. Both venues housed the film installation 'enclosure' – a purpose built wooden walled structure, containing the work and materials to work with as part of the workshop and response process. 'Props' and artefacts from both productions (baby dolls, empty wine bottles, bunting, paper, the chairs used in the work) were placed around the space and the trestle tables that feature in both Art of Attachment and In Loco Parentis productions were repurposed as the table around which participants sat. The materiality of the staging was key to the emotional responses of workshop participants, one of whom described it as 'making the invisible, visible'. Sitting at the same table, using some of the materials and being within a similar aesthetic space as the women and professional performers in Art of Attachment, created a tangible feeling of proximity and connection to the work between audience and performers. The paper which dominates the opening scene of Art of Attachment was reflected in piles of paper used in the workshops for craft activities. Lumps of air-drying clay were available to be squeezed and moulded by participants while watching the material, serving a regulating function as well as a creative one, and building an ongoing 'exhibition' of pieces made. Chewy sweets and lollies to suck were also available for sensory fulfilment while in the space. Along one wall were five smaller screens with multiple headsets which screened short contextual pieces on a loop, including interviews with three of the women from Oasis reflecting on their experiences of making Art of Attachment.

All workshops were facilitated by a member of staff from VDT, supported by me in a research capacity. Each workshop was two hours long and followed a similar structure. Participants were welcomed and invited to sit around the table. Ethical procedures had been digitally completed in advance of the workshops, but issues of consent and anonymity were revisited and checked at the beginning of each session. Participants were given evaluation booklets to complete by hand, devised by VDT primarily for their own evaluation purposes but also embedding useful research questions and designed to capture the feelings of participants 'before and after' being in this exploratory, creative space. Initial sections were completed at the beginning of the session, capturing participants' emotional states and expectations. We all watched a short film in which Vincent introduces Art of Attachment, describing how the project came about and how the work

Figure 3.1: Art of Attachment film installation and engagement space at VDT's studio, New England House, Brighton

Source: Photography: Charlotte Vincent. Copyright: Vincent Dance Theatre.

on film had been produced. Everyone was then offered a lump of clay to hold, squeeze and shape as they wished while watching the (39 minute-long) Art of Attachment on film through personal, sound-cancelling headphones. This sense of viewing communally but with individualised audio created the strange disjuncture of feeling simultaneously together in a collaborative space and isolated, experiencing the work in one's own personal space. Following the viewing, the facilitator checked in with participants and allowed everyone time to process, supporting participants to do simple craft activities using paper or clay (see Figures 3.2, 3.3 and 3.4). Instructions were already on the table for making origami hearts or crafting houses out of paper. They included suggestions for writing reflections or messages in the completed hearts or houses. People were able to either work in silence or speak with those around them. Many participants welcomed the opportunities provided by the craft activities. One person noted in their evaluation booklet that it was 'powerful to have opportunity to provide message to baby – have done similar tasks as a therapist in sessions but to do it myself was very helpful – jolted me inside'.

Participants appreciated that the craft-based activities were an invitation for them to attend to themselves and their own emotions, providing sensory regulation and a welcome 'excuse' for silence. As one person

Figure 3.2: Art of Attachment clay crafts

commented in the evaluation booklet, 'Tactile distractions help to reduce stress of difficult conversations.' These 'tactile distractions' are an important part of the creative and research process. They can be comforting, enabling people to 'do something' in the context of what can be an overwhelming sense of being unable to act. The printed instructions were retained by some practitioners who recognised that just as they benefitted from the focus on folding, creating and crafting, so could people they work with. Although many social workers do not see themselves as creative

Figure 3.3: Art of Attachment origami crafts

Figure 3.4: Art of Attachment origami crafts

practitioners, they often do a great deal of everyday creative work with clients. These craft activities prompted comments relating to the lack of funds and resources for social workers to buy craft materials. Making origami hearts and crafting paper houses require only a piece of paper. Once completed, participants were invited to either take their artworks with them or to leave them in an ever-growing gallery within the installation space. New clay sculptures and paper constructions took their place next to ones from previous groups, and people would look at and read other participants' offerings before adding their own to the gallery, making connections between different groups.

The live and creative methods in the form of the combination of watching/listening to the film, crafting, and discussion enabled participants to feel the experience in embodied ways. One noted that 'The film reveals more than live performance. I see expressions more fully. Doing these tasks afterwards means I can leave a message of gratitude. Talking about it brings it alive in my body' (Evaluation booklet).

Bringing it 'alive in my body' gets right to the heart of how sensory methods can enable embodied forms of knowing. Together with the previous comment that the origami task 'jolted me inside' we see clearly that sensory responses were elicited and reflected upon.

As the film ended, some groups immediately began talking about it. Others were slower, with more silences, and dialogue was fragmented as multiple conversations sprung up. After some discussion and crafting, participants were invited to watch other contextual short films. Many practitioners were interested in the interviews with three of the women involved in Art of Attachment in which they reflect on their experiences of participating in both the live theatre and film productions. The interviews provide insight into the impact of the process on these women and how being part of Art of Attachment has contributed to their recovery. Some listened to these, then returned to the table for more discussion and/or crafting; others stayed at the table engaged in activities and chatting. Towards the end of the session the facilitator drew people back together, shared final thoughts and sign-posted additional resources.

I joined in all workshops as a 'participant observer'. Workshop discussions were audio-recorded using a field recorder placed in the middle of the communal table. The audio recordings were later transcribed and anonymised. I made hand-written notes throughout the sessions. For the Coventry workshops I was supported by a research assistant, Carys Hill, who also took notes. Observational notes paid attention to emotions and embodiments, to how the room *felt*; people's movements, gestures, orientations and dispositions; their use of objects and props; expressions in sighs, laughter, gasps, silences. Photographs were taken of clay and paper artworks created in sessions, contextualised where possible by linking creative outputs with conversations. Audio-recordings were cross-referenced with notes to establish as complete a picture as possible of the conversations and activities in each session. Facilitators and researchers had a debrief meeting after each workshop, sharing thoughts and feelings about the sessions.

There were powerful moments in the delivery of and participants' engagement with Art of Attachment when it felt as though the different modalities of knowledge production brought physical, psychic, imaginative and visceral forms of connection and understanding together. Writing about sudden sensory moments of affinity in relation to kinship, Jennifer Mason (2018: 116, original emphasis) suggests that 'These moments, or these experiences, are heavy with something - *a frisson; a tantalising or exciting breach in our ways of understanding* perhaps … that do not usually bring together all these dimensions'. We saw instances of such breaches where participants were suddenly able to feel differently about a 'case' and where people recognised something of themselves or their experiences in the women and their stories, around patterns of attachment or coping strategies. In those moments of connection, people whose lives might appear very different and remote were brought suddenly very close. This proximity was enabled through the sensory methods generating embodied and emotional affinities. Mason (2018: 116) continues: 'at the very least, such moments constitute an unsettling of conventional binary divides in our modes of explanation, and enable us to glimpse the possibilities of connections, or parallel-goings on - ethereal or otherwise - that we can hardly imagine'.

The workshops created an engagement space where participants could not only hear and feel the women's stories in the film but also hear and feel each other's stories. Where groups of practitioners came to the workshop as a team, they brought the concerns and pressures of their work with them, entering the affective space with questions already half-formed. One member of the BTC team later reflected on the experience as follows:

> When we first watched [Art of Attachment] in full … it was shocking. It was like, oh my goodness … it's that powerful. But it was something that stayed with me as a positive. It reminds me, every time I work with parents; I remember how raw this is for them. This is real for them. You need to act empathetically. It was something that was painful to watch, triggering, harrowing even, but it's something that made me think in a different way. (Keziah, BTC staff interview)

VDT's core creative mission is 'to move people to think differently'. That these creative resources and methods enabled someone to 'think in a different way' is compelling evidence of their value. As well as the primary task of sharing these resources with people and generating their thoughtful responses and insights, Art of Attachment workshops offered compassionate spaces of interaction and support. This came to the fore one evening session with a group of women mature learners who were also practitioners in child-care settings, often juggling this work with caring for their own children. Unlike therapists or social workers, they receive no supervision or support. Nonetheless they related difficult, traumatic professional experiences, which had been made worse by the COVID-19 pandemic. At the end of the workshop, in which they detailed the effects of these combined pressures on themselves and peers, we talked about the importance of 'trauma-informed' services recognising practitioners' own trauma, not just that of their clients or service-users. This theme was to re-occur throughout the fieldwork and is paid analytical attention in Chapter 6. The attuned and sensory methods offered in VDT's Art of Attachment film installation and engagement space, together with careful and caring facilitation, provided these student/practitioners with a therapeutic space which is notably absent from other aspects of their training and paid labour.

As noted, one of the groups to attend an Art of Attachment workshop was the staff team from BTC. A Local Authority service, BTC work directly with parents who have had their child/ren removed from them by the state and placed for adoption. The Art of Attachment film installation and engagement space had a significant impact on them. Some of the stories told by the women in Art of Attachment resonated closely with the experiences of parents they work with. As a service they sometimes struggle to help other professionals understand things from their parents' perspectives. They saw potential in the powerful film resources and workshop activities for directly engaging with their parent client group. They also felt the materials would be useful for other professionals such as safeguarding social workers, adoption and fostering social workers, judges and midwives, for conveying how generational trauma can lead to the loss of children to adoption. A snatched conversation with their Team Leader at the end of the workshop established a connection from which the next stage of this research evolved. We promised to stay in touch to continue the dialogue. In this way, Art of Attachment set the scene for the next iteration of fieldwork: ethnographic work with BTC. The next section introduces BTC, considering what they do as a service and how they operate, before presenting the ethnographic methods used.

Breathe, Trust, Connect: introducing the service

BTC offers a therapeutic programme supporting parents who have lost a child or children to adoption, helping them understand what has happened and make informed decisions and choices about their current and future lives. BTC started out as a programme called Breaking the Cycle delivered by an independent adoption agency named After Adoption (for an account of the initial programme, see Gill and Lambert, 2019). After Adoption closed in 2019, and the programme was brought into Birmingham Children's Trust's core provision. It has been re/developed significantly since then. Two important changes are that in its initial formulation it recruited only mothers and ran as a time-limited (12–18 week) programme. It now works with mothers and fathers, individually or as a couple, and there is no absolute time-limit for engagement with the programme. This is an unusual and valuable feature which marks it out from other provision across the UK (see Cossar and Neil, 2010).[3] Another important feature of BTC is that all the work undertaken within the programme is underpinned by therapeutic principles and practices. In 2024, the service changed their name from Breaking the Cycle to Breathe, Trust, Connect. This change reflects a shift in seeking to resolve the complex structural problems of intergenerational trauma at the level of families and individuals and instead focuses on the critical and achievable work of embodied and relational connection necessary for any change to happen. I explore these factors in more depth in later discussions.

At the time of my research, BTC had ten members, of whom seven are senior social workers and three therapeutic support workers. All clients coming into the service are allocated a team of two, usually one social worker and one support worker. Support workers take the lead on practical tasks such as helping parents with benefits, housing, accessing medical or social care appointments, doing shopping, visiting food banks and so on. This every-day support is vital, not just for enabling people to function, but it is also key to the relational and therapeutic possibilities of the service, as trust and mutual understanding are built between workers and parents through spending time and doing things together. As well as this everyday activity based on need, parents have therapeutic sessions, building a folder of materials, mostly produced by the parent/s. There are also monthly coffee mornings for parents who do not have children in their care, and stay-and-play mornings for those who do. When I began research in September 2022 the service had 72 'open cases'. Over the next few months, I noted an increasing number of referrals relative to the number 'moving on' from the service. In addition, a new strand of recruitment was being introduced to enable pregnant care-leavers to access the service, even if it was their first pregnancy. Working closely with referrals from the local hospitals, this expanded the reach of BTC significantly.

As well as their direct work with their parent client-group, BTC staff train colleagues in related services, aiming to increase other professionals' understanding and empathy for birth families separated from their children, and supporting other services to use therapeutic practice models such as

Dyadic Developmental Psychotherapy (DDP) (see Hughes, Golding and Hudson, 2019) and PACE, where Playfulness, Acceptance, Curiosity and Empathy are the drivers for working with people (see Golding and Hughes, 2012). In the design and implementation of my research with BTC, I drew on these therapeutic framings. I reflect on what this meant in practice after presenting the range of methods used as part of the ethnographic research.

Ethnography with Breathe, Trust, Connect

Ethnographic work with BTC took place between September 2022 through to September 2023. Ethnography entails the researcher spending time partially immersed in the site of study, becoming familiar with people, systems and cultures. Building on earlier methodological discussion, ethnography was conceptualised through a feminist and queer lens that recognises the role of the researcher in the relational setting and is attentive to the generation and documentation of embodied and affective knowledges through diverse forms of data. Methods involved:

1. A day-long co-production event held with the BTC team and Sian Williams, then Participation and Digital Development Director at Vincent Dance Theatre. We reviewed the Art of Attachment film installation together and discussed the possibilities of using it with other professionals and with parents accessing the service. We also revisited the creative crafting tasks from the Art of Attachment engagement space to ascertain which might work with different groups. Joint decisions made on this day informed the development of bespoke film materials edited by VDT for use with parent and staff groups. I also shared formal research ethics documentation such as an information leaflet and poster and consent forms for staff and parents at BTC. We jointly agreed how best to inform parents about the research, how to invite them to participate, and how to ensure ongoing consent was fully informed.
2. Participant observation of relevant activities over the course of a year including selected team meetings; coffee mornings; stay-and-play sessions. This involved me attending these activities, participating where appropriate and observing and documenting what was going on. Observational notes were made in a fieldwork diary during or following the events. As with Art of Attachment workshops, my noted observations were attentive to embodied action such as movement, gesture, spatial and relational positioning, and emotional expressions made in non-verbal ways as well as through speech.
3. Individual semi-structured interviews were conducted with all ten BTC staff. These were audio-recorded and transcribed. All interviews were around one hour long. Two were conducted online, and seven in person at BTC's offices.

4. Participant observation of workshops with families and staff using bespoke workshop materials prepared by VDT following the co-production event described above. The first workshops, entitled Power of Words, were held with parents, and the second, Raw Emotions, with staff. Observational field-notes were taken during all workshops. Workshops were also audio-recorded and subsequently transcribed. Non-identifying photographs were taken of artistic outputs. Later in this chapter I describe the form and content of these workshops in more detail.

Data from ethnographic research with BTC thus comprises interview and workshop transcripts, field notes and photographs. These were all coded and analysed thematically before putting the materials together with those generated by the Art of Attachment film installation and engagement space workshops to identify themes which cut across both phases of the research. Ethical processes were integral. In the following section I consider what it means to undertake research like this ethically, remaining attentive to emotional and embodied ways of knowing and committed to social change and the political reform of adoption.

Power and emotions: researching with playfulness, acceptance, curiosity and empathy

To attend to people's experiences of adoption, whether they be parents or professionals, is ethically fraught work. In whatever form they are told, adoption stories are mired in complex emotions. As already established, methods designed and used for this research recognise that emotions provide a conceptual route to understanding how power inequities shape people's diverse experiences of adoption. This made the research feel 'risky' in terms of ensuring people and their stories were handled with care. Tiffany Page (2017: 14) highlights the ethical challenges of what she calls 'vulnerable research':

> As well as exposing the fragility of knowledge assembly, vulnerable methodology might be closely positioned with questioning what is known, and what might come from an opening in not knowing. This involves questions of ethics: the ethics involved in modes of telling, the sensory and affective responses to the material production of research, and the forms of violence committed in narrating the stories of vulnerable others.

Throughout the research, I sought to establish and maintain relationships with research participants in ways that minimised harm, amplified care and were attentive to power inequalities. Informed by a feminist literature on the ethical risks of 'giving voice' to people's experiences, I was mindful of the 'epistemic violence' that can occur in narrating others' stories (Spivak, 1988; Maggio, 2007). The research involved working with people with direct experiences of trauma as well as those working in traumatic contexts. The majority of those involved in workshops and/or interviews were social work professionals whose experiences were primarily supporting those directly affected by the loss of their child/ren to adoption. Their professional role and the training and support that came with this reduced power differentials between them as research participants and me as researcher and meant that there was mutual learning. However, I was the one shaping and recording their stories and held authority to retell them and 'make sense' of them.

Formal ethical approval for conducting this research was issued by the University of Warwick.[4] Trust was vital and the institutional processes of ethical protocol, while fulfilling university requirements, also offered reassurances about how data would be anonymised so that individual identities would be as protected as possible. Ensuring that consent was clearly given and genuinely informed at all stages of the research was of utmost importance. Ethical questions and how to address them were central to the collaborative conversations between myself, VDT and BTC. In our different settings – higher education, arts and culture, and social services – there are distinct norms and values around issues such as confidentiality and consent. For creative practitioners there may be an ethical commitment to *credit* producers or performers. It was important to ascertain we all meant the same thing and we worked in the interests of protecting each other and most importantly participants who were vulnerable.

Ethical concerns informed decisions made during the research. We had planned a series of three different workshops directly involving parents, using bespoke clips from the Art of Attachment film installation. I had also hoped to hold individual interviews with some parents. However, after running Power of Words workshops with parents we reviewed these plans. My observational notes document how even though these workshops were tightly structured, led by two BTC staff with the additional support of each parent's key worker, they were difficult for parents:

> This has been a really emotional day. All the parents tell the stories they want to tell, whatever the prompts are … My input is minimal, and I am just observing a BTC intervention. If I did interviews, I would be shaping the session for my own research ends and I would not be able to offer the intensive therapeutic responses BTC staff do. I have this strong feeling … that it would not be ethical to do the interviews one to one. Even the parents who have been processing this stuff for over twenty years display unprocessed grief. BTC staff have to work

hard to contain it in the space/time of the workshop. (field notes, Power of Words workshop)

Parents were keen to tell their stories and this felt positive. However, the stories the activities elicited were often distressing and it was evident that not only did staff have to work hard to support parents emotionally, drawing on their existing relationships and therapeutic expertise, but they themselves were finding it hard hearing the stories told in this format. Debriefing after the workshops, we all agreed that the resources were more emotionally triggering for some parents than we had anticipated. Instead, we agreed from a safeguarding point of view we would work on future workshops with staff only to develop resources for sharing with other professionals in different services. My notes also show reservations about interviewing parents. Although we had planned that key workers would accompany parents to support them during an interview, this workshop setting allowed me to think about how even 'unstructured' research interviews are guided by what the researcher wants to find out, and/or what participants *think* the researcher wants to know. BTC's way of working with parents is based on enabling and containing parents' emotional expression at their pace, on their terms. Although doubtless some parents would have welcomed the opportunity to have their stories heard, I could not be sure that the process would not do more harm than good.

The therapeutic underpinnings of BTC were also deployed in my ethnographic approach, specifically the PACE approach which was developed by psychologist Dan Hughes (see Golding and Hughes, 2012) as a parenting model but with much wider application. PACE is shorthand for the values of playfulness, acceptance, curiosity and empathy. These values are ethical and generative in research contexts too, where being able to hear and sense people's experiences and stories depends on the relational space that can be established. Although 'playful' approaches might seem most suited to working with children, the importance of play, including humour and creativity, are recognised as important political resources in queer and feminist activism (Leng, 2020) and research (Lambert, 2018; McWilliam, 2000). Curiosity is an established component of ethnographic research, enabling a researcher to be open to surprise. Acceptance and empathy are integral to caring methodologies and methods engaging with emotion. I am not trained as a therapist and did not at any point provide therapy; however, I do have an immersion in the relational approaches characterised by Dyadic Developmental Psychotherapy and PACE through my experiences as an adoptive parent. Adoptive parents are routinely trained and supported in these approaches to parenting (MacKenzie and Roberts, 2017). In this way, even if I did not make this explicit in my research encounters, these approaches cannot help but influence how I listen, engage and seek to understand other people, and the sense I make of others' relational and emotional expressions. In discussion with BTC staff, we also agreed that as these approaches are familiar to their parents, it made ethical and practical sense to use similar languages and framings in the research, where the intention was to better understand the complex and emotional stories they told.

Integral to these therapeutic framings is a careful temporality which by going at the person's pace can slow activities right down. As later analytical discussion details, unlike other services such as child protection or safeguarding, where timeframes are tight and work with parents is urgent and so often hurried, BTC work slowly, taking the time their parents need. Rather than the timeframes of assessment, the temporalities of grieving drive BTC's work. The research similarly needed to proceed slowly and carefully, giving me time to immerse in the service and get to know people and procedures, building trust and rapport by being around and having everyday encounters and conversations. In these ways, I embedded an awareness of trauma and how to engage therapeutically with traumatic knowledges into the research at all stages.

Use of creative methods at BTC

The creative methods used within the BTC ethnography were congruent with this slow and careful form of engagement. As with the therapeutic framing, there was alignment here between my research methodologies and BTC's routine ways of working. BTC staff think in a range of media about themselves, their service, their relationships with clients and areas of growth and development. It was of course this creative mind-set that led them to the Art of Attachment workshops in Coventry. They were not only interested in the content of the work, but also the use of movement and metaphor as therapeutic methods of life-story work, and film and craft resources as ways for practitioners and potentially families to understand more about trauma and attachment and process their own responses, using bodies, senses and emotions, as well as words.

BTC make extensive use of arts and craft as part of their everyday practices. Coffee mornings, held monthly for parents without children in their care, always have paper and pens for drawing and colouring available and staff offer an additional craft-based activity such as making dreamcatchers or painting stones. Paints, glitter, glue and clay invite people to make mess, feel different textures on their hands and express themselves in modes other than words. Staff are aware that many parents struggle to communicate using (just) words; art and craft activities not only make interactions easier, giving people things to do and activities in common, but also offer a way to communicate what they think and feel. When words feel inadequate or painful, creative activity enables interaction through sharing paints and passing scissors. Staff participate alongside parents, and dialogue and minimal embodied interaction is thus facilitated by shared activities: 'what colours are you going to use?', 'these metallic pens feel too harsh to me', 'has anyone got the glue'? Modelling behaviour, staff express their own feelings through creative forms, 'giving permission' for parents to do the same. The artworks might then be a basis for curiosity and discussion, as Rowan describes:

> I'm working with a mum at the minute who … [is] not very open at talking. But if you give her paint, and just a piece of paper, she'll do stuff, and then she'll be telling me what it … represents. Sometimes she'll do something and then say … 'that's a certain way, because I'm feeling this way.' (Rowan, BTC staff interview)

Staff recognise that opt-in forms of creative activity put parents in control of what they share, how far they go in communicating their stories and their thoughts and emotions about what has happened to them, or what they hope for the future. Artwork might prompt conversations about feelings, people or events. Or sometimes it might be the beginning and end of what is communicated, using the language of thumbs pressed into clay. It might be the language of paper, cut up, screwed up, marked or blank. It might be the language of colour, the red of blood expressing grief or rage, black ink on white paper making a strong or serious point. It might be the language of gesture, or movement, leaning onto the activity or away from it, making or resisting contact with others.

The two workshops undertaken as part of the BTC ethnographic research were attempts to explicitly trial creative approaches, using VDT's film materials as resources, and craft activities as ways to process emotions and ideas in embodied ways. The first series of workshops, devised by BTC staff, were entitled Power of Words. Six parents took part, one as a couple and five individually, all accompanied by their keyworker. They watched a short clip from Art of Attachment film installation and engaged in a creative activity in which they put their feelings about negative and positive uses of words onto labels and leaves. These were then hung together on a tree branch installed in BTC's office space. In the spirit of the Art of Attachment workshops, participants were encouraged to look at what others had done and add their words and stories alongside others in a collaborative art-form which was beautiful to look at (see Figure 3.5).

A later workshop, devised by BTC staff and entitled Raw Emotions, was conducted with me and five members of the BTC team. Raw Emotions was explicitly designed to trial a workshop which could be delivered by BTC to other colleagues in different services. Before the workshop, one member of the team produced a booklet for us to fill in during the workshop: a draft

Figure 3.5: BTC Power of Words workshop: tree branch with hand-drawn labels and leaves showing overall display

template for a document that could be used in future with other practitioners. Completion of the reflexive booklet during the workshop, together with group discussions on process, provided insight into how we were making sense of the film clips and managing the emotions implicated in watching difficult materials. Sylvia reflected on how writing in the booklet forced her to notice her own emotional response to the materials and how she was regulating herself. These comments relate to watching a scene from Art of Attachment film installation where Vikki recalls being sexually abused as a child and talks about the difficulties of escaping the memories of sounds and smells: 'Writing my own emotional responses … I actually took a really deep breath. So like straight away I was needing to regulate myself. Because even though I've watched this before, it was really powerful' (Sylvia, BTC Raw Emotions workshop).

This is an important part of thinking about how creative resources such as these impact on individuals, not just in terms of what they learn, but also how it can make them feel and the effect it can have on their embodied and physiological responses. Sylvia continued:

> Then I felt myself distancing from the story, almost like I could tune out. It was a conscious thing to actually *stay in the feeling* … I think it

was only because I was consciously thinking of writing down what's happening for me that I thought, 'actually my mind's already gone somewhere else'. (Sylvia, BTC Raw Emotions workshop)

Sylvia reflected on the fact that her mind wandering was partly a coping strategy, to avoid the difficult emotions generated by the material. Other participants agreed that it was hard to 'stay with the intensity of the emotion' as Olive put it. Olive continued:

> Where Child Sexual Exploitation [CSE] is so rife … you use … 'CSE' because actually it almost protects you from what it actually means … you don't want to immerse yourself in what's actually happened … the trauma that's there … you see it and you go to fix it.

Throughout the fieldwork, professionals reflected both on the uses of distancing language as emotional protection strategies, and the desire to 'fix' as a way of avoiding 'being in' the trauma. These issues are returned to in Chapter 6, but here I want to draw attention to the 'knowledge-production' implications of devising strategies that enable people to recognise these avoidances and work with them. At the same time as learning about their own emotional management, staff can reflect on how it might be for parents, or for other professionals engaging directly with these materials. Sylvia and Olive discussed how although stories of abuse are extremely common in their work engaging with parents, the creative format of the storytelling via material from the Art of Attachment film installation generates an embodied understanding of the stories which is different: 'when [Vikki] is pounding the dough and she's taking about the "white skin" and "heavy", and in my mind you know, "the next man and the next" … It brings it back to *your* body if you allow it' (Sylvia, BCT Raw Emotions workshop).

Sylvia explicitly names here the ways in which the knowledge of (sexual) abuse can become embodied through the combination of the words, action and materials being deployed in this scene in Art of Attachment. What she appears to describe is how feelings around the abuse move from Vikki's body to the viewer's body, moving from abstract or removed understanding about the impact of such abuse to navigating the effect in their own skin. Olive observes:

> It's very powerful, the washing hands bit. Just that feeling, connecting … I think it becomes quite overwhelming. So you want to try and shut down from it because it's like *you* can feel that *she* feels grubby and dirty, and to feel that somebody feels that and can't get rid of it.

You know, I think everyone can connect to that, when you feel, not through abuse, but you know, just needing to feel clean and you can't. And imagining if that can't *ever* happen. It's just, it's very powerful. (Olive, BTC Raw Emotions workshop)

The discussion demonstrated that the film materials and the systematic process of responding to them in the booklet used for the Raw Emotions workshop generated different kinds of empathetic understanding of the stories of, in this case, trauma caused by child sexual abuse.

Art of Attachment film installation analysis

As we have seen, VDT's Art of Attachment film installation viewed within workshops or re/viewed in creative workshops as part of ethnographic work with BTC, offered powerful resources and made different kinds of knowledge and understanding possible. The Art of Attachment project itself, facilitated by VDT in collaboration with Oasis, also informed my thoughts and arguments as the research and writing proceeded. I was not involved in this project, however the four women whose stories are told in Art of Attachment are not fictional figures: they are subjects actively engaged in the re/telling of their own and each other's stories, and their involvement extended beyond being part of the live and film productions. They produced additional documentary materials – interviews that were screened in the installation engagement space workshops – and attended workshops in an advisory and co-production capacity as activities for the staging of Art of Attachment film installation were devised. This 'real-life' aspect was of central importance to professionals and parents. Although the stories in Art of Attachment belong to Leah, Annette, Louise and Vikki, they had representational value: in Art of Attachment workshops, social workers often commented on the familiarity of the women's stories and how they echoed many of the circumstances of parents in their client groups. One parent attending a BTC Power of Words workshop began by asking of the film clip, 'Is it real? Or is it fake?' Had the accounts in Art of Attachment been fictional and/or represented by actors rather than featuring the women themselves, this would have undoubtedly reduced the 'authority' and thus the impact of Art of Attachment as a resource.

Providing continuity between different aspects of the research process and a cultural resource in common between research participants across all sites, Art of Attachment film installation formed a touchstone from which many of this book's conceptual and empirical pathways followed. It was an important resource for thinking critically and empirically about attachment itself. Attachment is a powerful political tool and there are compelling arguments for being wary of certain uses of attachment theory, as well as for embracing its political possibilities. In the following chapter I make a case for troubling attachment, drawing closely on how attachments are narrated and embodied in VDT's powerful installation. To do this, I undertook textual analysis of the film installation following completion of the other empirical methods. This timing meant that as I re-viewed the film and noted important themes, I had the wider data in mind, including audience responses and reiterations of the film in different research contexts such as BTC's Power of Words and Raw Emotions workshops described in the previous sections. This analytical attention to Art of Attachment also affirms its status as a significant cultural resource making important and unique contributions to understandings of attachment, loss, trauma and by extension, adoption. As established in the previous chapter, such a knowledge source deserves a place in a reformed adoption archive.

Mindful of the status of the women as both 'real' and representative of their own and others' stories, I re-watched the 39-minute Art of Attachment film, before undertaking close textual analysis of each scene and noting themes reflected in the wider data. I also noted the methods of creative delivery which in themselves provided alternative insights and interpretations of, for example, attachment or generational trauma. These methods included the literary translation of the women's stories through words into a poetic script, and the uses of music and movement. The Art of Attachment analysis informs discussion in Chapters 4 and 5.

Conclusion

With adoption knowledge production at the heart of this book, this chapter has explored methods for generating new knowledges around adoption. Resources already established in feminist, queer and live sociological scholarship are put to work in the empirical contexts of family intervention. Research decisions underpinning *Troubling Adoption* have been directed by the need to attend to experiences and stories which are currently marginalised if not hidden. The lack of visibility and intelligibility of certain knowledges may be because they are spoken by people (in this case, birth parents) whose voices and perspectives often go unheard. Such stories may not fit neatly into politically dominant narratives. They may be too heartbreaking to be listened to; they may be told in languages of emotion and embodied expression which are difficult to hear and understand through traditional methods. Current policy knowledges and frameworks that dominate social care are produced out of specific methodological traditions. While these produce knowledge of value, they are not enough. A more expansive set of knowledge production tools enables different accounts to emerge which may be difficult and contradictory but need to be included if we are to engage in meaningful change of adoption policy and practice.

How we listen shapes what we can hear. How we feel shapes what we can know. In practical terms, discussion here has explained how the epistemological and political commitment to listen and feel these different knowledges has led to developing ways of knowing that are slow and careful. Key to these has been collaboration with VDT, bringing an array of creative approaches and resources to the research endeavour. Distinct sites of empirical investigation have been detailed: the Art of Attachment workshops with professionals; ethnography with BTC, and analysis of the Art of Attachment film installation. Informed by the therapeutic framing through which BTC delivers its service, ethics of care and attention to emotion have been embedded in the research process. Hand in hand with a reformed archive, such methods are not just techniques for generating data but are integral to the politics and practices of reform itself. The varied data from across these empirical sites informs arguments made in *Troubling Adoption*. The following four chapters engage closely with this data, beginning in the next chapter with a troubling of attachment.

4
Re-thinking attachment theory and adoption

Introduction

Attachment theory is one of the most influential discourses around child development and parenting, not just in the UK but across many parts of the world (Duschinsky, 2020). It is a hot issue for adoption and any troubling of adoption policy and practice needs to grapple with how attachment is used, understood, translated into political discourse and everyday practice. A powerful body of critical literature demonstrates how psychological theories of attachment, translated into poorly understood 'brain science', are used to further socio-political agendas. In a pro-adoption political landscape, neuroscience is deployed in arguably problematic ways to justify early removal of babies, producing more 'adoptable' children and serving economic and ideological models of family and state (Wastell and White, 2017; Gillies, Edwards and Horsley, 2017; Kirton, 2019). Concurring with these arguments, this chapter asks, can other conceptualisations and applications of attachment do different political work? Rather than serving primarily as a tool for blaming and punishing individuals and families for social failings, can attachment theories be applied to complex lived experiences to enable greater understanding of people's relational behaviours? The discussion here draws on an alternative literature of social and cultural theories of attachment offered by Judith Butler and Lauren Berlant, applied to real life experiences embodied and expressed through art practice in the form of Vincent Dance Theatre's (VDT's) Art of Attachment film installation. Attachment is revitalised as a resource for thinking about and doing family intervention and adoption differently.

Directed and designed by Artistic Director Charlotte Vincent, made in collaboration with film maker Bosie Vincent, Art of Attachment film installation (see Chapter 3) anchors the empirical research undertaken for *Troubling Adoption*. It is a rich cultural resource offering insight into the effects of trauma on people's attachments to, and experiences of, other people, things and ways of living. Generated through therapeutic creative activities, emphasising movement and relational encounters, Art of Attachment offers different ways of knowing and understanding attachment, generational trauma, loss and repair. It engages directly with the removal of children from parents and the generational consequences of this. The evidence from this work was that the creative, affective and indeed political re/presentations of attachment offered by this work of art help people understand how childhood trauma plays out in adulthood as addictions, abusive relationships, broken families. Before turning to close analysis of Art of Attachment, conceptual groundwork is laid, turning first to consider traditional forms of psychological attachment theory, followed by critique of the powerful ways that bioscientific interpretations of attachment dominate political and common-sense discourse around family relations. The chapter then proceeds to think emotionally about attachment, using selected scenes from the film production of Art of Attachment to illustrate different understandings of parenting, loss and cycles of trauma through this conceptual frame.

Attachment and brain science

It is not possible to understand contemporary adoption policy and practice without examining the role of attachment theories, or perhaps more accurately, the role played by dominant versions of how attachment is (mis)understood. This is because attachment theories abound in adoption policies and practices yet their application in these contexts often relies on simplistic brain science. With its origins in child psychology, current use of attachment theory popularises the work of child psychiatrist John Bowlby. Bowlby's thinking around attachment, together with research experiments undertaken by Mary Ainsworth, have elevated attachment from a focus on everyday parent–child interactions to deeper and wider appreciation of the significance of relationships to human survival (see Bowlby's trilogy *Attachment and Loss*, 1969, 1973 and 1980; Ainsworth et al, 1978). Their research identified three categories of attachment behaviour in babies and young children: 'secure', 'insecure-avoidant' and 'insecure-resistant/ambivalent'. A fourth classification of 'disorganised/disoriented' was added later by different researchers (Main and Solomon, 1990). A 'securely' attached child is one whose behaviour indicates security in their relationship with their caregiver: they can seek reassurances and be comforted so that their play can continue. An 'insecurely' attached child is not so easily able to seek and accept reassurances or comfort from a caregiver. They may mask their distress through 'avoidant' behaviour, but an increased heartbeat, for example, reveals their anxiety. Or they might display insecurity through 'resistant' or 'ambivalent' behaviours as they attempt to take control of unpredictable situations in which they feel they cannot depend on their caregiver. Indications of 'disorganised' or 'disoriented' responses to situations supplement one of the previous three classifications: they were not intended to be used alone as a categorisation. Extensive research has been undertaken to test and develop these classifications over the decades since Bowlby proposed the theory (see the journal *Attachment and Human Development*).

Not surprisingly, a concept explored and researched across national and cultural contexts, on different species, within diverse disciplinary traditions using different methodologies, becomes stretched and strained, and meaning and complexities lost in translation. Varieties in cultures of child-rearing are often neglected, and there is empirical as well as conceptual work to be done exploring and rethinking attachment in contexts of multiple caregiving where the dyadic (mother-child) relationship is not so significant, and where what are assumed to be unpredictable, anxiety-inducing situations for some children may be unproblematic for others (Keller, 2013).

Despite these extensive critiques, attachment remains a popular and compelling concept. As Ainsworth wrote in a letter to Bowlby in 1968, 'attachment has become a bandwagon' (cited in Duschinsky, 2020: ix). It forms the basis of policy recommendations, educational and social programmes and legal decisions (Gillies et al, 2017; Keddell, 2017; Forslund and Duschinsky, 2021). More recently, the classifications identified above have been integrated into emergent understandings of 'brain science'. Brain science refers to neuroscientific knowledges about how our 'limbic system' is responsible for dis/connecting brain and body, seeking to understand how behaviour is determined by brain anatomy (the role of, for example, the amygdala and pre-frontal cortex) and chemical molecules (such as oxytocin and cortisol). These understandings – often patchy and partial, are not only put to work trying to understand and regulate children's brain-based behaviours, but also to intervene in 'the inner workings of the parenting brain' (Hughes and Baylin, 2012: 4). Psychologists Dan Hughes and Jonathan Baylin (2012: 6) argue that

> a wealth of neuroscientific research now makes it abundantly clear that parenting matters, and it especially matters early in a child's life when the brain is in a sensitive period for social, emotional learning and is vulnerable to stress. It is not an exaggeration to say, based on research across mammalian species, that good parenting sculpts the child's brain for emotional resilience and social competence while developing the child's capacity to trust other people and sustain positive, caring relationships. Sensitive parenting builds resilient, caring brains, and children who receive good care are better equipped to be nurturing and effective parents when the time comes to raise the next generation.

It is not surprising that these interpretations of attachment theory and neuroscience feature in adoption policies and practices. Key arguments suggested by Hughes and Baylin (2012), notably the significance of early childhood for brain development and the future consequences of negative and positive early parenting experiences, have become embedded into child welfare discourse. Such neuroscientific accounts underpin social policies concerned with child protection, providing justification for early intervention in cases where there is evidence of, or concern about, neglectful or abusive parenting (Wastell and White, 2017). They are also rallied in support of adoption itself, being used to bolster the narrative that while damage has been done to an infant's brain by poor parenting in their infancy, 're-wiring' can take place through 'brain-based' (adoptive) parenting focused on positive attachments (Siegel and Bryson, 2012).

In this way, selected versions of attachment theory, brought together with neuroscience to argue that early attachment problems affect babies' brain development, have become part of the apparatus of state, justifying implementation of policies around surveillance of families and removal of children for adoption (Hill et al, 1992; Schore, 2000; Gillies et al, 2017). Government agendas around family intervention and welfare link the 'well-attached child' not only to the good *parent* of the future, but more generally to the 'law-abiding citizen' whose productive capacities as a member of society are enhanced by the 'emotional resilience and social competence' that Hughes and Baylin (2012) highlight. A striking example of this is UK MPs Graham Allen and Iain Duncan Smith's 2008 report, its political argument summarised in its title: *Early Intervention: Good Parents, Great Kids, Better Citizens*. Despite Allen and Duncan Smith's status as 'laymen' who 'do not pretend to be neuroscientists' (2008: 56), they extract selective 'medical evidence' from a range of studies and re-contextualise it to support their argument for 'early intervention' in families deemed to be 'an underclass' or in their preferred terminology, 'a dysfunctional base' (Allen and Duncan Smith, 2008: 10). At the heart of this approach is parental (maternal) blame, linking growth in social dysfunction to a decline in traditional families and targeting mothers of new babies as the focus of intervention in the form of state surveillance and parenting instruction. The perceived financial benefits of this approach are highlighted: 'the 16 year old, banged up in a secure unit, at a cost of £230,000 per year often for want of a few hundred pounds worth of help to his mother on parenting skills 16 years earlier' (Allen and Duncan Smith, 2008: 15). Throughout their report the 'dysfunctional base' is characterised in terms of 'poorer communities': 'if we are to break the intergenerational cycle of underachievement in our poorer communities ... Early Intervention strategies have to be the standard' (Allen and Duncan Smith, 2008: 111). However nowhere do they acknowledge the structural impact of poverty for families. Instead: 'child poverty and income are only part of the picture. Building human capacities is at least as important and rewarding. Capable, competent human beings will almost always find their way in life, find work and raise happy families' (Allen and Duncan Smith, 2008: 21). With their scientific and empirical credentials, theories of attachment and brain development have proved malleable and persuasive in reinforcing this conservative political agenda. With the focus on the first two years of a baby's life as a critical period, they fuel pro-adoption policies by justifying removal of babies from 'dysfunctional' families to be adopted, endorsing foster-to-adopt or concurrent planning pathways (see Monck et al, 2004) and promoting intensive attachment-based re-parenting within adoptive families.

Critical responses

As we saw in Chapter 1, the numbers of such interventions, leading in many cases to permanent removal of children for adoption, are on the rise in the UK. A body of critical literature has built up in response to this deployment of attachment theory and neuroscience to justify early intervention in families. Many people are concerned about removal of children based on *risk* of *future* harm rather than *evidence* of *actual* harm (Broadhurst, Mason and Ward, 2022). Allen and Duncan Smith (2008: 56) talk of a 'future biopsychosocial profile' for identifying mothers perceived as potential risk. This profile is based on factors such as parents having themselves grown up in care and/or having had previous children removed. Race and class-based factors influence predictive concerns (Selwyn and Wijedasa, 2011; Bilston et al, 2017; Drew, Pierre and Sen, 2023). Allen and Duncan Smith's (2008: 17) report appeals to their imagined 'middle class readers, whose children imbibe effective social behaviour with their mothers' milk'. The narrative that if drastic pre-emptive action is not taken within the time-critical eighteen-month period, children's brains might be damaged, leading to attachment disorders and the reproduction of social disfunction, offers an emotionally compelling framework for justifying removal of babies from mothers, even when no instances of neglect have occurred. In their book *Challenging the Politics of Early Intervention*, Val Gilles, Rosalind Edwards and Nicola Horsley (2017) provide wide-ranging analysis of the ways in which neuroscience has been taken up uncritically and without full understanding and is being utilised for political means. They demonstrate that existing social, racial and gendered inequalities are reproduced and amplified by these policies. The target of blame and subsequent intervention is individuals, usually mothers. Gillies et al (2017: 152) argue that 'ideas about brain science and early intervention animate a "neurosexism" that assumes mothers as the "natural" environment for early intervention, and ultimately holds them both cause of and solution for the wellbeing of the nation'. Despite evidence of the relationship between poverty and child neglect (Ridge, 2013; Bywaters et al, 2016; Bywaters and Skinner, 2022; Webb et al, 2022) and other social and structural issues such as poor education, inadequate housing, racism and lack of access to mental and physical health treatments, these state and collective responsibilities are side-lined or ignored. Responsibility is shirked by government and laid disproportionately upon parents, predominantly mothers. At the heart of this political harnessing of attachment theory is 'family'. We return in Chapter 7 to consider the state's reliance on narrow, traditional forms of kinship as the basis for enacting neoliberal policies dependent on the private nuclear family as the site of social re/production and care. For now, what is important to note is how discourses of attachment are used to political effect in the surveillance and control of families and family relations.

I agree with the compelling arguments provided in these critical accounts. They demonstrate the problematic ways in which certain knowledges and ways of knowing gain power and authority because they suit political agendas. They also show clearly how this happens; scientific claims are made using 'careful and slippery wording' (Gillies et al, 2017: 50) which disguises the lack of scientific foundation; there are inappropriate extrapolations of evidence based on animals onto humans, and contradictory evidence is erased or ignored. A combination of deliberate cherry picking of some evidence and suppressing of other evidence, alongside poor public scientific literacy, allows those with political influence and power to produce and circulate claims which are then enthusiastically taken up in policy arenas. These accounts of brain development and attachment are repeated in influential contexts by influential people and communicated widely so that they become common-sense within and across different settings such as child protection, adoption training and education. The science on which they are based may be only partially grasped and is itself subject to dispute. For example, many question the status of research integrity and evidence that significant and irreversible damage is done to children's brains during the first two years of life (see Rose and Rose, 2016). Nobody suggests that neglectful or abusive parenting cannot harm children, or that babies' in vitro and early years experiences do not significantly affect their brain development. However, many do question whether claims about the impact of this on children's neurological and behavioural development are driven by evidence in service of supporting families and children or by political and economic interests. Gillies et al (2017: 65) map out the 'intricate web of vested interests and agendas that are woven into the fabric of children's services generally, and, more specifically, early intervention'. The enthusiastic take-up of neuro-scientific arguments about brain development and parenting is evident across political parties and across nations, feeding into a powerful ideological project with market interests at the forefront (see also Sen and Kerr, 2023c).

These valid critiques have led to hostility towards, and dismissal of, attachment theory and neuroscience from many sociological and feminist perspectives (Duschinsky et al, 2015). Inadvertently, this dismissal may cause us to miss important political possibilities offered by attachment theory. There is no indication that attachment will become less of a 'bandwagon', as Mary Ainsworth put it. Its persuasive and tenacious hold is not solely down to political influence but also the fact that attachment itself *feels* vital and binds us to life in complex and compelling ways. For workers supporting parents who lacked the 'secure base' of a consistent care-giver in their own childhood and now find themselves unable to safety care for their child/ren (see Golding and Gould, 2019) or for adoptive parents making sense of children's insecure behaviours (see Mackenzie and Roberts, 2017) the popular narrative of attachment theory *makes sense*. It can be used to enhance understanding and empathy, helping professionals and parents to understand how childhood experiences of trauma are not easily 'overcome' and can lead to cycles of destruction and chaos in adulthood (Perks, 2024). Where does this leave us in relation to attachment theory? Can important philosophical and psycho-social insights based on analysis of the primary scene of attachment (birth and early parent-child relationship) be extricated from the current *application* of attachment theory in family policy making and practice? Can different conceptualisations of attachment depart from the discursive use of attachment as a political tool for punishing the poor and marginalised? Drawing on a different set of theoretical framings, is it possible to understand how our attachments and desire for attachments shape our lives and offer possibilities for change? Might such understandings help us think differently about what families and parenting might look like, enabling us to formulate new demands for the state/family relationship? In short, might a critical but expansive engagement with attachment theory contribute to a radical reform of family intervention? These questions are explored here and in subsequent chapters, foregrounding storytelling and emotion in the generation of new knowledges and developing interdependencies in political and personal relations. The following section considers different conceptualisations of attachment which are a useful resource for addressing these concerns.

Thinking differently with and about attachment

Drawing on work by queer theorists Judith Butler (1997, 2004) and Lauren Berlant (2011) I stake out a political and optimistic role for attachment, which strengthens critiques of 'neuro-policy' with alternative ways of conceptualising the complex ways in which we are bound to life in given social, political and economic circumstances. At the same time as feeling the hopeful influence of these theories, I have been immersed in VDT's Art of Attachment. Both the conceptual framings offered by Butler and Berlant, and the empirical and creative openings provided by Art of Attachment take us to the affective scene of attachment (birth) and the primary relationship between child and caregiver. For Butler (1997: 6) the 'passionate attachment' of a subject to those they are dependent on marks the beginnings of our subjection to others' power:

> this situation of primary dependency conditions the political formation and regulation of subjects and becomes the means of their subjection. If there is no formation of the subject without a passionate attachment to those by whom she or he is subordinated, then subordination proves central to the becoming of the subject. (Butler, 1997: 7)

Butler's interest here is demonstrating how power operates through psychic as well as social processes. Their account is a reminder of the egalitarian ways in which we all emerge as human subjects bound to life and with capacity to sustain our lives through attachments to others. Of course, our *experiences* of attachment are far from egalitarian. Referring to instances where babies or children are subject to 'radically inadequate care', Butler (2004: 45) reflects on the 'bind' that attachment is crucial to survival and that

> when attachment takes place, it does so in relation to persons and institutional conditions that may well be violent, impoverishing, and inadequate. If an infant fails to attach, it is threatened with death, but, under some conditions, even if it does attach, it is threatened with non-survival from another direction.

Here the impossibility of 'not attaching' is spelt out. An infant's desire to survive is strong, even when levels of subordination are abusive. This desire is not just a feature of a child's dependency but 'that subordination provides the subject's continuing condition of possibility' (Butler, 1997: 8). That is, striving to survive and be recognised as a subject remains key to our ongoing existence. Butler (1997: 20) talks about this in terms of our fundamental vulnerability as human subjects:

> if the very production of the subject and the formation of that will are the consequences of a primary subordination then the vulnerability of the subject to a power not of its own making is unavoidable. That vulnerability qualifies the subject as an exploitable kind of being. If one is to expose abuses of power ... it seems wise to consider in what our vulnerability to that abuse consists.

This pre-disposition of vulnerability, applicable to all human subjects, is an important starting point for understanding how and why people end up in all kinds of trouble and for grasping the mechanisms of (psychic, social, political) power which enable abuse to occur, continue and be resisted.

You might be wondering at this point in what ways this account of attachment could be considered optimistic or hopeful. The kind of hope articulated here is a queer kind, in line with the troubled and troubling approach taken throughout this book. Butler (2004: 31) notes that although our primary scenes of attachment make us vulnerable to the power of others, we are 'also vulnerable to another range of touch, a range that includes the eradication of our being at the one end, and the physical support for our lives at the other'. To recognise our fundamental dependence on others' 'touch', 'signifies a primary helplessness and need, one to which any society must attend' (Butler, 2004: 32). Against the individualising politics of current discourses around self-sufficient or dependent families and good or bad parents, from Butler's account of attachment follows an ethics of human interdependence and social and political responsibility. This argument is developed in Chapter 7.

A more explicit optimism is named by Lauren Berlant (2011: 125) who describes their own childhood attachment experiences as taking place in a context of 'disappointment, contempt and threat':

> I salvaged my capacity to attach to persons by reconceiving of both their violence and their love as impersonal. This isn't about me. This has had some unpleasant effects, as you might imagine. But it was also a way to protect my optimism … Out of this happy thought came an orientation towards fidelity to inclinations of all sorts, including those intellectual and political. Attachments are made not by will, after all, but by an intelligence after which we are always running (It's not just 'hey, you!' but 'wait up!').

'Hey you!' refers here to an example provided by the Marxist scholar Louis Althusser (1972), describing a moment of identity formation in which recognising ourselves in another's (in his account, a policeman's) interpellation subjects us to (state) power. Hailed in the street, 'hey, you!', we turn or freeze (or run?) and in doing so take up the subject position imposed upon us. It is not hard to identify the relentless ways in which parents whose children are removed from them experience being interpellated and positioned by the state as failed parents. However, in contrast to the disciplinary 'hey you!', 'wait up' suggests a different power dynamic, in which future temporalities open with the movement of 'always running' after attachments not fixed by the past (Duschinsky et al, 2015). Bringing Berlant's (2011) 'wait up!' into the picture helps us to understand the lure and promise of attachments that people make; the optimistic investment that keeps them hanging on, even when such attachments appear to yield more harm than good. 'Optimism is the only thing that keeps the event open, for better or ill' says Berlant (2011: vii). Although such attachments allow for liveable worlds, and are necessarily optimistic in their orientation,

Berlant (2011: 2) is attentive to the 'cruel' optimism that drives us towards attachments which are not necessarily good for us:

> optimism is cruel when the object/scene that ignites a sense of possibility actually makes it impossible to attain the expansive transformation for which a person or a people risks striving: and, doubly, it is cruel insofar as the very pleasures of being inside a relation have become sustaining regardless of the content of that relation, such that a person or a world finds itself bound to a situation of profound threat that is, at the same time, profoundly confirming.

It is easier to think about such attachments in concrete examples, and throughout the discussion that follows we encounter many, providing insight into why people make and sustain damaging attachments – to people, lifestyles, substances, and so on. Time and time again, the stories of families who have children removed for adoption are littered with narratives of 'poor choices', specifically women staying with violent or abusive male partners, and parents addicted to alcohol and/or drugs. Thinking with Butler and Berlant, we can instead attend to (cruel) relations of attachment which enable people to remain bound to life even in extremely damaging circumstances.

The Art of Attachment: thinking emotionally about attachment

These damaging circumstances, and attempts to survive them, are presented to us in VDT's Art of Attachment which translates and represents the stories of Annette, Leah, Louise and Vikki. As described in the previous chapter, these four women worked with VDT on Art of Attachment through their involvement with Brighton Oasis Project, a service for women in recovery from addiction. Their experiences were shared and scripted over a nine-month creative process leading to the production of a one-off live performance in 2018 and film installation in 2021 (see Vincent, 2023 for details of the creative process including ethical and therapeutic aspects of the work). Artistic Director Charlotte Vincent (2023: 122) notes how:

> *Art of Attachment* offers an opportunity to discuss the medical, ethical and attachment issues encountered within the fields of substance misuse, domestic violence and childhood sexual violence and to think about attachment, birth families, adoption and fostering differently – from an emotional as well as neurological or scientific point of view.

I present analysis of Art of Attachment, moving through key scenes to consider the empirical manifestations of the themes of attachment developed in the chapter so far.

Figure 4.1: Still image of table scene from Art of Attachment film installation (2021)

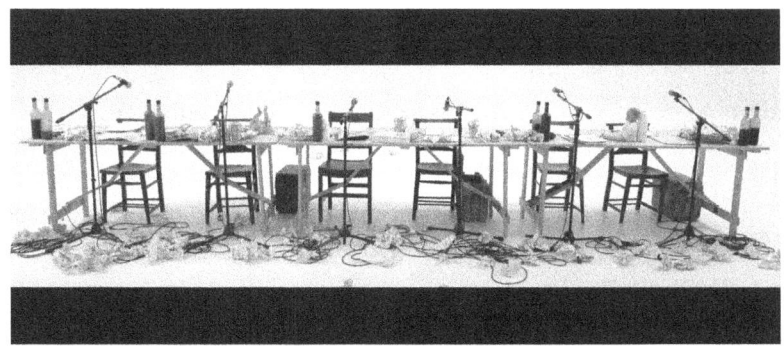

Source: Photography: Bosie Vincent. Copyright: Vincent Dance Theatre.

The film opens with the image in Figure 4.1: three long wooden trestle tables in a row, with six wooden chairs behind, and microphones on stands in front. Wires and sockets tangle with screwed-up, discarded paper, littering the floor and tables. There are also neat piles of white A4 paper – forms, scripts, medical reports – half-drunk wine bottles, and baby dolls. A hum is building. Six people sit on the chairs at the desk, dressed in black and white, moving papers from left to right and right to left, from one pile to another. A clock ticks. They pick up biros and scrawl on the papers, editing, crossing things out, marking the papers, not looking at each other, but focused on their work. Whispers overlay the hum and ticking as the sound intensifies. Each person takes the paper they are writing on, screws it up and throws it forwards, and the camera catches the paper balls flying and landing. We hear distant screams. We see the source of the screaming, as the camera moves close to a woman in labour, held by a man whose face is off camera. He is behind her, holding her hand. His hand then gestures as if to puncture her rounded stomach/womb which pops like a balloon as blood seeps through her hospital gown. Her hand goes to the blood, as he steps away, registering distress, holding the new-born baby (doll). He cuts the cord with office scissors, the blooded baby held against his white shirt and black tie. He remains at a distance from her, with the baby in a nurturing hold, while she reaches out towards him crying 'my baby!' and curls up in a foetal position, hauling a long umbilical rope back through her legs as if trying to pull her baby back towards her. But only the frayed end of the rope appears, as her baby is not attached.

In these opening scenes of Art of Attachment on film, bureaucracy and emotion are entangled. There is efficiency (the ordered desks and chairs, the piles of papers, the attempts to process it) and chaos (the scrawling, the screwing up and throwing of paper). The ticking clock gives us a sense of order and urgency. The hum and the screams register anxiety and distress.

There is much about this birth scene that remains unclear, ambivalent. Who is the man; what is his role? The initial supporting hold briefly suggests he might be her partner, but his actions soon position him in a different role, forcibly removing her baby and refusing to let the mother hold it. His own demeanour registers some distress, some resignation, but his emotions are flat and hard to read. With his suit and tie and office scissors he is a symbol of bureaucracy, an 'official', incongruously efficient and detached in the face of pain and grief. The woman's distress is palpable in the graphic representation of the removal of her baby. This is the separation so often referenced in court papers and social work files, where the mess and sorrow are absent. We are reminded of the critical literature on baby removal in the UK, drawing attention to the increasing numbers of newborn babies targeted for separation from their mother at birth due to anticipatory risks, and highlighting the trauma and lack of support for those mothers (Bilson and Bywaters, 2020; Mason et al, 2023). The emotional encounter forces us to recognise attachment and loss from the mother's perspective as well as the baby's, while the framing of bureaucracy, paperwork and surveillance locates this scene as not only an individual's experience but one with social and political significance.

Reflecting on the process of working as an Integrative Arts Therapist for the Art of Attachment project with Brighton Oasis Project, Jo Parker (2019: np) observes that working with people in recovery 'is not a clean business … it involves working with trauma, chaos and pain and loss; it is neglecting, violating and violent. It is messy and it is not in the securely attached world … the way the arts fit in with this has also been complicated and multi-dimensional'. The opening scene takes us into the affective scene of chaos and pain, enabling us to experience, briefly, what it might look, feel and sound like to be 'not in the securely attached world'. Workshop participants watched the film wearing sound-cancelling headphones which made the experience immersive (see discussion of Art of Attachment workshops in Chapter 3). It was a scene to which participants returned repeatedly in workshop discussion. They were affected by coming up so close to the mother's loss and despair. They felt the complex ambivalence of the male figure taking the baby. They were shocked by the graphic representation of process and paperwork counterposed with the material realities of giving birth:

Participant:	the way they were all sitting behind the desk, it was as if it was just a conveyor belt, waiting for the next one … [lots of overlapping 'yeahs', 'I said that', 'I thought that']
Participant:	it made me think of *panel*, and *court*, and *processes*/
Participant:	and just being another case/
Participant:	and the write up/

Participant:	and it just being another case, like it's not real: it's not happening to a real person

(Art of Attachment workshop)

As we see in later chapters, working within, as well as pushing against, the constraints of a 'conveyor belt' system of cases and processes is part of the everyday labour of many professionals working in family services. As one trainee social worker put it: 'All the paperwork, continually moving the paper over. You got into social work for the right reasons, to understand people holistically, but realistically there's so much paperwork and such high caseloads. You can't do what you came into social work to do' (Art of Attachment workshop).

As noted in Chapter 2, paperwork is shorthand here for something negative, opposed to the 'holistic' work of engaging directly with people. The 'high caseloads' together with the conveyor-belt image from above, invoke the constrained temporalities of social work practice. Responses such as those above from participants were often expressed with feelings of responsibility, even guilt; they recognised themselves in the representation and that generated uncomfortable emotions. This scene of the row of tables (see Figure 4.1) is returned to throughout the film, anchoring the women's stories in the paperwork. This paperwork symbolises processes such as assessments, panels and court hearings which produce documentation about the women and their lives. These official stories are entangled with alternative stories told by and between the women themselves. The first story is Annette's.

Desire for absent attachments

The screen is split into two and on one side Annette sits on a wooden chair looking at the camera. Behind her a pile of wooden chairs appears precariously balanced, casting their shadows up the wall, evoking an unsafe and threatening domesticity (see Figure 4.2). On the other side of the screen, VDT's professional collaborator Antonia (Toni) Grove stands with her hand resting on an empty chair. To gentle piano music, Toni then takes Annette by the hand and with Annette remaining seated, a tender partnering sequence follows. The voiceover (read by Vikki) tells us about Annette's history and the information is factual, clinical:

Age: Unrecorded.
Parental Information: Maternal: Still alive
Paternal: Unknown
Adopted: Foster Care (Sexual Abuse)
Race: Unknown
Sexuality: Unknown.

Substance Abuse: Multiple. Alcohol. Cocaine. Cannabis. History of Self Harm.

Other: Patient has two children but is now sterilised. No partner. Previous partner's whereabouts unknown.

> (Art of Attachment script, based on medical records, written by VDT collaborator Wendy Houstoun)

Figure 4.2: Still image of Annette and Toni partnering, split screen, from Art of Attachment film installation (2021)

Source: Photography: Bosie Vincent. Copyright: Vincent Dance Theatre.

Although the words themselves allude to a life punctuated by abuse and drug misuse, the movement of their bodies is tender and nurturing. Annette and Toni take turns to bear each other's weight. The scene elicits empathy, in contrast to the cold list of 'facts' of her life, many of which are 'unrecorded', 'unknown' gaps that we are left to imagine. We are told that she

> Expresses belief of being bad (i.e. Bad Mother. Bad Person).
> Verbally displays visible signs of loneliness and isolation with associated symptoms (shame, sadness, powerlessness). Multiple reports of feeling 'different'.

And her 'problem list' is long:

1. Birth mother rejected her.
2. Passed on through fostering and adoption.
3. Sexual abuse between age of 7 and 14.
4. Unable to read as a child.
5. Experienced racial taunts.
6. Drank and self-harmed at young age.
7. Eating disorders.
8. Two children in abusive relationship.

9. Early sterilisation (Age 26).
10. Mental health issues.
11. Lost court battle for children.
12. Substance abuse (drugs and drink).

> (Art of Attachment script, based on medical records, written by Wendy Houstoun)

This fragmented account of Annette's life pieces official recordings of her history as documented in files and court case notes together with professional observations about her behaviour and what it indicates. To the professionals participating in Art of Attachment workshops, Annette's story was a familiar one; defined by rejection, moves through the care system, struggles with poor mental health, addiction, abusive relationships, and loss of her own children. Annette gets to speak for herself when she lists her 'positives' directly to camera:

1. Stopping substance abuse.
2. Desire to be loved.
3. Desire to be happy.
4. Desire to be a good mother.

> (Art of Attachment script, written by Annette)

Aside from 'stopping substance abuse' Annette's positives are hopeful expressions of subjectivity: desires *to be*. Her desire to be a good mother is set against the fact that she had two children in an abusive relationship and has subsequently 'lost the court battle' for these children, suggesting they have been adopted. Her 'early sterilisation' tells us she will not have future birth children. On one reading, her attachment to positive motherhood seems 'cruel', to use Berlant's terminology. However, we see in subsequent chapters that there can be possibilities for positive parenting and positive parent identification, post adoption. In Annette's account here, whether such 'good mothering' can be achieved is not addressed, but her desire to attain the 'good mother' status is presented as a strength, perhaps speaking back to the shame of being (seen as) a 'bad mother' (Sharpe, 2015; McGrath et al, 2023). A nurturing 'good mother' version of Annette is portrayed in the movement of bodies. Annette moves to the floor where Toni lies curled, and she gently rolls her over, tenderly stroking her back. While the words paint her as victim, we also see a nurturer, with great capacity to love and care. The whispered voice-over tells us she

> Repeatedly affirms a belief in her own badness and expresses the idea that something is missing. Has developed protective coping strategies which she refers to as wall building.

> While she has reported multiple painful life events she continues to affirm desires:
> To recover, to feel valued, to be happy and to love.
> She has drawn pictures of a bird, a flower and a teddy bear on her notes.
> The pictures are soft, gentle and in pencil.
>
> (Art of Attachment script, written by Wendy Houstoun)

The final observation calls to mind case notes with their authoritative black on white type, with her gentle pencil drawing in the margins. It reminds us, as we saw in Chapter 2, that margins are full of meaning and value, and people are much more than the words said and written about them. In this short sequence, we have been offered different perspectives on Annette, the formal documentation of her life providing partial understanding of what she feels and what her potential might be. Annette's story illustrates that we might attach to things that harm us but, as Ben Anderson (2022: 7) puts it 'the objects of attachment might be "negative" in the sense of 'absent' – lost, partial, problematic and fraying – and yet still affect the present and are held onto'. This fraying but nonetheless persistent feeling of attachment makes sense of the experiences of families whose children have been removed from their care, as well as adopted children and adults' attachments to birth families they have little or no contact with. Such 'absent presences' are forms of attachment that, while the absences persist, must be lived in bearable ways (Lambert, 2020). We explore this in more detail in subsequent chapters when we take a close look at the therapeutic work of Breathe, Trust, Connect (BTC). For now, we turn to Louise's story in Art of Attachment.

Making life bearable: the ambivalence of damaged attachments

> Even when it turns out to involve a cruel relation, it would be wrong to see optimism's negativity as a symptom of an error, a perversion, damage, or a dark truth: optimism is, instead, a scene of negotiated sustenance that makes life bearable as it presents itself ambivalently, unevenly, incoherently. (Berlant 2011: 14)

What Berlant (2011: 14) describes as the 'complexity of being bound to life' is illustrated in Art of Attachment through all four women's stories but is best exemplified in the account of Louise's conflicting attachments to alcohol and to her children. This was performed by Louise herself in the stage production and by professional understudy Anna Avarez who stepped in for Louise for the consequent film installation. It takes the form of a partnering sequence between Anna and VDT Artistic Associate Robert (Rob) Clark, in which she is torn between nurturing and holding a wine bottle and her baby. Against a stark white infinity wall backdrop, the performers and the two objects move backwards and forwards in a dance of attachment and detachment, love and rejection. Over the music there is collective whispering from the rest of the cast, as if the voices of friends, family, professionals, wider society, her own inner voice, all merge in their pleading:

> Don't do it! Stop! Put it down.
> You don't want it. Stop. It's not worth it. Put it down. Think of your kids. Think of your children. You can do without. Think of your children. Stop. Put it down. Don't do it.
> Put it down. Please! Think of your children.
> You've done so well. Stop. Put it down. You don't need it. Think of your kids!
>
> (Art of Attachment script, devised by the cast)

And Louise's voice tells us:

> Incy Wincy spider climbing up the spout, down come the rain, completely washed him out and then the sunshine comes out dries up all the rain and then what does the Incy Wincy Spider do? He climbs all the way up again. That's me [pause] climbing up [pause]. Then I have a drinking binge. The hangover's gone. And then what does the Incy Wincy Spider do? He climbs all the way up again. Climbs all the way up again. He climbs all the way up again. Climbs all the way up again. I was happy climbing up that spout. Yeah, it was hard work, but it was fine. I was managing. But then came the [PHOOF sound]. It takes control, doesn't it? That's why it's an addiction.
>
> (Art of Attachment script – transcription of Louise talking to the group, edited into soundtrack by Charlotte Vincent)

Throughout the partnering sequence, composer Jules Maxwell's music is gentle, reflective, and the dance both harrowing and beautiful, a graceful exchange where baby and wine bottle are deftly passed, held, removed. As in the opening scene, Rob's role is ambivalent – he is the caring social worker, disapproving, responsible, stepping in, giving her a chance by handing the baby back, but not much of one, before the baby is out of her arms again and in his. The bottle and the baby take on an equivalence: similar sized objects that she cradles and holds with seemingly similar love and devotion. The repetitive temporalities of addiction are embodied in the sequence, and Louise smartly reflects that addiction is 'bigger than you, it's bigger than your own being, it's bigger than your soul as such'. Vikki's voiceover interjects in the background, asking 'Aren't I enough for you, Mummy?' and we can imagine the scene Louise paints through the following fractured dialogue devised from group conversations captured and edited by Vincent:

Woman 3:	Just have a couple of glasses of wine.
Woman 4:	Mummy. Mummy.
Woman 3:	I was like, 'yeah, I'll bounce on the bed with you!' Next minute I was throwing up and I'm in bed.
Woman 4:	Mummy, wake up. Mummy, wake up
Woman 2:	And I did that for a long time. Just brush it under the cover.
Woman 4:	Wake up.
Woman 2:	Just brush it under the cover. Get on with it. Wake up, wake up. Get on with it. I had all the best plans
Woman 4:	Aren't I enough for you, Mummy?
Woman 2:	So, I stopped. And I stopped for so long. But then I got complacent. And I got back on it
Woman 4:	Daddy
Woman 2:	We wasn't [pause] other than the drugs, we wasn't that chaotic [pause]. We kept it to a routine. D'ya know what I mean?
TV sound:	'It's not fair!' SHOUTING, POLICE SIREN, DOOR SLAMS

The words evoke the banality, the everyday ways in which addiction and neglect take hold, interspersing play and care and routine with sickness and chaos. There are moments when Anna holds the baby with affection, and from behind Rob reaches and takes it away. She looks like she doesn't understand why. At the end of their sequence, the baby has been removed and Anna lies in a foetal position cradling a bottle. The voiceover says:

Woman 4:	Mummy wake up. Mummy wake up
Woman 3:	Daddy shouts at Mummy. Mummy gets upset. Mummy has a bad drink, Mummy gets ill
Woman 1:	It's kind of like not a happy story, is it?

        (Art of Attachment script/soundtrack, edited together from captured conversations with Oasis by Charlotte Vincent)

This rhetorical 'It's … not a happy story, is it?' resists solution-focused narratives of progress which, as we explore in more depth in Chapter 6, so often obscure the complexities of cyclical, damaging trauma and its effects. Despite it not being a happy story, Louise's story presents attachment to things which provide meaning and keep her bound to life even though these attachments are damaging. As Anderson (2022: 3) puts it 'We may be attached to things that harm us or things which simultaneously sustain and harm us, unsettling the line between sustaining/flourishing and harming/damaging'. Louise's words above illustrate this unsettling: the allure of a 'couple of glasses of wine', the optimism of Incy Wincey Spider climbing up the spout, which quickly slips into the chaos of alcoholism. As the then Director of Oasis notes, writing in the Wellcome Trust funding application to support Art of Attachment: 'A powerful, damning narrative exists about women who fail to achieve an idealised image of motherhood and public media responses to substance misusing women is rarely sympathetic, tending instead to be punitive and demonising' (cited in Vincent, 2023: 43). Art of Attachment offers a different narrative, and at the same time provides insight into how attachment might be understood as an optimistic reaching towards people and things and ways of life, even as those things are harmful. Such attachments are not one-off events or decisions but are imbricated in the subject's continuity and survival. Berlant (2011: 24) reminds us that

> What's cruel about these attachments, and not merely inconvenient or tragic, is that the subjects who have x in their lives might not well endure the loss of their object/scene of desire, even though its presence threatens their well-being, because whatever the content of the attachment is, the continuity of its form provides something of the continuity of the subject's sense of what it means to keep on living on and to look forward to being in the world.

Such a perspective exposes a punitive discourse of 'poor choices' as inadequate and unlikely to lead to the kind of support and intervention which women in Louise's situation need.

Taking steps: 'a bit of hope'

In the final scene of the Art of Attachment film installation, there is a loud bang, as if a gun shot, and blood appears on Toni, taking us back to the birthing scene at the beginning of the film. The music is sadder, gentler. Toni lies foetal, alone. Rob stands at a distance, alone. There is quiet grief. They come together in a duet which appears reparative and possibly hopeful. The four women emerge from behind the table and stand together in a line stepping slowly forward towards the camera as they speak:

Leah: The past is not enough to stop us, to stop or block our way.
Vikki: So watch us now, stand up, stand tall
Stand all the shit and let it fall.
We cry, we try, we fly into breath.

Annette:	Stop. Count 1. Count 2. Count 3. Count Death.
Anna:	Stop.
	To all our fights and flights–
	We stand.
	We strike.
	Strike out on our own.
Vikki:	Stop.
	Turn corners,
	Turn tricks
	Turn tables
	Turn heads
	Spin ourselves into care.
Leah:	Stop.
	Reach out
	to friends,
	to right directions
Annette:	To our kids with new affections
	Taking on the search for what we lost–
Vikki:	The cost we paid in full.
	Not that its laughter - or that happy ever after stuff -
	Just bits of hope, to cope
	to bend, not break,
	to reach, not ache,
	to weave and breathe.

(Art of Attachment script, written by Wendy Houstoun)

In this final sequence, while Toni and Rob duet together, falling, catching, holding, separating, and coming together, the women step towards a different space – close to the camera as though they might now move beyond it. As they stop, they state the need to take a breath, count, step again and again, move forward. Their message is one of measured hope: 'not laughter or happy ever after'. They take steps as if moving towards something, but without having an endpoint or resolution. The individual stories become collective as we see them in a row and Annette says 'We breathe'. Our attention is drawn to the intertwining of senses: 'an eye for how we might be feeling', 'an ear to what we might be thinking'. The movement of bodies and emotions is given rhythm and structure by the breathing. In one of the Art of Attachment workshop discussions, Vincent reflected on this final sequence as follows:

> the minute you say 'let's talk about attachment', if you've had your children removed – you're not attached; you've been

abused – you're not attached; you're free-falling actually a lot of the time, and so recovery is as much about grounding and landing. Hence the stepping ... if we can regulate breath; if we can step; if you just *move*; if there's a sense of movement towards something that's possible.

Here attachment as a feeling of security, being 'grounded' and 'landed', is set against the feeling of 'free-fall' with its sense of chaos and lack of control. Keeping breathing, feeling and moving may be the only meaningful possibilities, where words fail. Being moved keeps emotional and embodied possibilities alive, even against the odds. Movement also has a regulatory function. In the early psychological accounts of attachment provided by Bowlby and Ainsworth, the attuned caregiver uses noises, rocking, verbal reassurances and their physical proximity to regulate their infant's emotions. We have seen movement as regulation in action in the partnering work in Art of Attachment, and in following chapters we see it in the different context of BTC's direct work with parents accessing their service. In this way the steps and the breaths the women take are not just metaphorical, although the metaphor is important, but are a literal act of survival. The co-regulation enacted in the making of Art of Attachment itself constitutes a practical and therapeutic intervention for the four women, the professional performers, and for the audience and research participants.

This final scene provoked discussion in the Art of Attachment workshops. There was some frustration with the lack of concrete resolution, but most practitioners valued the politics of an ending which is open-ended, refusing solution or closure, but at the same time offering hope. Vikki's reference to 'bits of hope, to cope/ to bend, not break' resonated in its refusal of a 'happy ending' and recognition that healing childhood traumas is at best a partial and ongoing process. Rather than the grand gestural form 'hope' often takes as an abstract emotion, 'bits of hope' captures the messiness of hopefulness as it is lived. Participants from BTC connected this with the contingent and fragile ways that 'hope' manifests in their service:

Participant (BTC):	... hope for the future, hope to be a parent
Researcher:	Do you think hope is quite important?
Participant:	Absolutely, but I don't think you can have hope until you've processed what's happened to you.
Researcher:	OK, why?
Participant:	Because you just don't feel safe. You don't feel worthy of experiencing nice things that happen to you. So from an attachment perspective, a lot of the parents that we work with would see

> themselves as worthless, helpless, hopeless, just … not worthy of being fixed.
>
> (Art of Attachment workshop)

What is this relationship between hope and attachment? What does it mean to tether these two grand terms to each other and to the materialities of lived experience? Berlant (2011: 14) suggests that attachment is promissory and optimistic: 'optimism is … a scene of negotiated sustenance that makes life bearable as it presents itself ambivalently, unevenly, incoherently'. We saw this in Annette's story. Her feelings and expressions of low self-worth were evident, but from the security of the physical partnering sequence developed with Toni, she was able to articulate 'positive' attachments, desires to have and to be the things that have been denied her through the damaging circumstances of her life. Significantly for Berlant (2011: 2) such optimism might not *feel* 'optimistic' in the sense of being accompanied by 'positive' affects.

> All attachment is optimistic, if we describe optimism as the force that moves you out of yourself and into the world in order to bring closer the satisfying *something* that you cannot generate on your own but sense in the wake of a person, a way of life, an object, project, concept, or scene. But optimism might not *feel* optimistic. Because optimism is ambitious, at any moment it might feel like anything, including nothing: dread, anxiety, hunger, curiosity, the whole gamut. (Berlant, 2011: 2, original emphases)

For women with life experiences like Annette, Leah, Louise and Vikki, or for parents with experience of losing their child/ren to adoption, such as those accessing BTC, hopeful attachments may well be experienced as shame, anger, grief or 'nothing'. This affective complexity will be returned to in Chapter 6, but we note here the potentiality of thinking of hope as an optimist attachment which, by virtue of its relational quality, has 'force that moves you out of yourself and into the world'. Such hope has a temporality that refuses stasis, as captured in the final scene of Art of Attachment, and as such, in Anderson's (2022: 9) words:

> opens a valued future – whether of continuity from the present, or return to a lost past, or of something better – and enables the present to be better navigated and rendered more habitable. Attachment works to organise the present in itself and in relation to the past and future in a way that offers something to the subject held in the attachment.

Against the reductive accounts of attachment used to enforce narrow political and economic agendas, highlighted earlier in this chapter, here we can see a generative role for these more expansive conceptualisations of attachment. The discussion here demonstrates the value of bringing theoretical insights on attachment together with empirical connections made by creative and social practitioners. Both recognise the importance of movement in pursuit of hopeful attachments. The work of Vincent Dance Theatre and Breathe, Trust, Connect reminds us that movement is only possible from a place of safety, and we see in later chapters how safety can be generated strategically via therapeutic input to move people from hopeless situations towards more positive attachments.

Conclusion

Thinking with the creative content of the Art of Attachment film installation and practitioner responses to this content in workshops directs our critical attention towards the emotional and embodied scene of attachment, represented graphically in the opening scene of the work. This chapter has drawn on theories which do similar productive work, in particular the work of Butler and Berlant. Their starting point is also the affective scene of attachment, from which they develop ways to think about how power operates to structure lives, subjecting us through infant dependency on others' care and offering subject positions into which we might be forced – 'hey you!', or enticed – 'wait up!' In the empirical material examined throughout this book we see numerous examples of both 'hey you'! and 'wait up!'. The discussion here has provided insight into how attachment works in powerful ways to keep us bound to life in forms that can help us flourish as well as damage us. It has also set up the possibility that our attachments, and desire for attachments, offer possibilities for change. Such possibilities are not limited to what might be broken or fixable within brains, but incorporate embodied ways of feeling, knowing and acting in the world. These possibilities are represented powerfully in the final scene of Art of Attachment, which offers realistic forms of hope.

Attending closely to analysis of empirical data from Art of Attachment together with data and insights from ethnographic research with BTC, the next three chapters cultivate arguments established here. The conceptual insight that our primary attachments and relational dependencies shape all aspects of our lives is put to work in developing a case for greater interdependencies between families, and family and state. An enhanced understanding of how cruel attachments might lead us, through a need to remain bound to the world, to make apparently poor life choices, offers a different framework for thinking about therapeutic and practical support. In the next chapter, the importance of being moved, emotionally and physically, is elaborated with a focus on the generative power of telling and listening to different stories which might trouble and change dominant narratives and political discourses around adoption.

5

Telling adoption stories in new ways

Introduction

The dominant story told about adoption is a positive one: adoption is rescuing children from bad situations and providing security and good outcomes for them; it is about creating happy families. These narratives have sustained over time, underpinning policies and their implementation within and across nations, developing and becoming powerful through repetition and normalisation. With their authoritative structural form, they influence popular and political discourse as well as the paper/work of family intervention (see Chapter 2). The production of specific narratives of parents and families as 'failing', 'deserving' and so on, is at the heart of how child protection and adoption policies are put into practice. Social workers are required to produce accounts of parents' problems in highly standardised ways that tell a specific story for a specific purpose, such as justifying the removal of a child from their parents and placing them for adoption. Parents can feel that the stories told in court, documented in official paperwork, are partial and unfair. Such stories can have significant impact on their ongoing sense of identity and emotional health (Memarnia et al, 2015).

Similarly, for adopted people it can be challenging to construct a coherent life story out of a history of severance from family who retain an ambivalent and contradictory presence, as we saw in Chapter 2. Understanding the story of your own life – your 'origins' – is a powerful drive leading to 'archival fever' for many care-experienced and adopted people (Pugh and Schofield, 1999). The importance of having some coherence around your individual 'life story' is recognised within contemporary adoption culture, leading to the production of life story *work* and life story *books* (Rees, 2009; Rose, 2012). However social care and adoption archives are often inaccessible, and/or full of gaps and redactions. Stories are missing or incomplete, with emotional and material consequences for those seeking answers (Goddard et al, 2008; Condit-Shrestha, 2021). We can see how from the macro level of national state and institutional discourse through to the intimate psychic dynamics of belonging, stories are involved. And in all these multi-layered iterations of storying, power is at work. Extreme imbalances of power determine which, and whose, stories are uttered, validated, silenced. Of all stories about what it means for children to be removed by the state from their families and placed with a different family forever, those least heard are those of birth parents. Legally, their accounts have come to not matter as the story shifts to one of hope for a child's future in their adoptive family (Rushton, 2003; Deblasio, 2021). In this chapter, parents' perspectives are amplified using data from the Art of Attachment film installation, together with Art of Attachment workshops with professionals, and Power of Words workshops with parents designed and facilitated by Breathe, Trust, Connect (BTC).

Chapter 2 argued for the generation and inclusion of a wider range of archival materials and different conceptualisations and practices of archive to expand the range of stories and knowledges available. Recognising that it is not enough to simply add more, new stories, but also increase possibilities for storytelling, the discussion in Chapter 3 established the importance of finding and utilising alternative ways to listen and narrate people's experiences and knowledges. These include embodied and emotional forms of knowledge production, in which movement and making create space for communication. In this chapter, creative approaches to knowledge generation enable a diversity of adoption stories to be told. These stories may be fragmentary, told in languages of emotion, embodiment and movement as well as words, and the knowledges they express may be ambivalent, complex, troubling. In thinking about the diverse forms that adoption stories can and should take, and the potential of stories to enact change at individual and collective levels, this chapter draws on an interdisciplinary literature. Narrative and storytelling are recognised as central to our sense of ourselves (Frank, 1995; Plummer, 2019; Cavarero, 2000; Squire, 2020). Echoing and extending the discussion around attachment in the previous chapter, storytelling is understood as integral to our identities as formed through relational encounters. We need our stories to be heard and validated by others: we become a 'narratable self' in the social and political world through this dependency and through our desire to have our stories told and heard. This relationality is what makes storytelling, like attachment, political (Cavarero, 2000). Ken Plummer (2019: 151) highlights the political potential of this power in hopeful terms:

> stories can damage, destroy, dehumanise. But above all they can inform, influence, inspire. They are the beating heart of good education, therapeutic culture, social activism, humanitarian aid, Truth and Reconciliation Commissions and much more. Stories can bring hope and the power of transformation at personal, practical and social levels. As we engage in narrative interactions and build narrative communities, we share stories that may change the world … stories can remould lives even as they raise political challenges, provoke change and set new political agendas.

In the following discussion we see examples of stories that damage as well as those that transform. Damage and transformation do not happen 'out there' in words and texts but are emotional and embodied processes. Plummer (2019) addresses how stories work when people act in relation to them, what he calls 'narrative action'. Such action in turn informs new stories, creating *movement*, which is of course affective, embodied and political. We saw an example of this at the end of the previous chapter, drawing on the final scene of Vincent Dance Theatre's (VDT's) Art of Attachment film installation: acts of breathing and stepping forwards were interspersed with words that articulate 'bits of hope' to keep going. Artistic Director Charlotte Vincent talks about this in terms of 'the rehearsal of alternative narrative, taking confident steps in a different direction' (2023: 43) and being able to narrate new stories, or relate old stories in new ways. This chapter attends to the generation of alternative or re/narrated stories focusing on their connectedness to movement and action as necessary for social change. Returning to the storytelling in the Art of Attachment film installation, together with empirical reflections from the associated workshops and creative research activities undertaken with parents at BTC, the discussion demonstrates that reworking the *form* of dominant stories, as well as creating new ones, is an important aspect of a reforming agenda.

The chapter begins with the process of creating Art of Attachment, generated from emotional stories out of which different forms of narration become art. The chapter then turns to consider workshop material from parents accessing support at BTC. The power, and difficulty of words, both spoken and written, is explored, paying attention to validation and hope in enabling stories to be expressed through creative methods. Such methods allow for emotional and embodied forms of knowledge to be articulated and made culturally intelligible.

Translating and trans/forming stories

Laurel Richardson (1990: 129) states that

> People make sense of their lives through the stories that are available to them, and they attempt to fit their lives into the available stories. People live by stories. If the available narrative is limiting, destructive, or at odds with the actual life, peoples' lives end up being limited and textually disenfranchised … New narratives offer the patterns for new lives. The story of the transformed life, then, becomes a part of the cultural heritage affecting future stories and future lives.

In the previous chapter, we saw how cultural resources such as Vincent Dance Theatre's Art of Attachment creates and shares such new narratives, providing possibilities for movement and forming of new attachments. Art of Attachment is structured around four women – Annette, Leah, Louise and Vikki – who tell their own, and each other's stories. Charlotte Vincent recounts the intention to separate stories from people to protect the women from being exposed by telling their own story. However, they wished to narrate some of their own experiences. In the production, distinct narrative threads connect Annette, Leah, Louise and Vikki with their own life stories, but there is also blurring of voices and experiences. Vincent (2023: 39) describes the process of generating stories as follows:

> The first six months of this project were spent listening, gathering ideas and stories from the women ... sometimes we brainstormed ideas about attachment, drawing in charcoal on large rolls of paper sprawled over the floor ... the material was dark and challenging, their voices clearly expressing many years of pain, grief, abuse and loss.

Vincent (2023: 40) found that in the early months, 'unexpressed hurt and anger from childhood and intergenerational trauma dominated our discussion', and that the women struggled to tell 'coherent stories about their past':

> Chaotic and unsafe patterns of attachment repeated themselves, manifested in unsafe feelings and behaviours and were reflected in incoherent stories. The process of finding ways to tell these stories is very much one about attending to disordered attachment and ordering it, in some form.

Part of this 'ordering' took the form of a 'layered artistic process' which involved collaborator/writer Wendy Houston being sent stories in the form of interview transcripts, notes from workshops, and medical records, with notes from Vincent, and bringing them together as poetic and performative texts. In this way the generation of stories was not just an act of listening and re/telling but of artistic translation. The craft of the film adds new layers of translation, reauthoring individual stories to produce what Vincent (2023: 41) refers to as 'an alternative script':

> Understanding the weight and influence of these negative, inherited narratives, carried so heavily throughout life, made me wonder whether the process could 'rewrite' or 'reauthor' their individual scripts or at the very least articulate their experiences so precisely that our production might offer an alternative script.

The idea of alternative scripts is powerful, nodding as it does to the intentional act of creating not just one-off stories, but a form of storying that can act as a template. Scripts demand being performed and this in turn demands an audience: scripts are stories to be actioned, repeated, listened and responded to. This process of scripting shifts the story from being an individual concern for the storyteller to something 'outside of themselves'. To enable this for the women participating in the Art of Attachment project Vincent (2023: 59, original emphasis) describes setting 'creative tasks'

> so the women could start to imagine creatively 'staging' their experiences, thoughts and feelings into a visual image, a set of gestures, a duet, a monologue, a list: something *outside* of themselves that could be performed for an audience to 'bear witness', to understand them better, judge them less.

Finding new and diverse forms through which to tell their stories enables clear connections to be made between the women's traumatic early experiences and problems they have experienced as adults, including addiction, domestic violence and the loss of children. The repertoire of possibilities for storytelling expands far beyond the use of words, exploring other forms of expression and communication. The reordering of experiences and writing of new scripts draws on a range of creative media: metaphor; aesthetic devices such as props (wine bottle, baby doll, fake blood, paper); black and white visuals; the use of whispering to layer voices in the work, and so on. Annette, Leah, Louise and Vikki were encouraged by Vincent to 'craft their experiences and feelings into a shape that would be bearable to repeat, that could be more objectively witnessed' (Vincent, 2023: 36). At the same time as making the stories bearable for the women to repeat, the eloquent and compelling art form also makes them bearable for audiences. Meaning is conveyed in layered words, images, sound, movement – engaging multiple senses: these forms take on an equivalent value, which runs counter to the usual hierarchy of knowledge production, where words are king, and written words king of kings. As the form changes, so does its possible reception: audiences do not just hear stories in the form of spoken language but also draw on a range of senses to witness and understand the experiences being communicated. Social workers participating in Art of Attachment workshops recognised that in Art of Attachment they were seeing, hearing, sensing and feeling familiar stories in different ways:

> It's the format and the intensity behind it. It's not necessarily *new* stories: we've heard similar things in terms of the work that we do, but it puts it in a whole different way. (Participant, Art of Attachment workshop)

> I could reflect on a lot of the cases that we are working with that have very similar experiences to these women and I was just thinking about

[how] we used terms like 'the child's been removed', 'the adoption order's gone through'… but when you *watch* the cord representing the umbilical cord and the severing of that relationship and that attachment, it's so powerful and hard hitting. It kind of really hits another note than what happens when you read it off a report. (Participant, Art of Attachment workshop)

The limitations of words to convey emotional and embodied experiences came up repeatedly throughout the fieldwork. Parents reflecting on their experiences also recognised that words are not only inadequate but can harm, or as Annette put it, 'get in the way'.

Words that get in the way

At the beginning of the film production of Art of Attachment Annette makes clear that although she wants to talk about difficult things that have happened to her, words do not help:

> Difficult. It's difficult. I am difficult.
> I was difficult.
> But words get in the way.
> Words I couldn't read get in the way.

Speaking directly to the audience, Vikki invites us to 'picture this', and the words she offers paint a series of pictures depicting the women's lives.

> Words like:
> Birth. Reject. Birth. Reject. Repeat. Birth. Reject.
> Alone. Alone. Miles from Home. Evil man. Abuse. Death. Grieve.
> Reject. Reject. Reject. Dope. Coke. Dope. Coke. Battle.

Whole life stories are presented in a series of disjointed words, spoken here by Leah:

> Escape. Bedsit. 16. Loner. Man. Older. Control. Children. Two children. Escape. Alone. Refuge. Fighting. Courts. Lose. Family. Gone.
> (Art of Attachment script)

It is a life reduced to defining, traumatic events. We are left with a clear impression of the women's lives, but simultaneously, we feel the failure of language to enable the women to tell their stories or communicate their feelings and their needs. The women recount emotions of loneliness, sadness, self-loathing: 'I am stupid', 'I am mad'. They tell of the impossibility of expressing these emotions and the things they have done with words available, words which they can't read or 'don't even wish to say'. Words are not only difficult but obstructive and damaging. The women narrate generational cycles of trauma from birth through multiple instances of rejection punctuated by drugs, drink, violence, death and grief, children and the loss of children and family. These are not coherent stories, but nonetheless they convey recognisable sequences of life events which are all too familiar to anyone with lived or professional experiences of family intervention.

Participants discussed the use of 'sanitised language' which can obstruct understanding. Even if a parent *can* read the words, their meaning might not be clear. Lyn Charlton et al (1998: 4) noted in their study with mothers that

> Birth parents are desperate to understand their rights. Given the emotional crisis caused by the removal of their children, parents often fail to assimilate information at the same time it is given ... Clarity of written information is crucial because the legislative process ... is difficult to understand alongside primal feelings of fighting for one's child.

Parents reported being confused about court proceedings and 'humiliated' that they didn't 'know the words' (Charlton et al, 1998: 19). Conversations in Art of Attachment workshops echoed these findings as social workers reflected on their use of a 'permanency medical' which implies that a child will be placed for adoption ('permanency') imminently, however this might not be clear to birth family. The language of loss is bureaucratic and obfuscating. What one participant described as 'professional jargon' can strip empathy out by using technical terminology. This is captured in a later scene in the Art of Attachment film installation in which one of the performers represents a social worker explaining that 'There's been a process. A rigorous and thorough process. Do you understand? If you don't understand, you can ask me and I'll explain that to you again and again and again until you do understand, OK?' (Art of Attachment script).

Professionals' control over what parents are allowed to know and understand is demonstrated here. If 'you' (child, or parent) don't understand, the explanation, the same words, will be repeated 'again and again until you do understand'. The burden of enabling understanding is not on the professional, beyond their pedagogy of repetition, but on the child or parent who 'with the right support' will 'grow to understand the reasons'.

That many parents who have had their child/ren removed from them for adoption *lack clear understanding of what happened or why* is a social justice issue that resonated with social workers. BTC participated in an Art of Attachment workshop as a team, and as detailed in Chapter 3, they were particularly struck by overlaps between Annette, Leah, Louise and Vikki's stories and the stories told by so many of the parents accessing their service. During my ethnographic research with the BTC team, this scene when Annette talks about the difficulties with words was used in BTC's Power of Words workshops, designed to facilitate parents' reflections on the role of words in relation to their own experiences of losing their child/ren.

The Power of Words

Each Power of Words workshop, facilitated by BTC, involved a parent (or couple) watching the film extract together with their support worker, followed by a craft-based activity where words and phrases were written onto paper labels and leaves. These were hung together on a branch which looked beautiful and which others could see (see Figure 3.5). Just as Charlotte Vincent devised creative tasks during Art of Attachment to make telling difficult stories bearable for the teller, while producing something aesthetically engaging to make it bearable for the audience, this activity used creativity with similar aims. In a practical and meaningful way, the workshop was designed to enable parents to name and challenge words that 'get in the way', as Annette put it, as well as those which enabled them to speak back and have their own words and stories validated and displayed (see Figures 5.1 and 5.2).

Willow, a parent accessing support with BTC, had her own story about how words were used against her in written reports. She suggested if people were to read these reports they would 'get the wrong idea of what has actually happened … They [social workers] don't word it properly. They word it like it was something else than what it actually was' (Willow, parent, Power of Words workshop).

Using the phrase 'they don't word it properly' several times, Willow wrote 'What was written was not true!' on her leaf. This led into discussion of the power professionals have to 'word' a parent's life and the consequences of this. Willow's recollection of why her children were removed is patchy:

> I was sixteen, seventeen, I never had any parents there to help me. All I had was social services and they should have done more. They should have done more to help me. I failed my [parenting] assessment with my oldest one … And then I had my daughter, and in one assessment I passed it, and they moved me from one to another one … and they failed me. So it was very unfair. Yeah. What? What? What was I failed on? I have no idea. Maybe they explained it to me, and I can't remember now. (Willow, parent, Power of Words workshop)

Similarly for Ivy, words written about her in documents had lasting impact and as Ivy put it, 'It takes away your competence'. She talked about how

Figure 5.1: BTC Power of Words workshop: labels written by participants hung on tree: *Hard to find the right words*

having been judged as 'mentally unstable' and having her first child removed made her feel 'I'm just not good enough' and 'not supposed to be a mum'. Ivy has three children; the first has been adopted, the second is in foster care and visits her, and her third is currently in her care. She told us:

> Because of the first time [when child was removed] I always said to myself, 'I'm not supposed to be a mom'. But when I have both kids,

Figure 5.2: BTC Power of Words workshop: label written by participants hung on tree: *What was written was not true*

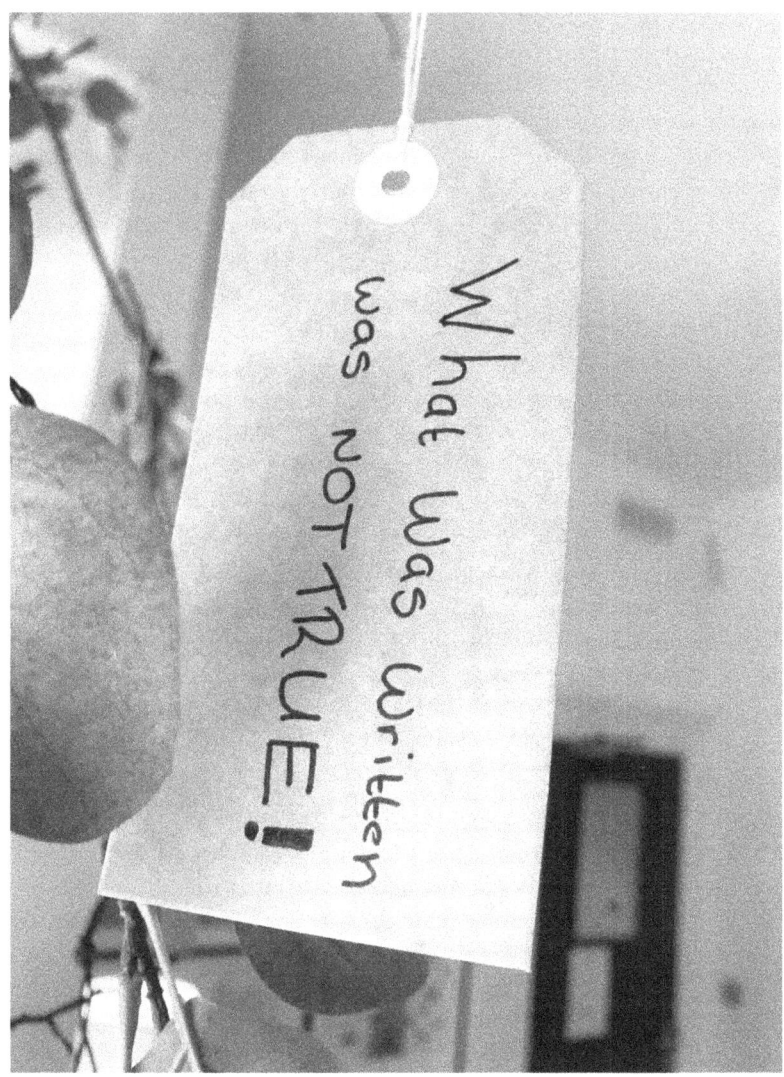

I have like better contact or when I have both kids in my care, [I feel] I am supposed to be a mom. (Ivy, parent, Power of Words workshop)

Not surprisingly, Ivy's feelings of identification with motherhood and her sense of entitlement to claim 'being a mom' follow from her ability to perform this role. This echoes findings from other studies paying attention to the impact of child removal on parents (see Charlton et al, 1998; Memarnia et al, 2015;

Mason et al, 2023). While losing her first child to adoption made Ivy doubt herself, positive parental feelings followed from being able to actively care for her other two children. Ivy wanted to state her feelings about her first experiences of pregnancy and loss to adoption. She told us: 'I don't know how to write this. What I was wanting to write … I just thought like I was just a surrogate. Just someone who was there to have a baby for someone else.' Ivy was helped to write this down on a label (see Figure 5.3) and hang it on the tree.

As well as having these words displayed for others to read and acknowledge, BTC staff amplified Ivy's own positive words (see Figure 5.4) in the workshop:

> I want you to think of the positive things that you shared. You are a good mom. You are doing great … We all feel that and we're glad that you can see that … I love this one: *I'm supposed to be a mom*. I love it. I want you to take ownership of these beautiful powerful words and hang them on the tree. (BTC staff, Power of Words workshop)

Just as the words shared by the four women in Art of Attachment were made beautiful by VDT's devising and scripting process, this simple creative activity of writing on leaves and labels and hanging them on a tree branch validates the words and stories, giving them value not just through the dialogic reassurances but also the aesthetic form. In all the workshops parents struggled to articulate what had happened to them and why it had happened, despite in some cases many years having passed since they had lost their child/ren. What are the consequences of living a life where you don't understand or cannot articulate what has happened to you? Evidence from both Art of Attachment and from parents at BTC shows how parents carry trauma, feel the weight of the words attached to them, and often experience the material impact of life events (homelessness, abuse, losing a child) *without* understanding, or with a very partial and often damaging understanding (see also Syrstad and Slettebø, 2019). This is not due to any lack of intellectual or emotional capacity in the women whose stories are being told. The women who participated in Art of Attachment display high levels of reflexivity and empathy for their own and each other's life stories. Additional documentary materials produced with Annette, Leah and Vikki, where they reflect on the process of making Art of Attachment and its impact on their lives, show how the physical, embodied and relational processes of sharing and exploring experiences through movement, have enabled different and expanded forms of understanding. Similarly for parents accessing support through BTC, different words, and knowledge developed and communicated in different forms, has enabled understanding of themselves and their situations. The issue is not parents' lack of capacity to understand, but rather systemic failures to communicate practical and emotional decisions, outcomes and consequences.

Figure 5.3: BTC Power of Words workshop: label written by participants hung on tree: *Just a surrogate*

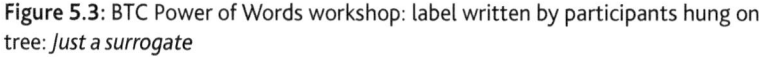

The creative processes described here can be part of enhancing people's understanding of their own lives, as well as offering powerful ways for people damaged by the ways words have been used against them to challenge those scripts and produce new ones. Offering the means for those scripts to be enacted, performed and documented is also important. It widens the expanse and variety of stories available, which is vital. Their inclusion also endorses and makes these stories intelligible in important ways. A member of staff from BTC noted that

Figure 5.4: BTC Power of Words workshop: labels written by participants hung on tree: *I am supposed to be a mom*

Leah [one of the women in Art of Attachment, interviewed by Director Charlotte Vincent and film maker Bosie Vincent about her experiences of participating in it] talked about being a 'role model'. This [Art of Attachment] is an *artwork*. It shows that people want to listen to other people's stories. Many of our service-users feel afraid to tell their stories. We genuinely want to listen. (BTC staff, Art of Attachment workshop)

The fact that the stories the women tell in Art of Attachment – experiences which resonate for many parents accessing BTC – have been made into a public and high-quality art form, gives them value. That Art of Attachment was a public live performance, attended by 300 people, and is a beautiful and compelling film installation, seen by many hundreds more, attests to the fact that people are interested in these stories and want to hear them. They want to listen and understand but rarely get the chance.

Telling hopeful stories, or storying hope in different ways

In one of BTC's Power of Words workshop Elowen, a parent, wanted to talk about words 'used against her', and how they made her feel. This is an extract of the conversation while she was writing words on labels:

Elowen:	[There's] too many words in my head. How do you spell 'violent'?
Staff:	However you would spell it.
	…
Staff:	OK, let's talk about the words that you've chosen, that literally just poured out completely! So we've got 'children will hate you'. Is that all children or your children?
Elowen:	Mine.
Staff:	Your children will hate you. Who's telling you that?
Elowen:	Like everybody. Even professionals.
Staff:	So you feel that from everyone. And do you think you tell yourself that as well?
Elowen:	Sometimes.
Staff:	[reading words] 'Heartless'?
Elowen:	Everybody.
Staff:	'Worthless'.
Elowen:	Everybody.
Staff:	'Failure'.
Elowen:	Everybody, especially my ex-partners; my associates.
Staff:	'Bad role model for my children'.
Elowen:	Everybody.
Staff:	'Scum'. That is a very powerful word. And can you write on this one how all these words leave you feeling inside?
Elowen:	I don't know how to spell it.
Staff:	Spelling doesn't matter. How does that leave you feeling about you?
Elowen:	I don't know how to spell it.
Staff:	[reading] 'Suicidal'.

This exchange opened up conversation about Elowen's suicidal feelings related to losing her children. This was not the first time she had talked these stories or feelings through with BTC staff, but it was the first time she was able to write the words and feelings down and have them documented in this different format.

Elowen:	Two years ago, just before I came here [to BTC] I phoned Samaritans and said 'I'm gonna go' … I was so frightened. And then to find out I was pregnant. I thought 'right, I'm gonna pull my finger out' but in the next [moment] I thought 'I'm gonna lose my kids because of my past, because I'm a druggie'. Sorry to use a word like that.

Staff:	Any word you want to use today is fine. You just spoke about that 'not wanting to be here' feeling, like wanting to end it, and everything feeling too painful …
Elowen:	And that's why I used drugs to try and numb the pain, but obviously it doesn't numb the pain.

Elowen had lost previous children to adoption and had a baby that died. When she became pregnant again with the baby she is now caring for, she was understandably stressed about what would happen to the baby and what the impact of this would be on her own mental health:

Elowen:	I said 'I'm gonna lose her' and when I found out I was pregnant, at first I was thinking abortion.
Staff:	I remember having that chat with you. So why did you think about abortion? What was the feeling inside you that made you think that?
Elowen:	I couldn't do it. I couldn't deal with the heartache, because I said to everybody, 'If I lose her I'm gone' …. In the next scan, my heart said 'I gotta keep her, you can do it'.
Staff:	It was painful. There was a little bit of hope. But there was so much fear.
Elowen:	That's when I asked [BTC keyworker] 'can I do the therapy with her in my belly?'

Elowen asked BTC to be able to undertake the kind of Theraplay[1] which parents usually do with a new baby to support attachment and connection. She engaged with 'prenatal Theraplay' and with ongoing support currently cares for her baby.

Elowen:	I said 'please, just let me a little bit'. Because something was telling me I wasn't going to lose her …
Staff:	There was so much fear and so much anxiety but really wanting to hold on. Really scared to love her.
Elowen:	Of course I love her. She's my child. I couldn't have loved her more … My heart was telling me 'yeah, you can do it, you know, you're getting a second chance.' But my mind was like 'no you're not'.

Staff tell Elowen they want her to hang her words and phrases on the tree: 'The reason I want you to hang them is other parents have gone through similar things and might see your label and think, "I've been through similar stuff".'

The story Elowen can tell here is full of ambivalence. Countering the certainty of written reports and the power of the 'words in my head' that she wrote onto labels in black marker pen, the dialogue that followed showed the complex negotiations she had engaged in, balancing fear and hope, heart and mind. Like the ending of Art of Attachment, detailed in Chapter 4, when the four women take steps forward, hope here is fragile. It is embedded in, and affirmed by, actions such as doing pre-natal therapy. These actions help change the damaging script of her life, in small steps which do not always proceed in linear and uncontested ways.

The reminder from BTC staff that although her story is unique, others have 'been through similar stuff' is validating, replacing judgement with empathy and implying that in telling and documenting her words in this way Elowen might benefit others. This capacity to help others through storytelling was enthusiastically noted by other participants of Power of Words workshops. Linden said 'It's nice my voice is going to be heard … I would love to help all the people here', and Willow was keen to put her feelings into words: 'I'll tell them. I'll put it down [on paper] … If I can make a difference, I will make a difference. And I hope this does make a difference. Because there's a lot of people out there that do need a lot of help' (Willow, Parent, Power of Words workshop).

Sharing stories in this agentic way contributes to transforming individual, often shameful stories into collective narratives where recognition and transformation are possible. The next section considers how stories are not just told in words but are written on bodies, enacted through affective and embodied inter/action and movement.

Embodied and movement-based ways of telling stories

We have seen how words are important to telling stories. The women's re/scripting of their own stories in Art of Attachment as well as parents' outputs in BTC's Power of Words workshops show possibilities for challenging how words are used and using them differently. At the same time, as Julietta Singh (2018a: 21) puts it, 'materiality and language cannot be parsed' or as she states so graphically and beautifully, 'I can feel my fist thinking' (Singh, 2018a: 109). That our fists can think, and our hearts know, is key to making sense of many adoption stories. Singh's (2018a) insights are developed from her experiences of giving birth, which 'critically recalibrated my relationship to my body, and in a real sense made me open to thinking and feeling in ways I had not thought to access before' (Singh, 2018a: 45). Taking us back to a discussion about listening in relation to knowledge generation in Chapter 3, Singh (2018a) draws our attention to the ear as

> the orifice that listens and stabilizes most acutely. The part of the body that modulates social cacophonies, that sometimes selects what it allows in and at other times cannot help but to metabolize the noise

that surrounds it. The unexpected place where the body's equilibrium is produced. (Singh, 2018a: 105)

These insights are astute reminders of how our bodies, feelings, thoughts and intellect are not separate or even entangled: they function together.

Linden is a parent who has been supported by BTC since having her daughter removed from her and adopted over two decades ago. In a Power of Words workshop Linden enacted and vocalised pain, felt in her back, which holds in one place a physical disability she experienced from birth, abuse she has received throughout life because of her disability, and the birth and loss of her daughter. At the time of the workshop, she was struggling to get her doctor to take her 'trauma pain' seriously:

> I'm suffering through trauma ... the GP is referring me back to the gynie [gynaecological department] so we can get some of this trauma pain, so I call it, trauma pain sorted ... When you go through childbirth, and you've still got that pain. Even when I had my hysterectomy, you've still got your trauma because you've had a hysterectomy: your womb's given birth to your child. An obviously, your mom's given birth to you, so it's like a three way system ... I've still got that trauma pain going on. (Linden, parent, Power of Words workshop)

Just as removal of her womb has not reduced the physical pain, the removal of her daughter from her care as a toddler does not mean she is not felt as an ongoing presence for Linden, who talked about being unable to legitimately grieve or adapt to the changing realities of her growing into an adult (Fravel et al, 2000). The reference to her own birth alludes to generational trauma, associated in Linden's mind with the act and pain of birth. The account in words necessarily lacks coherence but the pain, for Linden, has explanatory power and her frustration is that others, in this case medical professionals, cannot understand the story this pain tells. If they could hear it in its totality and understand the connections over time as Linden can, perhaps it could be treated differently. Her account reminded me of the dying migrants whose stories Yasmin Gunaratnam (2012, 2013) attended to using the concept of 'total pain'. Taken from palliative care and articulated in the work of Cecily Saunders (1964), total pain 'interpolates, and at times creolizes, physical, social, psychological and spiritual pain ... It also gives recognition to pain that is accrued over a lifetime' (Gunaratnam, 2012: 109). Like the sociologist Pierre Bourdieu's (1999) idea of 'social suffering', recognising radically different forms of suffering as pain experienced simultaneously, can bring structural injustices and individual experiences into the same frame of a person's embodied life over time. Pain is often seen as a 'destroyer' of language (Gunaratnam, 2012: 110; see also Scarry, 1985); however, 'total pain' points towards pain as a *different kind* of language. Thinking of Linden's pain, some aspects of her physical pain might be treatable with medical attention; other facets of her grief and loss might not be so easily resolvable but attending to them in Linden's terms – *as pain* – might enable them to be lessened. At the same time, being able to hear and encounter another's pain as knowledge widens our understanding of different experiences of adoption. Singh's (2018a) work also helps us think about how such pain-as-knowledge might be accommodated in archival form or as archival practice.

We see how this capacity to be with parents' pain is a core part of BTC's relational work in the next chapter. There is need to incorporate pain-based knowledge into adoption scholarship. The extreme mental distress of mothers following removal of their children is well documented (Neil, 2013; Morriss and Broadhurst, 2022). Karen Broadhurst and Claire Mason's (2020) study notes psycho-social damage to mothers following the removal of their child/ren. In these accounts pain and trauma is evidenced, but how this pain might be felt and known as an embodied experience, in the way Linden evokes above, remains implicit. Research critical of removal of babies at birth (see Broadhurst and Mason, 2013; Broadhurst et al, 2015; Bilson and Bywaters, 2020) details some of the stresses and injustices of this painful severance. As Paul Connerton (1994: 72) notes, 'memory is sedimented, amassed, in the body'. Memories might be experienced in sensory ways but not made sense of, perhaps cannot be made sense of, in language. This is recognised in popular psychology and 'self-help' books (Van der Kolk, 2014; Menakem, 2017; Mann and Rabin, 2024) and informs attachment-based parenting. Children do not need cognitive memories to remember early traumatic experiences through embodied and sensory recall (Elliott, 2013). However, binary separation of mind/body and mental/physical pains and treatments dominates mainstream understanding and provision of both physical and psychological services and the development and validation of research methodologies and evidence.

What the Art of Attachment film installation and work with BTC showed was that *moving* was a key component in preventing stories becoming 'stuck', like Linden's 'trauma pain', in bodies. The collaboration with Vincent Dance Theatre was vital in being able to see and feel what 'being moved', both emotionally and physically, could do in terms of shifting traumatic knowledges and stories into forms which could be shared. As Vincent (2023: 83) explains 'There is a reciprocal connection between movement and meaning. Both movement and metaphors can bridge an individual's inside world with the outside, and vice versa enabling invisible realities to be made visible.'

The crafting of clay and paper in workshops likewise enabled participants to shift feelings held inside to an external form, and to bring thoughts back into embodied form through activity. In Art of Attachment, as we saw in detail in the previous chapter, movement constitutes a powerful form of storytelling. Partnering work demonstrates the interdependency of humans making meaning through attachments and detachments. For the women involved, the process of learning to move in this way was a new way of being in their bodies and relating to others. It took time to build trust and confidence. In one of the scenes, Vikki is told to 'get on your feet. Stand up on your feet now!': there are echoes of 'stand on your own two feet' as an indicator of taking responsibility and being independent. The partnering work permits *not* standing on your (own two) feet, showing how important and perhaps inevitable it is to sometimes fall, and allow others to fall. This theme is taken up in consideration of vital interdependencies in Chapter 7.

Stories need to be heard and validated, whether they are expressed in words, or embodied action. Creative interventions enable grief to be articulated and heard, on its own terms. It is widely recognised in adoption literature that the losses experienced by both parents and children are experienced as 'disenfranchised' (Doka, 1999; Geddes, 2021; Mason et al, 2023). Deblasio (2021: 55) notes that 'With adoption there is no physical or psychological ending. The birth mother is catapulted into bereavement and loss: the grieving process starts but may never end'. This feeling of never-ending grief was articulated clearly by parents: Linden told us

> I've got a friend … and she says to me, your child is still alive, it's not like mine, dead, and I said 'hold on a bit. I'm sorry for your loss, but at least you can go down to their grave and visit the grave, and that's trauma, I understand that, but at least you can do that'. I can't, I can't put a lid on mine. (Linden, parent workshop)

Not only can Linden not 'put a lid on it' but she describes how, 'you constantly got it with you all the time, you know what I mean? … you can't really switch off'. It not possible for her to mourn the loss of her child, and there are ongoing griefs associated with the attachments she has to her now adult daughter. Linden's own metaphor for the layers of complex grief is that it is 'like a cabbage … when I came to BTC years ago, I didn't know where to start to unravel the cabbage'. Being able to tell the stories of loss and trauma are part of that unravelling.

Conclusion

The discussion here lends weight to the belief that stories are powerful and that telling and hearing them can have important and often positive effects. However, it also troubles some of the common-sense notions of storytelling, emphasising the ambivalent and risky nature of speaking and representing trauma. At the same time, the multi-modal use of words, sound, props and bodies to re/present stories in Art of Attachment draws attention to their constructed nature and the value of non-verbal modalities as methods for communicating lives. Arts interventions not only enable a different type of storytelling but they problematise accepted norms and tropes of and around storytelling in relation to trauma. In the wider political context where any heartbreak is silenced and disenfranchised griefs are disallowed, re/framing experiences of adoption as heartbreak is a radical act.

Further, the analysis here seeks to understand what knowledges about adoption can be articulated and heard through emotional and embodied experiences. Michelle Caswell (2020: 155) observes that

> we can simultaneously hold the existence of facts and validate the epistemic importance of feelings. It is not either/or. It is both/and. But it is always an issue of the stories we choose to tell. It is always an issue of how we deploy the evidence to tell stories.

Allowing heartbreaking stories to be told and heard, and re/presenting experiences of grief and loss through any media, is risky work, raising questions of ethics and power. Although it can seem that the telling of stories redresses power imbalances where people and their experiences have been rendered invisible, storytelling is not inherently liberatory and can make vulnerable people more vulnerable in certain contexts. As addressed in Chapter 3, methodologies underpinning the research on which this book draws were mindful of these vulnerabilities and used strategies for minimising risks. These included a slow, patient approach to build safety, making use of methods that enabled participants to tell their stories in ways that felt comfortable to them, using movement and creative materials. In Vincent Dance Theatre's work, movement-based processes facilitate relationships of trust and reciprocity. There is a focus on partner-based work, experimenting with relations of power, vulnerability, intimacy. In this way communicating with bodies and movement precedes or runs parallel to verbal communication. Movement is again generated in the following chapter with a focus on emotion. Building on the arguments that heartbreak and hope are both vital for generating knowledges that move our understanding and fuel possibilities for political change, Chapter 5 attends empirically to the routine work of supporting parents undertaken by BTC.

6

The emotional complexities of adoption

Introduction

Troubling Adoption considers emotion as an *epistemological* and *political* resource and concern. Emotional knowledges need to be made intelligible and validated. Affect and policy making are inseparable, and their interconnections must be taken seriously (Jupp, 2022). Previous chapters have demonstrated the importance of using methods able to generate and make sense of emotions whether communicated in words or embodied actions. We need to attend to emotion in our analyses and explicate the role of emotion in relation to political power, whether that power be used to dominate and control, or for social transformation. As Gargi Bhattacharyya (2023: 111) claims:

> For those of us dreaming and hoping and scheming for a better world, heartbreak must have its place. We cannot afford to sideline grief, both the grief of human loss and the heartbreak of wasted or disrespected lives. Somehow, we must both resist the push to manage and fix heartbreak and also make a politics that seeks to render heartbreak a thing of the past. Heartbrokenness might be seen as the complex grief of a broken world, necessarily resistant to therapeutic interventions because there is no reasonable response to what we know of the world other than heartbreak.

Heartbreak needs to be at the heart of any project of reform (see also Eng, 2010; Carland and Cvetkovich, 2013). 'Who can imagine another world', asks Bhattacharyya (2023: 15) 'unless they already have been broken apart by the world we are in?'

The discussion here explores the everyday enactment of social work practice with parents, enabling close attention to be paid to the emotional complexities of breaking and making families through adoption. Research demonstrates that adoption results in grief and loss which endures over not just lifetimes but generations. For an adopted child, separation from their birth family leaves a traumatic legacy which cannot be 'managed and fixed'. For parents whose children are removed from them, their loss is not a one-off traumatic event but something they must live with and navigate for the rest of their lives: it is part of who they are and shapes who and what they can become. We saw in the previous chapter that such griefs are disenfranchised, lacking narrative validation and recognition. The work of supporting parents who have experienced this loss, such as undertaken by staff at Breathe, Trust, Connect (BTC) is emotional work. The discussion in this chapter considers different emotions involved in social work, offering analysis of data generated through ethnographic research with BTC (for an account of BTC's service and the research undertaken with them, see Chapter 3). It demonstrates the complex emotional labour of sitting with, and walking alongside, people who are heartbroken. It also provides insight into the emotions involved in other aspects of family intervention including the removal of children from families. It shows how the temporalities of being with grief in this way are (and must be) different to the usual (fast) pace and (tight) timeframes of social work interventions. This empirical analysis lays groundwork for pragmatic suggestions about reform and intervention within social care and children's services in Chapter 8.

Alongside this detailed discussion of day-to-day practice, a more abstract argument for the central role of heartbreak in adoption reform is articulated. This politics of refusing to either ignore or rush to resolve and repress heartbreak is evident in the embodied actions of BTC staff and their relational work with parents. It is also part of a bigger picture in that a reformed vision and plan for child protection, and the role of adoption within that, needs to hold onto the knowledge heartbreak provides. Any plan for change of current practice that does not do so ignores vital understandings about contemporary adoption which take the form of emotional knowledge. The discussion turns now to the importance of practical support and relational connection in establishing safety as an essential foundation on which other therapeutic work builds. The different temporal demands this makes are considered. The importance of clinical supervision for enabling BTC to operate as a therapeutic service is addressed: this not only enables their own work but means they can support colleagues. A case is developed for resourcing services that not only support parents directly but by enabling safety, relational connection and empathy in colleagues, influence outcomes for children and families.

Establishing safety: the interconnections between emotional and practical support

When parents first come to BTC, the focus is on establishing 'safety' for them. This refers to both physical and emotional security, recognising that they are intertwined. Safety is the basis of all other work: being able to build a relationship, making practical changes, accessing therapeutic support, reflecting on the past and making decisions about the present and future. Ayla gave me an example of a mother who was new to the service:

> [I asked her] 'what do you need me to get for you, for you to get here?' ... she was very much 'I'm not getting the bus. I don't feel comfortable'. So it was fine, I told her 'I'll get you a taxi'. And then I asked her what kind of snacks she's wanting or what she needed, in terms of her feeling safe and comfortable, so that we really enjoy meeting, and she said, 'I really enjoy knitting'. So that's what I got, some wool and some knitting needles ... She started knitting on the way back home and sent me a video of it. And I've ... had the conversation about 'is it easier for you to be doing an activity and talking to me?' And she said 'Yeah ... I'd rather have something in my hands'. (Ayla, BTC staff interview)

Here the attention to helping meet parents' practical needs (the taxi for transport) extends to what will enable this parent to feel 'safe and comfortable'. These are not peripheral issues: if mum is not feeling safe and comfortable, she may not attend or be able to fully participate. Ayla also notes wanting her to 'enjoy meeting' – this simple relational care being central to the development of safety and trust on which other things depend. We see here the importance of asking (rather than assuming) what people want and need and find pleasure in and responding to that without judgement. The knitting is not only a regulatory activity but also enhances the relationship between them, providing a talking point and a prompt for ongoing communication via texts and videos.

Sylvia told me about one mum 'who couldn't sit down' and how identifying a mechanism for her to self-regulate was key to her being able to engage in her assessment: 'When she first came to meet me, I think thirteen times ... she stood up, left the room, walked around. [She] ... physically couldn't sit still ... Over a number of weeks we were able to start to be safe enough to be in the room together.'

What made a difference was having drinks and sweets which enabled sensory regulation as well as possibility for taking some control in a context where parents have very little power:

> Having a can of fizzy coke really, really helped ... [and] if I actually took a sweet first and modelled being able to regulate as I chewed on this sweet, that's something that could really help. Like modelling taking a breath and [saying] 'gosh, that's really hard'. And then *she'd* be able to take that breath ... This was all over a period of time ... By the time it got to the initial Child Protection Conference, she could take those skills into that meeting ... 'This is my drink; this is the drink that helps me. And then in those moments, I can have a drink' ... That meant

that that Child Protection Conference was a very different experience. (Sylvia, BTC staff interview)

We see the power of modelling behaviour to show how a simple sensory activity (chewing a sweet, sipping a cold fizzy drink) could provide essential emotional regulation, which in turn meant this mum could stay still, be in the meeting room, and engage with the process. These strategies may seem small and easy to implement, however they are dependent on the ability of staff to work 'over a period of time' to build trust and safety. There were many such examples shared during interviews and observed during my time with BTC: detailed, concrete illustrations of how modelling coping strategies, and identifying the practical, achievable mechanisms for parents to regulate their own emotions, led to much better outcomes for parents. What these examples have in common is attention to sensory aspects of regulation, and the time necessary to undertake this work. These outcomes were not achievable through verbal instructions – 'just sit down and stay still during your meetings!' – and the modelling of strategies such as taking a breath, chewing a sweet, sipping a drink happen through patient repetition, not instruction. Patient, repetitive, slow: these are the qualities necessary to achieve these outcomes.

The work of BTC is underpinned by recognition that vulnerability is a necessary starting point for parents to do the difficult work of reflecting on what has happened to them in their own childhoods, in their relationships and their role as parents. As Sylvia put it, 'Parents need support; parents need somewhere safe to be vulnerable. How can you be brave and courageous if you can't be vulnerable? Because the two things aren't separate'. Without being able to be vulnerable, as we see in later examples, parents cannot regulate their emotional responses and often struggle to move beyond defensive emotions such as anger and fear. For any of us to admit vulnerability we need to have a degree of safety. For BTC staff, this commitment to 'cherishing parents' – echoing John Bowlby's (1951: 84) claim that 'if we value our children, we must cherish their parents' – involves difficult and painful work, creating and maintaining space and time for parents to feel safe so other outcomes can be achieved. Such work makes significant emotional demands on staff as individuals and as a team. They need to work actively to maintain their *own* emotional regulation if they are to be the support that grieving parents need. As all services, the team operates within the requirements and regulations of the wider social care system. At the same time, they navigate these systemic limitations and possibilities while holding emotional regulation at the heart of the service:

> We've developed a model that recognises where people are at when they come in through the front door. So rather than ... asking somebody to

go right back to think about some really painful trauma that's happened in their own childhood, we have recognised that unless somebody really has established safety with us, that we're asking them to do something that's not ethical … and isn't safe for either party for that to happen. (Laurel, BTC staff interview)

This model informs the progression of work from practical relationship building through to more in-depth therapeutic interventions. Laurel recognises that when people first access the service, they

> might have lots of chaos surrounding them. They might … [be] about to be evicted. They're up to their eyes in debt. They're really isolated … They might have serious mental health issues that aren't being addressed by the relevant services. So a connection and integration service stabilises a person, the main aim of which is to establish safety for them. To remove the danger from their life as much as we can do, so that they're then in a place to be able to emotionally start to think about their own needs. (Laurel, BTC staff interview)

This 'stabilisation' can take time, both in terms of addressing practical needs (housing, debt, poor mental or physical health) but also building the necessary trust for them to feel safe. Once such stability is in place 'actual therapeutic interventions' can be made. In Laurel's words these involve 'Theraplay, Prenatal Theraplay, Circle of Security Parenting course, the parenting pathway and therapeutic life story work, which is looking back on the past and mourning the losses'. There is no automatic progression to this kind of therapeutic intervention, rather for some parents

> therapeutic life story work comes way down the line, because they're not ready for that. Because if they're focusing on having a safe pregnancy and going on to keep their baby, that's not the time to start going right back to … abuse and trauma … But that [work] will come. (Laurel, BTC staff interview)

Initially, practical support may be the priority. There were many examples of the kinds of support needed and offered. Basic survival needs, such as for food and housing, were frequently being unmet. My research notes from a stay-and-play session document how

> Sara has a 13-month-old. She was talking to a member of staff about getting hold of a food voucher. She said 'that would come in very

useful at the moment. We haven't got any food. Nothing to eat tonight. I feel like a bad mum because I can't provide. We haven't got money for the electricity'. She was getting upset and rocking, and her leg was shaking. She kept repeating, 'it's doing my head in at the moment, going round and round in my head'.

Many families who have a child or children removed by the state experience other social problems such as poverty, homelessness and poor health (Skinner et al, 2023; Featherstone and Gupta, 2023). For parents accessing support through BTC, their most urgent preoccupations were often material. They were unlikely to be able to engage with therapeutic work if they could not secure enough food for themselves or their family or were struggling to access transport or find adequate housing. Therapeutic Support Workers' primary role is to help parents identify and navigate these concerns. For support worker Ayla, the priorities were '"Let's go shopping together" or "let's go for a walk together". I've got one mother doesn't go on a bus; she only uses the taxis and even then, she's frightened. So, you know, "let's do this together"' (Ayla, BTC staff interview).

In recognising this mother's practical needs around transport, Ayla notes the emotions involved – 'she's frightened'. Similarly, Olive recounted work she is doing with a pregnant mum, acknowledging the negative emotional blocks to doing ordinary activities:

She's 16 weeks pregnant, and she's had two previous children removed. She's very anxious about the upcoming pre-birth assessment. And she just finds day-to-day living quite difficult … so I'd go shopping with her and help her do her meal planning. And we've got a diary with all her appointments in, and I support her to go to those appointments, sit with her at the hospital, go to scans with her … She doesn't have any friends. She doesn't have a family … She knows she's going to have to go through a Children's Services Assessment. She's scared … It's just being that person that's at her side, really just walking alongside her. (Olive, BTC staff interview)

Olive names the anxiety and fear experienced by this mum. She also recognises that without family and friends to take a supporting role, she has a need for someone 'walking alongside her'. *Walking alongside* is very different to sitting in a judgemental or assessing role and both these roles should be available within a child protection encounter. To walk alongside involves acceptance and a willingness to 'be with' a person as they navigate complex experiences. This idea of 'being with' extends to difficult emotional connections at later stages of the relational work but begins here with basic tasks and support. Ayla similarly recounted:

> I've got two moms that I've worked with before they had baby and … I'm still working with them. So then the support has been very much 'let's go to play groups'. You know, baby's unwell, 'let's go to the GP together' … That work really does continue for mom. (Ayla, BTC staff interview)

The repetition of doing everyday things together, in what Ayla calls 'bite-size' chunks, gives us insight to the kinds of minimum support necessary for many parents. A parent who has previously lost their child or children to adoption might struggle with attending play groups and taking their baby to the doctors. Having someone do these things with them is time and resource intensive but enhances the possibility of the family staying together.

Another key struggle for parents was around housing. Inadequate housing and the stress caused by constantly moving were raised frequently by staff and accommodation worries came up in conversations with parents. Many parents were living in sub-standard accommodation which was unsuitable for their own or their family's needs. This could become a critical factor if a mother was pregnant and being assessed. Hazel noted that when someone's pregnant

> they don't need that worry. They think 'if I haven't got a property, they're going to take my baby off me'. Even now Ash doesn't really want to say 'I'd like a two bedroom property'. Because she's like, 'well, they're gonna think I'm refusing the one-bedroom property. And then what about my child?' … [She] can't see it logically, because she's just scared. (Hazel, BTC staff interview)

Being scared in this context is an understandable and arguably proportionate response. Hazel was aware that lack of adequate housing is 'a contributing factor to someone not being able to parent their child'. The stakes are clearly high for parents in this precarious position. However, resolving their housing issues is not always within a parent's capabilities. In turn this puts pressure on social workers. As Hazel continues, social workers

> don't prioritise housing, but it's probably to do with their caseload, because the majority [of parents] are experiencing some sort of housing issue. Applications, they do take a while. So, I think it's something to do with time and capacity as well.

In the current context of a national crisis in housing, with limited social housing and affordable private rented accommodation available, the most vulnerable people in society can be left struggling to access a safe and appropriate home (Spratt, 2023; Hagen and Ahmed, 2025). This crisis is compounded by the fact that social workers are not routinely able to support struggling parents with issues such as housing because of excessive caseloads and more urgent priorities (Murphy et al, 2024). We see here the practical, sometimes banal labour necessary to support parents. Everyone needs safe housing, the ability to travel, to make and attend appointments, go shopping, and so on. Without these things, is not possible for parents to manage their grief and create liveable lives for themselves after losing their child/ren to adoption, or to demonstrate their ability to successfully care for subsequent children (Philip et al, 2020). We see the vital interconnections between emotional and material safety and stability. As identified by wider research, intensive support to help parents develop these skills – Featherstone et al's (2014: 96) 'ordinary help' – can pay off. Many BTC staff recounted a process whereby they model skills, then encourage parents until they can do things independently. This process of 'walking alongside' parents may take years, and their progress from helplessness to independence may not always be linear.

Time and space, rhythm and pace

BTC are unusual as a service in offering an open-ended, flexible timeframe for parents to engage. Most services and programmes are time-bound, with activities or goals against which to mark time (DfE, 2020; Jondec and Barlow, 2023). Although it is understandable that under-resourced services would put time-limits on accessing support programmes such as this, the findings here highlight the importance of taking time and slowing things down when doing this kind of emotional work. Rowan told me:

> A lot of teams or services are like, 'you get six weeks of this, or this is what you're doing on week one, two, three'. Whereas here … we're not going to rush you … it's your pace. We'll try stuff. If you don't like it, we'll try something else. You know, it's that flexibility, which is important because everybody's different … On this team someone will say 'I've just done that session, and all we've done is talk about this' and it's like, *that is the work* … it sometimes doesn't feel like work … just give them that space and that time, and that's part of the work. (Rowan, BTC staff interview)

Staff spoke frequently of the need to abandon pre-conceived outcomes and create and hold space to be with parents, to often simply witness and acknowledge their feelings. Olive talked about her work with a pregnant mother and the example illustrates the importance of time to being able to access a different 'version' of a parent in crisis. Olive highlights what this mum was like when she first accessed BTC:

> she made comments like 'well my other kids got took off of me because they were really cute and social workers were on commission' ... [It] was easier for her to believe those kinds of things.

Three months later, things are very different:

> now in our sessions, she understands that she made some difficult decisions. I mean, she was very young, and she didn't have a lot of choices available to her, but she made some poor choices and she's able to accept those now, and she's trying to make changes so that doesn't happen again ... It's only been fourteen weeks, and she's moved this far. And I think it's more that she *knew* it before, it's just that her defences were up ... now, she could be more vulnerable with me. So she has moved along, and I keep thinking, with the right support ... I am a holder of hope that she can do this. (Olive, BTC staff interview)

There are several important points raised here by Olive. Through a trauma-informed lens, Olive can see this mother's initial defensive stance as necessary protection: she was unable to be vulnerable enough to acknowledge such painful things at that stage. As the mother's levels of safety increased, she could recognise what had gone wrong previously, a vital step in being able to do things differently if she is to be able to keep her baby in her care. The other significant thing in Olive's account is the recognition that this mother has 'moved this far' in 'only' 14 weeks. Of course, Olive is right that fourteen weeks is a small amount of time for a significant shift in thinking and behaviour. However, it also highlights the difficulties with the tight timeframes of parenting assessments (Alrouh et al, 2022; Broadhurst et al, 2022). It is possible to imagine a very different scenario for this mum: without the patient, hopeful support of BTC, an assessment of her stuck in that early defensive mode would have been unable to judge her capable of taking enough responsibility to adequately parent her next child. Keziah, speaking more generally about pre-birth assessments, noted the impact of the lack of time:

> For a parent to relax and trust, they need to build a relationship. A social worker comes in, and ... it's a short time. Sometimes they're not starting [assessment] until weeks before the baby's born. They don't take into consideration postnatal depression and the trauma of just giving birth, the fact that this parent is aware that they're being assessed or it's triggering old emotion of when they had the last child removed. It is

> ... processes and assessments and processes and assessments ... they are assessed beyond humanity. (Keziah, BTC staff interview)

Echoing findings from a wider literature, Keziah expresses the impossibility of working empathetically and building trust within the short timeframe and structure of assessment, highlighting conditions prescribed by assessment processes, compounded by high caseloads and emotional pressures on assessing social workers (Harris, 2012; Murphy, 2023). Such workers must often make high-stakes decisions to safeguard children. BTC staff were keenly aware that they themselves do not need to make such decisions, a factor which significantly impacts on their ability to build trusting relationships and remain non-judgemental about parents. In contrast, assessing social workers *are* required to judge, and provide appropriate evidence to support that judgement, within tight timeframes. For the mother in Olive's example above, we can see how important it is for her to be able to access BTC in order that a different kind of therapeutic space and time be generated alongside the assessment. Whatever the outcome for this mum, the assessment will be fairer for having given her chance to acknowledge what, as Olive highlights, she knew all along, but was unable to articulate.

There was also recognition that the 'slow' model of sitting with parents' grief and working at their pace is not only undoable in urgent assessment situations but that some front-line social workers, used to the 'adrenaline' of the crisis, find it frustrating and unproductive:

> we've had members of [front-line] staff that have come to our service and hated it and said 'I can't work at this therapeutic level. What are you doing? We're not doing anything! I need to have the cases. And I need to be on the front-line. And I like the adrenaline of it being really, really busy'. (Keziah, BTC staff interview)

'Front-line' was shorthand for colleagues working in safeguarding teams whose primary responsibilities are to safeguard children and whose relationship with birth parents is therefore characterised by assessment and the pressure to make life-changing decisions within tight time frames. Differences between the kinds of emotional work undertaken by different social services personnel were regularly commented upon by BTC staff. BTC are conscious of being a therapeutic service and benefiting from clinical supervision. They considered their therapeutic responsibilities as not just being towards their parent clients but also towards each other and towards other colleagues, particularly those on the adrenaline-fuelled front-line:

> you're dealing with ... heartbreaking situations in people's lives ... it's hard to make assessments and make difficult decisions. For example,

children have to be removed. But in a way, that adrenaline … kind of makes that doable, maybe. But when you've got to just sit with it, then, you know, how do you manage? (Holly, BTC staff interview)

With her rhetorical 'how do you manage?' Holly draws attention to the impossible emotional demands on professionals working with parents whose children have been taken away from them by the state. She hypothesises that the 'adrenaline' of front-line work, the urgency of needing to safeguard a child, makes the act of removal 'doable', but without the urgency or adrenaline, 'you've just got to sit with it'. Together with 'walking alongside', 'sitting with' parents and their grief surfaced many times as central to the work of BTC, invoking not just the practical labour of being with a parent in their time of emotional distress but also the emotional labour of being able to be with another person's unbearable grief. As we see in the following section, being able to sit with grief and sadness rather than rushing to fix problems prioritises what BTC consider the most important aspect of social worker labour: emotional regulation.

Emotional regulation and relational connection

Writing on the political significance of heartbreak, Bhattacharyya (2023: 27) highlights the importance of 'travelling with sadness' rather than sidelining or trying to fix it. Parents' grief at losing their child/ren to adoption does not always manifest as a problem that can be 'solved'. This can be challenging for professionals working with them, who have become social workers expecting to problem-solve. It demands a different perspective on birth parents and a different kind of emotional labour to work with them. In interview, Olive provided a more detailed account of this:

> I've been a social worker for a long time. I've been involved in child protection … where sadly children have to be removed for safeguarding reasons. And so I thought that I knew what it was like for the birth parent and what support I could offer. But now being on the other side of that … [I am] working with a mum who's had her two children placed into foster care because of her difficulties. I've been that social worker, that's had to take those children to their placement. But I've never been the person that sat whilst mum falls apart, and she's completely broken and [I've] had to sit through that pain with them. And that's a very different feeling. It's, you know, it's social work, but it's very, very different. I mean, I've seen parents become upset. I've seen people in court. I've seen people distressed, but I guess it kind of made me realise that I've never sat through that pain with them … This role now shows you exactly what they do need. And that isn't a

number for a crisis mental health line. It's someone to listen to them and to sit with them through those moments.

I have quoted Olive at length because this example is important in highlighting the difference between statutory support and 'sitting with' people through their pain. Distinct from the removed witnessing of grief – 'I've seen parents become upset' – this role demands *being with* emotional distress, without the relief of resolutions. What positive 'outcomes' or consolations can be documented here? In instances like the one Olive describes above, common to their daily work at BTC, travelling with sadness needs to be recognised as constructive, not offering easy or immediate answers or transformations, but allowing sadness to be acknowledged for what it is.

This is incredibly hard for anyone working in family care services. There is an (understandable) tendency to rush to solutions and positive outcomes (stepping down a child protection order, placing a child for adoption) which might provide temporary feelings of closure for professionals and others involved, but can mask ongoing issues and create new ones. Olive reflected on a positive outcome for a parent, whose child was allowed to remain in their care:

> I went to a Child Protection Conference … It was stepped down and the message was very much like 'we don't want to see you again', like 'well done' … you know, 'we've fixed this now. Don't be coming back' … and it's just not reflective of life, or trauma, because it is going to be triggered again at some point and people that have had child protection involvement from when they were babies or even before they were born, they're likely to at some point have children's service involvement again but … they become so afraid that they don't ask for help and it becomes harder and harder … The problem doesn't end. It's not fixed. (Olive, BTC Raw Emotions workshop)

Olive's reflections here do not take away from the positive outcome of removing a child protection order and enabling a child to stay with their parent/s, however they challenge this outcome as an unconditionally positive solution, pointing to the need for ongoing support for parents to make change sustainable. This challenges the 'fixing' approach to complex problems. To see such problems through the lens of trauma is to recognise that the whole idea of fixing is flawed and calls for very different models of understanding and validating successful outcomes. As Sylvia noted in interview, a shift in thinking is needed from 'There isn't an answer but we're going to find one anyway' to 'There isn't one. To coming back to slowing down and listening, to breathing, and that regulation … That is where there is hope'.

Figure 6.1: Origami heart produced by participant in Art of Attachment workshops: *If you never recover, I understand*

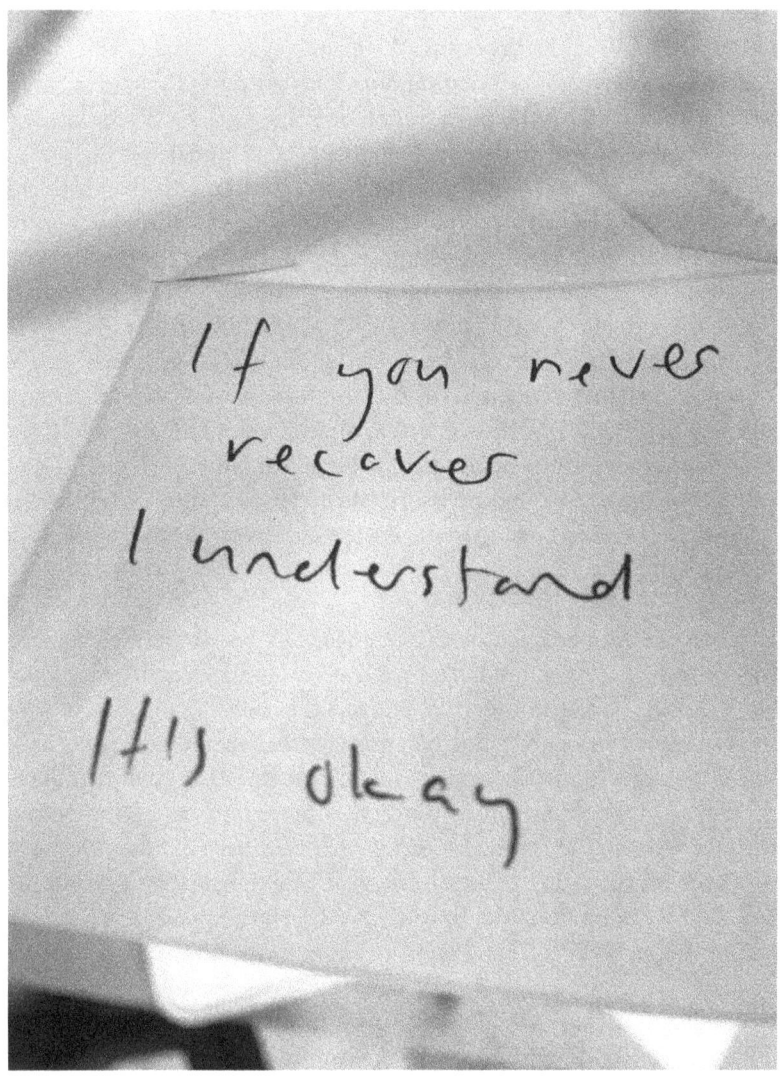

What that might look like in practice was described in detail by Sylvia when she talked about a mum she was working with, who after having lost previous children to adoption was being supported by BTC to care for her new baby. Sylvia describes their work in Theraplay sessions:

> This mum was completely disconnected. So much pain that she wasn't allowing; she was so blocked off, because that's how she had to be to

keep herself safe, just to carry on breathing and living her life. And that baby just reciprocated that blank face herself … I increase sessions to twice a week, because there's a significant level of need. You come in every single week. And yes, it's painful for me to sit there and share this feeling of [breaks off].

Sylvia broke away from the example, in a manner that displayed the conflicts of the scenario, before saying 'I just want to pick up this baby and hug her myself'. The painful feeling remains unnamed. Although she just wanted to hug the baby, a quick and immediate response which would have made Sylvia feel much better, she knew this was not what mum and baby needed. She demonstrates being torn between intervening, and the knowledge that separation of mum and baby would also be the wrong outcome. Instead, Sylvia needed to work on her own pain at watching the difficult interactions so that she can 'sit aside this mum for long enough to then be able to get to where we need to get to'. For Sylvia, this was only possible because she received clinical supervision to discuss her own feelings and be reassured of her strategy of continuing to build trust and supporting mum to emotionally engage with her baby herself. In another example, we can see and feel close-up the specific emotional demands placed on BTC staff and the kinds of infrastructural support needed in terms of time and supervision. Sylvia told me how

> I did a Theraplay session … when she was bottle feeding … The little one must have been about seven or eight months at this point. I can still feel the activation within my own system of how uncomfortable this was to watch. If you can imagine, basically mum's holding the bottle at the wrong angle. So the little one's gulping in air. Mum's not aware of this and baby is like squirming, spluttering. [It was] really, really uncomfortable to watch the level of mis-attunement.

When Sylvia relayed this memory, she was taken back to the feelings of intense discomfort, and listening to her I could feel it too, experiencing the urge to quickly intervene and adjust the position of the bottle, to end baby's and our own discomfort. However, Sylvia knew that this quick feeling of relief for her and the baby would do damage to the fragile relational connection she was building with the mother. It would also have taken away the mother's own capacity to notice and resolve this situation herself. Rather than 'jumping in to rescue or to judge' Sylvia recognised that

> I had to regulate myself, to be like, *this is happening every day. This is how this mum feeds her baby*. So how I respond to this matters, because if I shame her … and make this about you feeding her wrong, then it's going to be a rupture [in our relationship] that we might not get

over. And this is really, really sensitive. But this is how you feed your baby. And this is partly why she's so uncomfortable. And this is why baby's not settled, and then completely shuts down because their mum is [shut down]. So you can just imagine … this cycle.

In a different social care setting, without the therapeutic framing and emotional attunement of the worker, this realisation that mum is not feeding baby properly could be handled very differently and with very different outcomes. Here the difference between BTC and other social work professionals is highlighted:

We're not assessing this mum. So I'm not going to write down and report that to anyone because no one needs to know. The person that needs to know is mum. And mum needs to know that *safely*. So … how I respond and how mum experiences [my response] will have the biggest impact on the child.

In a culture driven by assessment and judgement and a heightened sense of fear of risk, these insights by Sylvia are incredibly powerful. She is completely aware of how serious this is for baby and has the baby's interests at the forefront of her concerns. She also knows that improving things for the baby not just in this session, but beyond it, depends on how she handles the situation. She needs to enable mum to become aware herself and change her feeding method 'safely'. The trust between her and mum would be damaged by her taking the bottle and feeding the child herself, shaming mum in the process. Sylvia's decision was informed by her belief that the outcomes for that baby will be better if mum continues to access support from BTC with the longer-term aim of being able to keep her baby in her care. She continued:

The answer isn't to whip her out and give her to a foster carer, and then another foster carer, and then another foster carer, and then she might go on to adoption … That isn't the answer. Actually, no one is going to meet this child's need like her mum, if we can make it safe for her to be there … The role we have is ultimately about regulating. It's about having a workforce that can regulate themselves enough not to bring in the judgement, not to bring in the rescue, not to bring in the 'this is a better way' … 'I'm going to write down everything you're doing wrong'. But to keep it about relational connection. Because I wanted to … feed baby myself. But mum would still have gone home and fed her the same way.

Sylvia's explanation here provides evidence of the vital importance of small, careful and caring practice, enacted within the 'bigger picture' of crisis and dysfunction in family intervention. What Sylvia describes as the 'rich relational connection' between her and this mum was made possible by the time allowed for the relationship to develop and the freedom Sylvia had to 'follow her instincts' about what this mother needed. The consistency in this relationship was vital: 'I need to be the consistency, that carries on', hence the need to avoid rupture. Timeframes are long, and pace of work is slow. The baby was around one at the time of my interview, and the mum was still seeing Sylvia weekly as well as attending stay-and-plays with the child. As Sylvia reflects: 'It's taken all this time … it's just amazing because that would have been a baby that would have been removed'. Sylvia's capacity to regulate herself in that instance, to not just hug and feed the baby, is enabled by clinical supervision that can recognise the emotional impact this has on her. This is an expensive and time-intensive resource which BTC benefit from.

Clinical supervision for staff: being a therapeutic service

Located in a wider service that aims to be trauma informed and foregrounds relation-based practice, there is much to be learnt from the journey BTC have been (and continue) on, to practice therapeutically. At a time when 'trauma informed' has become something of a buzzword (Cherry et al, 2023) it is more important than ever that if the aspiration to take trauma seriously is real, the support, time and care be put in to enable it to happen (Perks, 2024). Receiving clinical supervision was cited by many members of staff as critical for processing their own emotions. Olive described how

> you can bring those difficult feelings … just kind of untangle them, your own emotions, because it feels hard, especially when things don't work out. You're left as a practitioner thinking 'Did I do enough?' Because actually the children have still ended up being removed, mum's actually still in a really bad place. (Olive, BTC staff interview)

As well as providing staff themselves with a place to 'untangle' complex feelings and thereby look after themselves emotionally as individuals, clinical supervision also supports their emotional connections as a team. This sense of building safety as a team comes right back to the primary work undertaken with parents in their early engagement with BTC. Staff also need to develop this feeling of safety in relation to each other, to enable an openness to being vulnerable. Linnea talked about how clinical supervision

> has really helped with being able to be vulnerable with each other. And I think that's really important … that the care that we provide to our parents, that we provide it to ourselves as well … The work that we do

is really hard sometimes, and we do get kind of emotionally involved with our families. And then when things happen that aren't nice for families, you really feel it personally. (Linnea, BTC staff interview)

Clinical supervision was also highlighted as key to staff being able to support clients adequately and fairly. As Laurel explained,

It's all the kind of unconscious bias stuff. It's there. You can't, unless you're having really reflective supervision, where you're being challenged, actually think about your *own* feelings, and what does this person evoke in you? You know, is there any transference happening here? What are the barriers between you and mum? Or you and dad? (Laurel, staff interview)

Such transference and counter-transference[1] is part and parcel of working with people in emotionally challenging circumstances but is not a straightforward thing to understand or resolve without meaningful therapeutic support. Most social work staff do not get anything like this level of emotional support. Linnea talked about how she had been supporting social work apprentices

who were just so stressed. And then I got this email to say 'mandatory training for a whole day on relationship-based practices'. And I thought, well, yeah, that's really important. But actually, do we not need to spend the day to nurture our staff and start with *us* first, like *be* relational, you know, *within* … Why aren't *they* getting clinical supervision? Because they work with the same parents, with the same trauma as we do. (Linnea, BTC staff interview)

When I asked Linnea 'so why aren't they?' she replied, 'I don't know. It's expensive'. In the context of high caseloads, training requirements as noted by Linnea not only induce stress and possibly resentment, but they are also likely to fail, as it is not possible to care for others adequately while neglecting your own emotional and practical needs (as the 'oxygen mask' theory goes). Undoubtedly the financial costs of clinical supervision, combined with the time required to do it, would burden Children's Services if it were implemented more widely. However, given the existing and well-documented concerns around staff recruitment and retention, and the effects of burn-out on staff well-being, there are economic as well as human benefits to taking a longer-term and more holistic approach (see Samuel, 2024; Social Work England, 2024). In the absence of therapeutic support being more widely available, BTC consider an important part of their role supporting colleagues in different parts of children's services. Sometimes, as the following example shows, this takes the form of practical support based on their therapeutic training. In the following extract Sylvia describes in detail how BTC staff used their therapeutic skills to support staff involved in a supervised final 'goodbye' contact session between parents and their child who was leaving foster care for adoption:

> [The parents] physically needed [help]. They'd missed a couple [of contact sessions] so we were like 'Would you like a lift? Would that help if we get you there?' And it did, that did make the difference … But then how it ended up, is that we were then also needed in the [contact session] room … You've got the contact worker, at the back of the room, writing notes. I have been that worker, so I understand … And a foster carer also in the room, whose heart is breaking because the child is just screaming for the foster carer and won't go to mum and dad. So you've just got all of this pain within this room … By going in open, engaged, using some of our Theraplay skills … [we] see how we can facilitate that relationship … [with] the child between the foster carer and mum and dad. (Sylvia, BTC staff interview)

Final 'goodbye' contact sessions between parents and their children are necessarily emotionally challenging events (see Deblasio, 2021: 128–133). A foster carer would not usually be present, but in this case the child would not leave them, adding to the difficulties of creating a positive-enough relational space. With their therapeutic training, Sylvia and colleagues can see the problems with the relational dynamics in the room and how hard it is to manage them. What Sylvia describes above will be familiar to social workers and parents who have experienced formalised contact in such settings. As will Sylvia's description of the physical space and set-up:

> We were in … a room where you might sit and do training … you've got like radiators down here, the tables that are still set up in a square, and then there was space to do contact in this like corridor … There were no toys … So just us going with some basic bits … one book, a small ball, some blocks …paints and canvas … the difference that that made. And just *accepting*. This isn't about assessing parents, this is about establishing a moment of connection, if we're able to have that. Because this is the time that none of them will get back, including the child. It's not about sitting in the corner writing notes and being judgemental about if they managed.

This detailed description of how a contact session was transformed from a difficult, painful experience to a session where parents were able to play and connect with their child/ren, points to the wider value of having therapeutically trained professionals able to support not only the parents in their service but other professionals too, in this case a contact worker and foster carer. In an ideal situation, contact workers would also be therapeutically trained and be able to create and hold the space to make it feel safe for all parties. The spaces themselves would be less like assessment centres or meeting rooms and be arranged to facilitate connection and play. Working with institutional multi-purposes spaces, BTC staff are skilled at transforming a room using toys and crafts. They know what works from creating and maintaining their own therapeutic spaces for their families. The critical component that BTC bring to this specific encounter, but which has wider resonance, is to displace the role of judgement, symbolised by the contact worker distancing themselves from the family and taking notes, and instead focusing on acceptance. Although, as noted elsewhere, there are pressures on social work staff who must fulfil important assessment responsibilities, there are times when assessment is not necessary or appropriate. There is a risk that 'assessing' becomes a dominant frame through which parents are viewed, regardless of what they are doing (Drayak, 2023). The example above provides a case for reviewing assessment as the default framing and seeing what becomes possible when acceptance and connection are prioritised.

Supporting colleagues doing front-line work: the role of empathy

Different types of social work labour have differing emotional demands. One of the important things to come out of the research with BTC was insight into the difficult emotional work undertaken by front-line services. As Rowan said in workshop discussion: 'In this job … we sit with people's pain, but if you did that in front-line … you can't do that in front-line'.

Although front-line and BTC staff were often working with the same parents, there could be differences of opinion regarding processes or outcomes. BTC staff expressed respect and empathy for front-line colleagues doing very difficult tasks, with high caseloads and limited support. Many of the BTC team had worked in front-line safeguarding teams, and/or fostering or adoption teams, so they understood the challenges. There was a strong desire to be able to work closely with these colleagues in better supporting parents and where possible bringing about different outcomes for them.

The role of empathy in relation to birth parents was frequently raised, noting the importance of empathy in making fair decisions in compassionate ways. For BTC staff, empathy is at the heart of their relational engagement with parents. They are keen for other practitioners to have more empathy towards birth parents in a context in which birth parents can be seen in a negative light and subject to pre-judgement (Broadhurst and Mason, 2017;

Deblasio, 2021). However, there was recognition that sometimes empathy was not possible or even desirable when undertaking a difficult safeguarding role involving the removal of children. In BTC's Raw Emotions workshop (see Chapter 3) staff discussed the 'limits' of empathy, using the example of the scene of the court room in which a social worker is required to make a case for a child to be adopted. Olive noted:

> You have to make big decisions, and as much as you feel for somebody and their experience, if their child isn't safe, you do have to go to court and say it. And the way that it's designed in court, you are sitting there and kind of feeling you're almost attacking the parent as well, because, you know, you have to put a case across. It's really hard then, if you immerse yourself in their experience, because then you are part of their pain as well, aren't you? Not what's caused it, but you're part of that and I guess you have to have some separation. You're there to protect the child as well.

Drawing on her own front-line experiences as well as working alongside social work colleagues, Olive makes a case for some 'separation' or 'distance' from parents' emotional pain. In her continued discussion, she brings in the difficult feelings incurred by social workers in this context:

> It's not nice. I've been there, to sit in a witness box and say, 'I don't think that this parent is able to safely parent a child, and I recommend adoption'. It's not a nice feeling when you've got the parents sitting there breaking down in front of you, but you've got to do what you've got to do. It's really hard. I think you have to have a bit of distance, otherwise I don't think you can cope. (Olive, BTC Raw Emotions workshop)

Olive reminds us here that in the affective space of the court room – or any other space of family intervention – there are a range of difficult and painful feelings being experienced by those present. Keziah responded to Olive's point by emphasising that there remains scope in the *way* things are done:

> Rather than ... presenting a case where you're saying 'this parent is not safeguarding her child' ... all that labelling ... you'd be going in saying ... 'we know this mum really would love to parent her child' ... there'd just be more empathy in the delivery of it, I think. (Keziah, BTC Raw Emotions workshop)

These discussions point to the emotional complexity of this labour, navigating how much empathy is enough or too much, how best to narrate a devastating outcome to both protect a child for whom you are professionally responsible, without further compounding the distress experienced by parents, as well as protecting yourself. Dissociation was recognised as a sometimes-necessary emotional strategy. Olive noted that as an assessing social worker

> You're always seen as the bad person … you get the abuse and that defensiveness, and sometimes I guess that's easier to deal with, being sworn at and shouted at and have chairs thrown at you. It … dissociates it … it's almost easier to deal with anger than it is to deal with the pain. (Olive, BTC staff interview)

This is an important insight. It echoes discussion in Art of Attachment workshops from social care professionals working in other services who acknowledged that *too much* empathy for clients could make their work unbearable, and ultimately undoable. Reflecting on her own practice, Idra talked about the immense pressure to make the right decisions when assessing a parent at risk, 'because there's a potential risk of harm … There are some children who are at real risk of harm, and they can't stay with their birth parents'. She continued:

> When you do that to somebody, when you take their child, and you are traumatising them, I think there's something in social workers that you switch off, you have to switch off a bit of yourself, because otherwise, how do you do it? How do you live with that? Like, even though you can rationalise, it is still such a hard thing to do that I think you end up putting birth parents in a side of your head that's like 'the other'. And that's how you can get through. (Idra, BTC staff interview)

Echoing Olive's thoughts on staff 'dissociating', this reflection is important by attending carefully to the labour of child removal. We can see how assessing social workers may be required to turn their empathy dial right down, to 'switch off a bit' to do what they must do and keep a child safe. John Radoux (2023: 164) comments that 'While some level of dissociation is probably necessary – it would likely be intolerable for any individual to be fully in touch with the pain and distress they will come across during a career in the care system – the pendulum often appears to swing too far in this direction.'

Crucially, Idra followed up her point above by arguing while dissociation may be an important coping strategy for a social worker required to remove a child, this does not mean that the birth parent should not receive empathy and support. What it means in this scenario is that the assessing social worker is not the person who is able to do it. To be able to sit with parents' pain and offer meaningful support requires a different person, with a different role, such as provided in this instance by BTC. However, access to empathetic support from a different professional, is not available routinely to parents in this traumatic situation. If parents are to be treated fairly and social workers supported to make fair decisions, this needs to change. There was recognition that as well as the emotional labour of urgent safeguarding actions, the conditions of front-line labour could lead to emotional burn-out and a need for self-preservation to keep doing the job. As Laurel put it, drawing on her own experience of being a front-line worker:

> You're seeing the same thing day in and day out. So working with neglect on a continual basis, you start to become quite negative; it becomes a little bit entrenched. You start to lose that non-judgemental practice, non-discriminatory practice. I think the nature of being a front-line worker, is that it wears you down. And I think that's when you start to lose that empathy, you start to lose that kind of connection …

This can impact on outcomes. Laurel continued:

> I can remember a manager pretty much saying to me 'this is an easy adoption, it's a done deal'. And I was in court all the time, staying up all night writing [the] statement, and not actually knowing the family … a statement based on a couple of visits. How do you know someone if you've only done a couple of visits? … If the expectation is, 'this is what's going to happen' … If you've gone in with that, even unspoken, in your mind, what you see in those visits is going to be shaped by that, isn't it? (Laurel, BTC staff interview)

Similar examples were given by others from contemporary cases of parents they were working with. When workload pressures are high, and time-constraints tight, pre-judgement and expectations, whether spoken or unspoken, can play a significant role in outcomes for parents (Murphy, 2023). BTC staff saw their role as being able to undo and challenge some of those judgements and expectations, working closely with parents to better understand their situation, resources, needs and levels of risk. More empathetic understanding of parents might lead to the same or different decisions in terms of whether they are able to keep their child/ren. Either way, they provide a more robust basis for decision-making and ensure that parents have been heard and given a fair chance, leading to better outcomes for those parents and their children, even if the decision is adoption.

With the benefits BTC staff have of lower caseloads, working with people over longer timeframes, and clinical supervision, they are in a strong position to support colleagues in other roles to develop their therapeutic practice:

> When we are in a meeting where it feels like people are being quite critical of parents, or they're being dismissive of parents' views, or they're not allowing the parents to have a voice, or they're *fearful* of a parent, because the parent is getting really cross and angry – which sometimes is justified – we're in a position to be able to use ourselves as a platform, having been DDP informed, and having clinical supervision ourselves, to be able to change the temperature of a room and try and ensure that everybody has a voice in that room. (Laurel, staff interview)

Therapeutic approaches include looking beneath surface behaviours to see what emotions they might be masking. This is routinely practiced in, for example, fostering and adoption services, where the client group is children and young people. However, it can be overlooked when dealing with adults. Sylvia observed lower levels of compassion and understanding towards 'vulnerable young people and adults ... who've been in care, or have had adoption disruptions, or been brought up by a granny ... we don't have the same level of empathy. And our systems, our services replicate that'. Sylvia's insights here point to powerful social norms around childhood and transitions to adulthood that mean empathy wanes as children get older and become adults, resulting in 'adultification' of young people, with Black young people at increased risk (Bernard and Harris, 2019; Davis and Marsh 2020; Drew, Pierre and Sen, 2023). A therapeutic understanding enables these norms to be challenged, allowing more empathetic engagement with (young) adults. As well as advocating for empathy towards parents, BTC could sometimes offer direct emotional support to colleagues. Laurel talked about a time they had worked closely with safeguarding colleagues, and noticed

> just how stressed they were and how hard that job was, and that they had loads of cases ... By offering them opportunities to be regulated, to feel contained, to be able to offload, to understand that that is transference, that working with that mom is triggering you ... That made the biggest difference for everybody, including unborn baby when baby came along. So the power of relational based practices is huge. (Laurel, BTC staff interview)

The importance of relational practice and politics, established here in relation to social work labour, is developed in the next chapter with a focus on interdependencies between families.

Conclusion

While dominant narratives around adoption gloss over or sideline heartbreak and other difficult emotions, the examples here show that they saturate the experiences not just of parents but of social care professionals. This chapter has provided evidence of the kinds of emotional labour involved in family intervention, whether that be removing children from families for adoption or supporting parents who have lost their child/ren manage their grief. It has also provided evidence of the value of taking a trauma informed approach. Working closely with analysis of empirical data from BTC, we see that it is not enough to provide emotional support without also providing practical help. The two are interconnected in as much as practical difficulties such as lack of food and poor housing have a negative impact on parents' emotional capacities. It is not possible to engage meaningfully with emotional support if you are cold, hungry, worried about where to live or how to get medical help for your baby. Emotional support also depends on parents feeling safe. Emphasis is put on relational levels of trust and security with social work staff: feeling safe enables parents to be vulnerable enough to acknowledge what is happening and accept support. The discussion here supports the argument that all family social work staff, no matter what role they play, need emotional support. This provision is not just about adequately supporting staff but also ensuring fair outcomes for children and parents.

Although the emotions experienced by parents who have lost a child or children to adoption may seem exceptional, Bhattacharyya (2023) here reminds us that heartbreak needs to have a place in any hopeful political project. What Bhattacharya (2023) notes as the 'push to manage and fix heartbreak' has been explored in the context of BTC, where we have seen the problems with models of social intervention based on solving problems and framing positive outcomes in terms of happy endings. Instead, analysis in this chapter has demonstrated the importance – and skills – of walking alongside and sitting with grief and loss. The temporalities of this have been highlighted, both in terms of the slow, repetitive labour of sitting with grief without seeking to resolve and fix it, but also the attention here to making 'a politics that seeks to render heartbreak a thing of the past' (Bhattacharyya, 2023: 111). The past here could be the historical hauntings of adoption and state intervention into families as well as the generational traumas passed on and re/produced through entrenched social injustices and failings. In the next chapter, the importance of relational connection is further explored through a focus on interdependencies in the provision of care and support.

7

Interdependence in adoption policy and practice

Introduction

As human beings we are interdependent. This is not a radical or controversial claim. In discussion about attachment (Chapter 4) and the role of stories in making sense of our lives (Chapter 5) we have seen that relational encounters enable our development and survival as social subjects. In Chapter 6, relational connection between social workers and parents was demonstrated as foundational to doing meaningful work. From total dependence as infants on their caregiver, a person's capacity to flourish relies on being recognised, accepted, supported and cared for by others. Given these inter/dependencies, a socio-political system that understands and nurtures this fundamental human need should be a basic ethical requirement. Despite this, *independence* is heralded as a cultural and political ideal. We see this most clearly in the neoliberal construction of the ideal form of family as economically and socially independent from state support (Brockmann and Garrett, 2022). An ideological commitment to this idea of family underpins the construction and maintenance of some troubling aspects of contemporary adoption policy and practice in the UK, as elsewhere. Using empirical evidence from ethnographic work with Breathe, Trust, Connect (BTC; see Chapter 3 for discussion of BTC and methods) this chapter addresses some of these troubling aspects close-up.

This chapter takes the framing of interdependence to think critically about key relationships involved in adoption policy and practice. The first relationship to be explored is that between families and the state, specifically families who have their child/ren removed from them by the state for adoption. We have seen in previous chapters how such families are routinely impacted by material challenges such as poor housing and ill health, and they can experience oppression based on intersectional factors such as race and class (Allen and Osgood, 2009; Tyler, 2020). Using empirical insights from birth parents and the social care professionals who assist them following the loss of their child/ren to adoption, we see how (lack of) practical, material and emotional support compounds these other factors, making it extremely hard for parents to break cycles of trauma and deprivation, and removal of children by the state. Many such parents were themselves brought up in care, and outcomes for children parented by the state are not good (Nuffield Foundation, 2021; Sacker et al, 2022). Child protection policies deflect critical attention onto families and parents, subjecting individuals (usually mothers) to blame when they are judged as failing to fulfil their responsibilities to their children (Gillies, 2007; Allen and Taylor, 2012; Jensen, 2018). The discussion here unsettles notions of blame and responsibility, noting the injustice that parents are blamed and shamed while the state remains unaccountable for its failures. The analysis here calls for more equitable and transparent regimes of accountability from state agents.

The second relationship to be examined is that between birth and adoptive families. Although narrated and positioned by legal and policy framings as dyadic, distinctive units, these families are interconnected and interdependent in complex and often enduring ways. Birth and adoptive families, radically separated and distinguished from each other in the formal narratives that constitute the process of adoption, are inextricably entwined emotionally and often practically. They not only have their attachments to the same child or children in common but may also experience similar support needs over time. The insights from the research with BTC, amplified by a wider literature, demonstrate that *all* families need support; birth and adoptive families have many comparable needs and experiences, despite being set up as opposites in the playing field of adoption. A presumption of life-long support might enable more birth families to care for their children, thus avoiding the need for adoption; but where adoption is the outcome, the maintenance of contact between birth parents and child/ren and the provision of ongoing therapeutic life story work might reduce the desperate struggles that many adoptive families experience. In the current context of economic precarity, such ideas feel utopian. However, like other resource-heavy interventions early in a child's life, the economic as well as social benefits will almost certainly be felt down the line, preventing financial, social and emotional losses in the future. The chapter supports the argument that while short-term changes are urgent, a simultaneous dismantling of the contemporary idea of family is also required, combined with a radical re-imagining of the kinds of networks of care and kinship that might be possible and necessary.

'Ideal' families: power and responsibility?

Idra, a staff member at BTC, reflected in interview on the type of family the adoption process aspires to create:

> It's about … no state intervention … I was on an adoption [approval] panel recently, and a student social worker … said afterwards 'Oh isn't this wonderful that this is happening? … These children will no longer have this state involvement'. And *I* wrote that in reports. That's why you do adoption.

However, as Idra went on to note, aspiring to create family independent of state support does not help birth or adoptive families or reflect their probable needs and outcomes. In fact, it is becoming increasingly clear that adoptive families require high levels of support and adopted children go on to become adults needing high levels of input (AUK, 2023, 2024; Hillman et al, 2024; O'Marah et al, 2025). However, the power of the mythical ideal persists, aligning with a political and economic model of independent, privatised families responsible for their own welfare. An established feminist critique of family helps to explain political investments in maintaining this ideal. Like other institutions of the state, families are controlled and used by governments to achieve political, economic and social aims. Families are the primary unit responsible for the construction and maintenance of nation-state (Oswin and Olund, 2010). In fact, a good amount of what makes a society exist and function is laid at the door of families, made responsible for the literal re/production of members of society primarily via women's unpaid reproductive labour (Bhattacharya, 2018; Ferguson, 2020). Embedded by custom and repetition into daily life, most people accept this reproductive and caring work as their own responsibility for which they can expect very little in the way of economic support, social services, or time off waged work to complete. Kathi Weeks (2020: 583) notes that

> The privatisation of care is crucial to the economy of the family: the enormous amount of time, skill and energy devoted to childcare, eldercare, the care of the ill, the care of the disabled, self-care and community care, without which the economic system would not exist, is provided mostly free of charge, disproportionally by women, in the moments left outside of income generating work.

This necessarily entails highly uneven provision from one family to another. As the UK and other neoliberal economies reject a model of society with a strong welfare state, those families unable to either provide necessary care for their members or fund it privately, are vulnerable. Such families find themselves struggling and isolated, labelled as 'troubled' and 'failing' and subject to surveillance and stigma (McGrath et al, 2023). They are characterised by politicians – using UK MPs Graham Allen and Iain Duncan Smith's (2008) terms – as a 'dysfunctional base' of society (see discussion in Chapter 4). Some of these families find themselves subject to care proceedings and the removal of their child/ren by the state for adoption. These families comprise some of the most marginalised people in society, having experienced generational trauma enmeshed in, and compounded by, multi-faceted and intersecting social and economic deprivation in the forms of poverty, racism, unmet health needs and inadequate housing. The politically motivated policy framing of such families as 'troubled' (Hayden and

Jenkins, 2014) isolates and individualises these problems such that blame falls upon individuals and families rather than systems of governance and political agency. The evidence highlights injustices in current practice, where despite the lack of support, families are left with blame and stigma following removal of their child/ren, while the state as corporate parent fails those who depend on it but avoids accountability. John Radoux (2023: 129) argues that 'state intervention should be reframed as a life-long interdependent relationship based on need'. In the analysis and discussion that follows I endorse this argument. I demonstrate that not only resources but also responsibilities need to be more fairly accounted for.

The monopolisation of care within families is not just bad for these families but for the wider functioning of society. Michèle Barrett and Mary McIntosh (1982: 78) declare the family 'anti-social' as it 'sucks the juice out of everything around it, leaving other institutions stunted and distorted'. As well as providing private unpaid caring labour which exonerates the state from responsibility to provide public care, Weeks (2023: 440) asserts that 'the privileged family form cuts off its time-strapped members from alternative modes of sociality, which might provide anything from momentarily pleasurable encounters to powerfully sustaining forms of association'. Exhausted by re/producing and caring for their own, members of families are less able to contribute to community forms of caring. Sophie Lewis (2019: 119) notes that making children the family's private responsibility means that 'the babies we gestate are ours and ours alone, to guard, invest in, and prioritize', reducing our feelings of responsibility and even empathy for others' children.

The ideal adoptive family is constructed in this political context as an inversion of the 'dysfunctional' family, in a narrative that must justify removing a child from the family they are born into and making them a member of a different family. The ideal adoptive family closely aligns with the norms of the 'nuclear' domestic unit, which Weeks (2023: 438) describes as having the following three 'fundamentals' – 'a privatised system of social reproduction, the couple form and a bio-genetic-centred kinship'. Where these fundamentals are not precisely met, they need to be adequately compensated for: for example, a single adoptive parent will have free, local support offered by able-bodied, retired grandparents; a child will be 'matched' as closely as possible to their adoptive parents to look like them.[1] Processes of assessment and approval for potential adopters ensure that adoptive families adhere as closely as possible to the ideal socio-political family form already outlined. While adoption recruitment highlights the inclusion of same-sex and single adoptive parents, and sometimes specifies flexibilities with regards to financial status, the procedure is highly 'normalising' and 'successful' adoptive parents are those able to closely align with the features of the ideal neoliberal family unit: monogamous, educationally and emotionally literate, physically healthy and able bodied, financially independent, able to provide and pay for necessary support (Myong and Bissenbakker, 2021). The state's involvement in the social re/production of adoptive families is obscured by the legal severance of a child from their birth family. This severance creates an illusion of independence: the adopted child now belongs to this new family, and their birth family are kept at a distance with no rights or responsibilities for the child. However, as addressed in Chapter 2 in relation to life story processes and forms of ongoing contact, this independence cannot be sustained as birth family are an active (absent) presence in the life of adoptive families, regardless of the forms of contact they have (Lambert, 2020). The simultaneous destruction and creation of their families via adoption fuse birth and adoptive family networks in complex ways, connecting them together forever via a child or children to whom they are both attached. The closer we look at the evidence from lives as they are lived, via established literature and the empirical insights generated here, the more we see how many families, birth and adoptive, fail to live up to political and social ideals and are damaged in the process (Boddy et al, 2023). In the next section, the ideal of a family who have little or no dependency on state support is shown to be a problematic construction, while the analysis supports the argument that all families should have access to state support based on their needs.

The case for support for all families based on need

At this political moment, it seems barely necessary to say that more genuine support needs to be routinely provided by the state. The fact that family support systems, administered in the UK through a hole-riddled patchwork of local governmental and private services, do not meet need, is barely contested in academic, popular and even some political discourse (MacAlister, 2022; Sen and Kerr, 2023a). It was perhaps not surprising then that discussion about this (lack of) support featured heavily in conversations with BTC staff and parents. The intergenerational effect of lack of support is clearly articulated here by a parent, Willow, whose first child had been adopted and other three were in foster care:

> When I was 16 or 17 I never had any parents there … to help me, all I had was social services and they should have done more. They should have done more to help me …. My mom's no good … my other kids are in foster care. Hopefully I'll get them back. That's what I'm working towards, is to get my kids back. I've got a good understanding now … I wasn't a bad parent, but there were things that I should have done more of. But being a lone parent with four kids, it's hard. And that's where they need to put the support. (Willow, parent, BTC Power of Words workshop)

Willow talked in detail about the difficulties of parenting her children, particularly a son with extremely challenging behaviour. Willow felt isolated trying to manage him on her own during COVID-19 lockdowns where support was even more lacking. Staff echoed this urgent need for early help:

> I'd often look at Child Permanence Reports and think, if that support had just been put in place, maybe, maybe this wouldn't have ended up in adoption? ... The most heartbreaking thing is seeing children that are in care themselves go on to then have children removed from their care. Or children that were adopted, and you think life should have been better ... Mum herself came into care when she was nine and was in the system ... now her children [are] being removed at 18 and 19 and 22. And now she's on her fourth baby. You think ... where was their support? (Olive, BTC staff interview)

As well as practical support many parents need therapeutic input. As we saw in the previous chapter, parents accessing BTC have themselves experienced early childhood trauma which is likely to make them more vulnerable to poor mental health during and after the birth of a child (Fitzpatrick et al, 2023). Parents' own mental health needs *are* often recognised in family assessments and court hearings, but provision does not always follow:

> How many birth parents do we see who have multiple children removed from their care, where they say in court that the expert advice was that they need to have X amount of sessions of psychotherapy, or they need whatever type of therapy it is, but it is never ever provided for them? (Laurel, BTC staff interview)

It is not just an absence of therapeutic support; some parents feel that evidence of poor mental health can be used to build a case *against* them. Ivy, a parent, talked about her challenges with poor mental health being the basis for losing her child to adoption:

> There was just a case of 'this person, this mom, she's got something wrong with her. She's mentally unstable'. It's used *against* me, so it kind of hurt me, and it made me angry because having a mental health problem or disorder or something shouldn't stop you from successfully being a mom. (Ivy, parent, BTC Power of Words workshop)

BTC's core work of supporting people therapeutically takes time and patience, investing in regular, relationship-building activities to build trust and safety. Even if it is offered, for parents to *access* therapy following the loss of their child/ren, they may need the kind of practical and emotional encouragements and interventions detailed in the previous chapter: lifts, snacks and sensory distractions, a companion. Without this time, patience and practical assistance, the offer of help may be meaningless. Funding constraints means that where support is offered it is often short-term. Olive argued for the provision of long-term assistance to enable families to be kept together:

> sometimes I've worked on cases where *the services just aren't available to keep the children at home*. So for parents that maybe have learning needs, or parents that aren't able to manage ... they would maybe need a couple of hours in the morning for support to help get the kids to school, and maybe an hour or two in the evening to support them with that, and access to a service that gives them that emotional support. And it's not just short-term intervention for six months. (Olive, BTC staff interview)

Olive is conjuring here the everyday reality of families who love their children, are not a threat to them, and who want very much to parent them, but due to their own and possibly their children's physical, emotional or cognitive health needs, will struggle or be unable to safely do so without some *ongoing* support. The failure here is not in the family but in the lack of services available to meet the family's needs. A presumption that all families may need support, and some certainly will, possibly throughout their children's lives, allows for a recalibration of the relationship between support and assessment. It widens possible responses to the vital question, 'can this parent or family parent their child/ren?' Although such a recalibration would put short-term economic demands on cash-strapped councils, seen through a longer-term lens, there could be economic benefits. Investing in slow, long-term support for people has longer-term financial gains. As Laurel highlights,

> A pot of money providing that [therapeutic] service would potentially prevent all the other children that come after that ... And the savings to Local Authorities would be massive in comparison to a pot of money to therapeutically support people who have a right to have access to that specialist support. (Laurel, BTC staff interview)

It is routine to assume that adoptive families will need therapeutic and practical input to help their family thrive (Harris-Waller et al, 2018; Penner, 2023). This is evidenced by provision of a centralised support fund and the development of an industry of therapeutic parenting resources targeting adopters in the form of books, training programmes, therapeutic provision and so on.[2] Rowan, drawing on her experience of working with adoptive parents, noted that provision presumed necessary for adoptive families is not considered for birth families, for whom

> It's almost like they're assessed, and then that's it, the child will be removed. Whereas in adoption, the child will be placed, and they'll throw everything at it to make the placement happen. So why couldn't they have done that before the child was removed and given that birth parent that? ... If it can work in adoption ... there's a chance it could have worked with the birth parent, before we got to that point. (Rowan, BTC staff interview)

Noting that adopters are not a unique group but rather 'we're all part of the same story', Laurel talked about how

> Lots of adoption workers are trained in DDP [Dyadic Developmental Psychotherapy] and Theraplay, and Therapeutic Life Story Work and NVR [Non-Violent Resistance] and all the things that are out there at the moment that very much sit within the adoption world. But actually they sit here too, and they sit really well here. (Laurel, BTC staff interview)

Laurel highlights discrepancies in provision between different types of family. Staff such as Laurel, with experience of working directly in both adoption services and supporting birth parents, are uniquely positioned to not only point to the injustices of these discrepancies, but also to understand how the kinds of therapeutic support offered to adopters could really make a difference to birth families who are struggling. Therapeutic interventions such as those cited by Laurel are used to help people understand how their childhood experiences impact on their emotional responses and resilience when parenting their own children; they can help parents understand that children's behaviour communicates their emotional needs; they help parents develop their own skills and capacities to regulate themselves, rather than attempting to change their children's behaviours through traditional behavioural models (Elliott, 2013; France et al, 2024). Such therapeutic interventions work relationally with families, encouraging connection and play, supporting parents to develop strategies for managing challenging, sometimes aggressive and violent behaviours from children (Lyttle et al, 2024). We saw in the previous chapter that BTC utilise these approaches with their parents with successful outcomes (see also Morgan et al, 2019; Nolte and Forbes, 2023). Of course, by this point parents have already lost at least one child to adoption. What difference might it have made for some of these parents if they had benefitted from these therapeutic services at a much earlier stage?

'Unsupportable families' or failures in provision of support? A social model

In the light of current reality, where adequate support is not provided, there is urgent need for this failure to provide support to be acknowledged explicitly in social services' interactions with families and in the narratives and paperwork generated to justify state intervention and removal of children. Olive notes that the removal of children may only be necessary because the levels of support do not meet need:

> If we could fund those supportive services, then there'll be a lot more children living within their families ... It's really hard when people struggle, and we have to say, well, you *could* do it if there was this level of support, but there's never going to be that level of intervention available. So therefore, the only option is for us to permanently remove this child from their family of origin. (Olive, BTC staff interview)

The decision to remove a child in these circumstances is the 'right' or 'only' one given the lack of support. Linnea similarly emphasised the importance of thinking differently about where the problem lies to challenge the idea that there are 'unsupportable families': 'When we're looking at unsupportable families, it's not that the family isn't supportable, but it's like we haven't got the resources to support this family' (Linnea, BTC staff interview).

Despite Olive's despondence that 'there's never going to be that level of intervention available', it does not have to be this way: an alternative version of family and family support is called for here. Olive and Linnea's insights need to be at the heart of a reforming agenda for adoption. They point towards a social model where blame is not on the individual failure of parents and families but on the inadequate levels of state support. This also has potential to lift a huge burden of stigma and guilt from families. Under the current system, parents have their child/ren taken from them and they are left to bear the blame, of feeling 'I'm not good enough'. Not only is this a damaging psychological burden but it can negatively impact on parents' capacities to parent future children. Ivy talked about the ways she felt words were used against her in reporting on her poor mental health as a reason for removing her children (see Figures 7.1 and 7.2): 'They just said so many things, like I was *unsuitable, unfit* ... when you go on to have more children as well, you have all these things that they've said about you. You worry and you think, am I even good enough?' (Ivy, parent, Power of Words workshop).

Figure 7.1: BTC Power of Words workshop label: *I don't feel like I should be a mom*

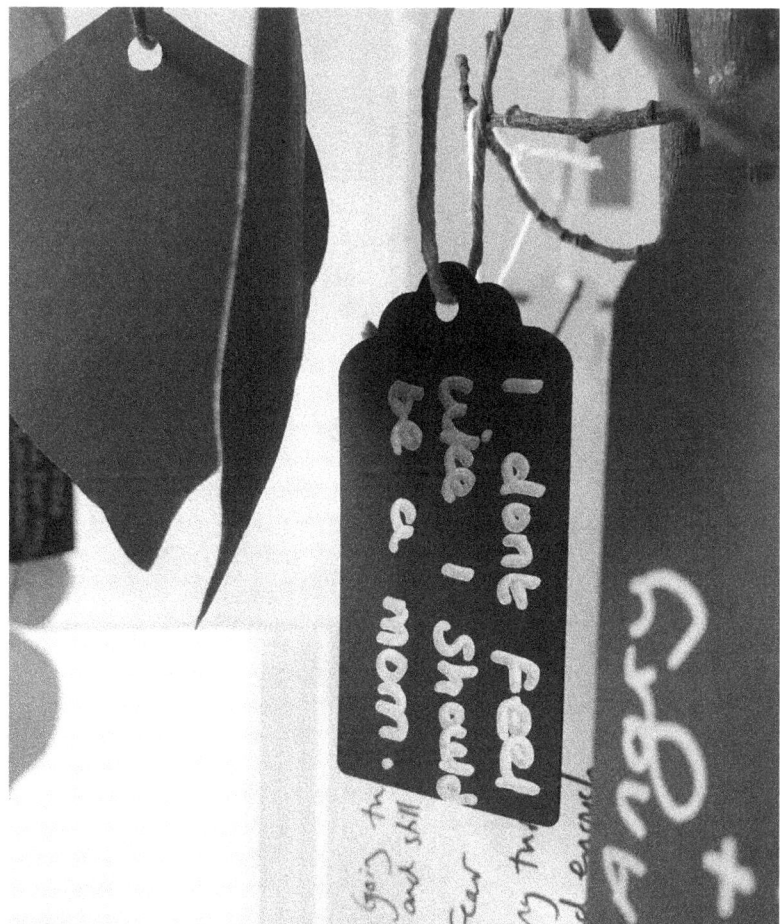

Contextualising what has happened to these families changes radically how parents are viewed (and view themselves). As Olive puts it:

> That reflects on the parent … 'you weren't able to provide good enough care to your child' … actually, you *would* have been able to *if* the support was there, but unfortunately, it's not. And then you have to think, well yeah, the failure is then on the state rather than on parents

Figure 7.2: BTC Power of Words workshop label: *I'm not good enough*

... some people just need that level of support, and they always will. (Olive, BTC staff interview)

To accept that some parents and families may always need support implies a different orientation to risk in families. Recognising that there are times when no level of support will make a home environment a safe place for a child, for most families this is not the case. The evidence from BTC's work, put together with wider research, demonstrates that where support can be put in place, changes can be made and sustained that enable children to stay with their families (Featherstone et al, 2014, 2018). Olive's reflections above make clear that child removal may be the only option available to social workers, but that is due to lack of an appropriate level of sustained support. Given the choice between leaving a child in a family environment with inadequate support to ensure they can be safely cared for, and removing the child for adoption, social workers must opt for removal.

As well as supporting a call for adequate, long-term support to be provided for families, the evidence here shows the need for a radical change in *accounting* for the lack of support when this is a factor in the decision to remove children from their families. Reasons for child removal should be more honestly reported and documented. If a parent might have a chance of keeping their child in their care with certain levels of ongoing support to meet their needs, but such support is not available, this needs to be documented. Removing from parents some of the damaging shame and stigma they currently bear, this is a practical measure by which the state can express responsibility and take blame where appropriate for its failings. Another factor with potential to reduce stigma is a growing awareness that more families than ever need 'parenting' support. As highlighted, many foster and adoptive families depend on ongoing support to cope (McQuillan and Taylor, 2014; Palacios et al, 2019; Brodzinsky et al, 2022; Lyttle et al, 2024). Social problems such as rising numbers of children and adolescents needing mental health support (Children's Commissioner, 2024; Bawden, 2025) and an increase in Child or Adolescent to Parent Violence and Abuse (CAPVA) indicate that many 'ordinary' families cannot manage without help (Holt, 2013; Coates et al, 2020; Rutter, 2023; Golm, 2024). Across different national contexts, the combined effects of social media use, the COVID-19 pandemic, conflict and environmental catastrophe and many other factors are leading to poor mental health in children and young people which in turn can lead to crises within families and communities. The evidence here supports calls from others for much greater interdependence between *all* families and the state. However, the challenge is that governments only appear to care about child protection when something goes wrong.

As well as improved provision, change is needed at the level of *cultures* of support. There is stigma around needing and receiving help. Within BTC, Hazel reflected on parents who say

> 'if I need … support with my housing or if I need support with a food bank, or I need support with financing … that could go against me'. Yeah. So, I think some of them are reluctant to ask for help … Jasmine for instance … She's had children adopted … She doesn't want it to be seen in a report that you've asked for housing help, or you ask for

household fund grants, or whatever, and that be seen as a negative. (Hazel, BTC staff interview)

Many parents in these circumstances lack trust and fear that anything can be used 'against them'. Peterson et al (2018) found in their study that mothers at threat of losing their children were more fearful of asking for help (see also Fitzpatrick et al, 2023). This is hardly surprising in a masculinised political culture in which asking for help is seen as weakness and coping alone is the 'gold standard'. As The Care Collective (2020: 23) put it: 'Dependence on care has been pathologised, rather than recognised as part of our human condition'. A shift in culture towards expecting *all* families to need help at certain times and offering and delivering support as standard, would help remove feelings of blame and shame and ensure parents in need access help. To make a presumption of ongoing, unlimited support for all families the norm requires a shift in political will and amounts to a re-imagining of the role of family in society. This re/conceptualisation of family need, and the possibility of offering meaningful support for as long as it is needed, are not within the power of individual social workers or perhaps even Children's Services. Current gaps in support are part of a wider systemic failure to invest in families and children and rethink the role of the state in relation to the labour of reproduction and care (The Care Collective, 2020). However, the fact that individual social work practitioners and services such as BTC can articulate and enact this vision in their daily practice offers evidence and perhaps hope that alternatives are possible.

State as poor parent: the impact on families and social workers

Not only are state failings in the forms of inadequate provision of support not acknowledged, but the state also takes inadequate responsibility for the poor levels of care it provides in its role as 'corporate parent'. While numerous reports and recommendations acknowledge poor outcomes for 'care experienced' people, with the MacAlister report (2022: 24) describing the disadvantage they face as 'the civil rights issue of our time', this does not translate into responsibility for the cyclical damage then done in neglecting to support care leavers who go on to parent and the subsequent harm their child/ren will experience if they in turn enter the care system. To justify removing children from parents the focus should not only be on the quality of care offered by the family, but what the alternative will be for children parented by the state. Being a 'looked-after' child comes with demonstrable risks. Thalia Drayak (2023: 92) argues that

> The entire care system has a narrative which focuses on parents as the problem. Parents feel as though they are perceived as being the locus of

greatest risk to their children. This is as stressful as it is inaccurate. It is vital that we have open conversations and explore a narrative that considers not only that children may be at risk with their parents but explores the risks to children of state intervention and exposure to the care system.

Existing research on the 'state-as parent' draws attention to what Claire Fitzpatrick and colleagues (2023: 13), writing about the criminalisation of care-experienced mothers, call 'intergenerational state harms':

> When young women ... feel ill-prepared for the challenges of parenting despite having been in care from a relatively young age, then surely some responsibility must lie with the state as parent. It is so easy to judge care-experienced girls and women with criminal justice contact as 'bad' mothers from 'problem' families. Far more challenging is any attempt to address the failings of the state, which requires wider structural change, and a recognition of the intergenerational state harms and intersecting gendered, racialized and class judgements that some women may face throughout their lives.

Children's Services act in ways that are arguably careless with their offspring (Stanley, 2015; Sen and Kerr, 2023b). Fitzpatrick et al (2023: 15–16) put the charge of care-lessness against the state in strong terms, highlighting the double-standards at play:

> A system that calls itself a care system but fails to recognise the harm it can cause may become a care-less and potentially negligent system for some. A state with the power to define what inadequate parenting looks like, but which fails to fully recognise its own inadequate parenting and its culpability in perpetuating intergenerational harm is a persistent offender ... we need to shift our view of care-experienced girls and women as problem parents and focus our lens instead on the state as problem parent. This can provide a very different perspective.

Staff at BTC work with parents in this situation of having been inadequately parented by the state, then blamed by the state for being a problem parent whose child/ren must be removed into state care. They are painfully aware of the ways these parents have been failed by their corporate parents. This awareness fuels their attempts to 'compensate' for these failings, often at emotional cost to themselves. In the previous chapter we saw the careful, slow, and often banal ways in which BTC staff work closely with parents, engaging them in practical and everyday tasks to help meet basic needs, build trusting relationships, and enable them to feel safe enough to engage in therapeutic work. This work includes 'modelling' certain behaviours, emotional responses and skills until parents learn how to do these things themselves. Modelling offers an appropriate and effective method for supporting parents who often lack appropriate role models, enabling them to learn strategies and behaviours in embodied ways through repetition over time. For staff, modelling is inseparable from the emotional labour of taking responsibility for the state's lack of care. Linnea gave an example of

> One of our parents that whenever she had to phone anyone, she would get so frustrated. So she would just put the phone down on them, like utility companies or other services. And kind of really slowly, but surely, we've really modelled … At first maybe I used to make the call and she would say 'can you talk for me?' 'Okay, I'll talk'. And then maybe we do the call together. And now there's no problems … we laugh about it now as well. (Linnea, BTC staff interview)

Linnea described this transition from doing something *for* someone to supporting them to do it themselves as 'having a bit of like a mothering role sometimes as well, like a parenting role. And then maybe moving on to kind of more like a sibling role'. Other staff said that modelling felt at times like taking a familial role, revealing that they held a sense of 'parental' responsibility. This feeling of responsibility was an empathetic response to working closely with someone whose support needs have not been met. There was also a more abstract sense of duty emanating from their professional role as an employee of the council, the branch of state with responsibility as 'corporate parent'. Holly captures both the everyday and abstract manifestations of responsibility:

> If I have a practical issue, I'll go to my brother, or I'll call my dad … whereas say, a child is in a foster placement up until they're 17, and then going into supported accommodation, you know, who do they call for that support? Or who do they call for a lift? They don't call anyone, because it's very likely that … it wasn't safe for them to have those relationships with their parents or their extended family … So I think it's only right that social workers have the responsibility to help with those things, because we – I mean, as the government, children services - we removed them and we cut ties with people that they would naturally have help from … We all need practical support. We all need emotional support, but we take that away from them. So we need to be responsible to put that back in for them … We are their corporate parent. (Holly, BTC staff interview)

Holly's use of both 'I' and 'we' here indicates the complex ways in which responsibility manifests in an individual social worker who imagines what it must feel like for people to lack the ordinary family support she has experienced but also feels that she represents or embodies 'the government, children's services'. These are the agents who, in removing children from their families, 'cut ties' and take emotional and practical support away from them. Holly indicates she shares responsibility: 'we are their corporate parent'. Linnea also talked about her feelings of obligation to nurture her clients:

> a lot of our parents were in care themselves. I really feel that we have that responsibility towards those children who are now adults, that were our children in here previously, and we need to nurture them. We're corporate parents. We're still corporate parents for them when they're adults, you know. The whole thing about that cut off [at age 25], I find that really hard with the leaving care service. Because, yes, they might be 25. But we know they're not the same as a 25-year-old who's grown up in a loving, caring environment and learned all the skills they needed to learn. (Linnea, BTC staff interview)

Even such a 25-year-old might still live at home, or benefit from contact and support from parents, siblings, extended family, resources are not available to most young people leaving care. According to UK Census data, the average age for moving out of the family home is 24 (ONS, 2023b). We noted the effects of 'adultification' (Drew, Pierre and Sen, 2023) in the previous chapter. As Fitzpatrick et al (2023: 14) note:

> Too often a lack of resources in an over-stretched care system means that responses to children in care, and decisions about where to place them, are reactionary and reactive in the short-term – sometimes for understandable reasons. But the care system could be so much more. And if we take a long-term view and consider the consequences of a system that fails to demonstrate what positive parenting might look like, and then ejects children to 'independence' at an early age, what is clearly revealed is a system that can become complicit in creating intergenerational harm.

Knowing that such services routinely and dramatically fail vulnerable people in their care, what does this mean that individuals feel – by virtue of their professional role – some sense of responsibility for this failure? This familial role was not a formal requirement of staff's professional duties but was a personal response to the political context in which they do their work. It is arguably a double dereliction of duty by state services that they not only fail the people in their care, being 'complicit in creating intergenerational harm', but also allow their staff to take on the burden of this systemic failure. Of course, however hard staff work to 'put that [emotional support] back in for them', as Holly puts it, they cannot compensate for damages done, leaving them with a sense of professional failure. There are risks that this might bring with it feelings such as guilt, and hopelessness, particularly if workers are not themselves supported therapeutically, as discussion in the previous chapter explored. Even with the therapeutic support BTC staff benefit from, the scale of 'parental neglect' enacted by the state as corporate parent can be significant and allowing oneself to take even partial responsibility for this might be to take on an unbearable weight. The actual corporate parent, in the form of the local government children's services, is rarely noted expressing responsibility or blame.

Of course, where state parenting is acknowledged as leading to poor outcomes (MacAlister, 2022) this can be used to bolster support for adoption. When parents are identified as struggling and children at risk, adoption provides governments with a much cheaper and quicker 'solution' than addressing structural inequalities and offering families adequate support. The flaws and injustices of this quick fix are becoming more apparent as the struggles of adoptive families and longer-term outcomes for adopted people are recognised and articulated (Palacios et al, 2019; Selwyn, 2023). Research not only points to the complex and overlapping roles of social determinants such as poverty, poor housing and exposure to a range of 'adverse childhood experiences' pre-adoption as influencing outcomes for adopted people, but also factors relating to adoption, such as separation from birth family, transition into foster care (Neil et al, 2020) and adoption itself (Brodzinsky et al, 2022). By prioritising adoption, governments not only neglect children by not offering adequate support for their families but arguably set such children up to fail by enforcing an irreversible outcome involving additional potential distress and trauma. This argument is developed as the overlaps and interdependencies between birth and adoptive families are examined.

Interconnection and dependencies between birth and adoptive families

> People are worried about working with birth parents. But actually, when you meet birth parents, and you get to know birth parents, and you see their vulnerability, you understand the journey that they've been on. And that, yes, they have made mistakes. And yes, they have caused harm, whether that be intentional or unintentional. Actually, they themselves in their own right are human beings that have not had positive experiences and healthy relationships. How do you deepen the empathy for somebody who has been part of intergenerational abuse themselves? How do you help somebody to understand that? The only way you're going to do that is if you build the bridges, and you

build the connections between the different parties affected. (Laurel, BTC staff interview)

While contemporary adoption practice in the UK does not endorse secrecy and promotes 'openness' around a child's origins, there is nonetheless complete legal severance from family of origin. The 'ideal' promotes a child's total belonging to one (adoptive) family, while maintaining links with birth family through life story work and in/direct contact, usually conducted via letters. This dis/connection can lead to what Sally Sales (2012) calls 'paradoxical' feelings for adopted people and their families. In Chapter 2 we considered the possibilities offered by these live practices of communication, and the archives of knowledges about adoption they generate. Here we revisit these practices to explore what interdependencies they expose and what improved relational possibilities they engender. As discussed in Chapter 2, 'letterbox' refers to the system of contact whereby a biannual or annual letter is exchanged between adoptive and birth parents. The system is managed by post-adoption social work teams, who act as go-between, checking and approving letters before they are sent. Although adopters sign a contract specifying frequency, dates, and any other details about letterbox correspondence (such as whether photos or celebration cards are to be included) these are not legally binding, meaning that once an Adoption Order has been granted, power as to whether contact takes place lies with adopters (Deblasio, 2021). BTC staff supported birth parents with a range of experiences:

> I've got examples where letterbox contact is really working well. And you know, they have it twice a year, they have photos, and that that's enough for [mum] to know that her child's safe ... But then I've also got others where adopters have just not sent any letters. I've recently chased one up today and the response I got back was, 'there's a note on the file to say we're not to bother the adopters' ... If that's their decision, then we have to accept it. (Rowan, BTC staff interview)

BTC staff see first-hand how vital any information about their children is to birth parents. Rowan talked about one parent with children in three different adoptive families: 'Two she hears from every year, but then one completely stopped after the first year. So she has no idea what's going on ... she writes her letters every year and saves them.'

We can imagine the emotional impact for this mother writing her letters and knowing that for one child they do not even get sent. Another mum, Willow, talked about her frustrations trying to maintain contact with her children: 'I felt after they took my kids, that was their job. That's what they was planning to do. And that's what happened. And then I got pushed to a side.'

When she tried chasing up to see if she had received a letter from the adopters, the service was bureaucratic and unhelpful:

> I wrote back to social services ... [they said] 'you have to go to another professional to sort it out for you'. Because they're not bothered, they're not interested. They're not doing what they're meant to do ... It shouldn't be like that. There should be people helping but they're not; they are pushing you to a side and leaving you ... It feels like 'Oh, we've got your kids. See you later'. (Willow, parent, Power of Words workshop)

The embodied feeling of being 'pushed to a side' describes the lack of power parents experience after they have lost their children. Even when they very much want to, writing letters can be difficult and the support of services such as BTC can be vital here. Linnea talked about the practical complications in some families' lives, such as moving house:

> It's just really hard to keep on top and keep in touch ... for all of our parents [letterbox] is such an important thing. And they do want to write back, and they do want to keep in touch. But sometimes it's just too difficult. And I think there's a real role there as well for a service to really offer [to] ... sit down with the parent in person and say 'What would you like to write? What would you like to say? What would you like to know?' (Linnea, BTC staff interview)

While parents accessing BTC have their support worker to help, most do not have this level of assistance. Staff talked about the content of letters and the difference it makes to parents to receive information or content that enables an emotional connection for them. There are blanket concerns about the exchange of photographs, linked partly to an (often unfounded) fear of birth family identifying children and compromising their safety, and/or to a concern that pictures will end up being circulated or posted online without permissions (Neil et al, 2015). However, Olive notes that

> The parents I work with would just love to see the back of their head, or you know, from a distance ... you couldn't really see ... significant characteristics ... Anything would still make it feel real; they would still be able to see that their child was growing. So many people I support now can't visualise their child as a 10-year-old. (Olive, BTC staff interview)

Visual evidence their child is growing, even if they can't see them close-up, enables the existence of their child to 'feel real'. This highlights the stark levels of separation between birth parents and their adopted children. Lacking ongoing evidence to the contrary, the reality of their child's life can feel tenuous. This point was echoed in one of the workshops where Linden talked about her daughter, adopted many years ago: 'With adoption, like when you've lost a child, it's like, I can still picture when she was three years of age. Even though she's [in her 20s] I physically can't picture she's a woman' (Linden, parent, Power of Words workshop).

This has contributed to significant distress for this mother, particularly when her adult daughter contacted her, and things did not go well. Strategies such as the ones Olive recommends could have supported her to develop a changing and developing sense of her child over time:

> Talking about, you know, what size clothes they wear, or what size shoes they are. And if [adopters] could put in, I don't know, a ribbon [and write] 'this is how we measured them, and they picked this ribbon, they touched it, and this is something for you to keep'... So much more that could be done to make it more human. (Olive, BTC staff interview)

Olive is thinking here about the materiality of a child's life and how to capture and communicate the reality of their (changing) existence in ways that are not just about words, or even visuals. Many parents talked about the difficulties they have saying what they want to say in letters. In workshop discussion Elowen (see Figure 7.3) described how:

Elowen:	I write to my kids twice a year. It is so bad, I have to put 'Hi, how is it going?' Do you know what I mean?
Staff:	Yeah, you can't write your feelings?
Elowen:	I want to write to my daughter to say, 'Mum's proud of you', 'I love you always' but [I am not allowed to] ... I can understand because obviously it might trigger her ... but give us a little. Like, let me know how she's doing maybe in another way ... a photo. I'm not *asking* for the address. I don't want to come to the house to see her ... I can't say how I feel to my child. I can't use my words.

This is a powerful exchange in which we see how letterbox might deepen grief and distress, as Elowen is forced to go through the motions of writing what is considered acceptable, burying her feelings. At the same time, her daughter does not get to hear that her birth mum is proud of her and loves her, both affirmations which *might* be emotional or confusing for her to read but would almost certainly be positive messages for her to receive, particularly as she gets older. We see that Elowen is reflective about the possible impact of her words on her daughter, not wanting to 'trigger' her. She also recognises that she is considered a risk to the adoptive family, someone who might 'come to the house'. As well as privileging adopters and their needs and priorities, the current system relies on this heightened assessment of risk that regards birth family by default as a threat to the safety of their children (MacDonald and McSherry, 2013). Although there are instances when birth family members *do* pose threats, this does not represent

Figure 7.3: BTC Power of Words workshop label: *I can't use my words*

most cases and there is little detail or nuance in considering such risks in relation to contact at the time of the adoption or subsequently. There is no mechanism for considering that both families' circumstances may change. Fear of birth family is built into the relationship between birth parents and adopters from the initial matching process when, as Olive puts it, 'you have to tell people about what's happened … why this child has come into care. And then I think that almost paints a picture of somebody that's a monster, somebody that could harm children' (Olive, BTC staff interview).

The narrative of risk introduced here has its origins in justifications for removing the child and the court proceedings where it has been decided it is in their best interests to be adopted. These narratives are expressed, often in formulaic ways, in Child Permanence Reports and other formal documents which are provided to adoptive parents and maintained in official records archives (see Chapter 2). We are reminded of the 'problem lists' presented for each of the women in Vincent Dance Theatre's Art of Attachment film installation (see Chapter 4). Olive notes the importance of considering other understandings about birth parents, which might provide counter-narratives to those of fear:

> Yes, the child is always paramount … we must protect and safeguard the child. But the birth parents love their children, and they want their children to be happy … The majority of our birth parents … if they knew where their child was, they wouldn't ever try and disrupt their life; they want them to be happy. They *would* like to be able to see them, or to know a bit more about them, but they would never cause them harm. And I think that's what needs to change within the system: that understanding, that recognition, and to take away that fear that is instilled. (Olive, BTC staff interview)

Talking about the 'one-off' meeting that sometimes happens between birth and adoptive parents, usually at the time a child is placed for adoption in their new family, Laurel notes that

> Every single [adoptive parent] that I … supported to meet a birth parent said 'I'm so glad I did that. That was really hard, but I'm so glad that I did that'. And what that then leads to is when you're writing to that person, you know who you're writing to. They're real. You have a relationship with that person … the adults can build that relationship and connect, and the difference that can make for the children is massive. (Laurel, BTC staff interview)

Such a relational encounter, even if only a 'one-off', can change, or add significantly to, what adopters know and feel about children's birth parents through reading paperwork about them (Neil and Howe, 2004; Neil et al, 2015). They encounter them as a 'real person', rather than the often stereotyped and narrow portrait of a person portrayed in Child Permanence Reports.[3] These relational possibilities are opened by thinking about doing letterbox contact differently.

Working so closely with complex families, all staff at BTC are aware of situations when it is unsafe for a child or children to remain in the care of their birth parent/s. Most felt that for the small number of children in this situation, adoption is the best outcome. *All* were critical of the closed nature of adoption, entailing as it does in most cases the severance of relations with birth family. All highlighted problems resulting from lack of contact, or poor experiences of contact, between birth parents and children. The views of these professionals, and those of parents accessing the service, resonates with a substantial research literature around contact, including recent policy recommendations (see MacAlister, 2022; Sen and Kerr, 2023a). Exposure to current research informed the opinions of many staff. For example, Idra told me she learned a lot from Beth Neil's previously cited work on contact. This research, together with her experiences of working directly with birth families, led her to ask

> Where is this severing of this relationship ever the right thing to do? … Does that mean that they can't ever see them? Or have any kind of relationship with them? Where do we get this 'Well, if [the children] keep seeing [their parents] they won't be able to build a bond with the adopters'. Where is that coming from? (Idra, BTC staff interview)

Expectations that birth parents pose risk to children and that any relationship with their children will negatively impact on the bonds children can form with their adoptive family are based more on 'the way things have always been done' than evidence. Despite the narrative of replacement family, birth family retain presence in the child's life, whether this is nurtured through contact and life-story work or not, often noted as an absent-presence in adoptive family life (Lambert, 2020). As they get older, birth family and children may make contact formally, or informally via social media (MacDonald and McSherry, 2013). Although adoption law is primarily focused on childhood, children become adults, and those adults must navigate familial relationships which may have been 'severed' legally but are still emotionally and often materially real. As Keziah notes, a system of genuinely open adoption would have benefits for everyone involved:

> A child would know who they were, where they came from, which would help with the whole separation and attachment issue; the parent

will be less anxious, because it would know that that child is safe and okay ... and the adoptive parents may have less issues with the child that's in their care. (Keziah, BTC staff interview)

Idra also had clear ideas for how a constructive post adoption contact system might operate in a way that improved things for everyone. At the heart of such a system would be the maintenance of a meaningful relationship between birth family and their child/ren. She talked about how you would need to have a dedicated team for family time or contact. Such a team would be responsible for risk assessments and offering support to birth families, as well as liaising with adoptive parents and the child/ren. At the same time as maintaining safe contact, therapeutic life story work with the child and the birth parents would be undertaken: 'imagine doing both of those at the same time, and then being able to bring that together'.

In current practice, direct contact post adoption is rarely put in children's plans. There is no statutory right for birth parents to have such contact and no legal obligation on adopters to follow what is put in a plan. It is perceived that adopters will be resistant to direct contact, and there is inadequate infrastructure or resource to train social workers and to support everyone and provide therapeutic life story work on an ongoing basis (see Deblasio, 2021). Rather than endorsing a binary disconnection between birth and adoptive families, Idra believed that such a model would be very much in the interests of both families as well as their children. Talking about adoptive families struggling, Idra noted that adopters have 'been put on this pedestal':

[Your children] weren't able to be with birth families. They couldn't keep them safe. They need to have a new family who can meet all of their needs. [Adoptive parents think] ... 'what if I can't [meet their needs?]? What if I'm not bonding with this child? What if this child's behaviour is like, really extreme? What if ... every strategy ... isn't working?' But you've taken them from their birth parents, because they couldn't look after them. 'What if *I* can't look after them?' ... Then it's like 'this is because I failed'. (Idra, BTC staff interview)

There are many reasons why adoptive families may struggle but severance from birth family contributes to distress and, in some cases, adoption breakdown:

what we've got is young people then being brought up with questions ... the missing parts of their identity because they didn't have that relationship [with birth family]. The young people that go off, and adoptions break down, because they've gone off to try and find the birth parents. And maybe that hasn't been safe, that hasn't been a good thing for them to do. But if they'd had more support, and more acceptance from their adoptive parents about some more direct forms of contact, for example, this might not have happened. And so I think so much has to change in how the system is set up, and *who* [and] *what* are we doing this for? (Idra, BTC staff interview)

Idra's comments here resonate with wider evidence (MacDonald and McSherry, 2011). Maintaining ongoing contact with birth family would bring added responsibilities and challenges for adoptive families. However, supported well, openness has sustained benefits for birth family and for children, who would have a better understanding of their histories and identities. This would potentially lead to fewer behavioural and emotional problems for children, which adoptive families can be left dealing with in guilt and isolation (AUK, 2024; Lyttle et al, 2024). Adoption policies are predominantly focused on the lifespan of children (in the UK, until they reach legal adulthood at 18). Narratives attaching to adoption are about babies needing homes, children needing permanence, families needing stability. The support offered to adoptive families, mirroring the child welfare system, offers support until children reach legal adulthood (18, 25 in some cases) but then is gone. Birth and adoptive families can find themselves navigating complex relationships with children and each other long after the state has relinquished its responsibilities. The complex connections between their families, centred around the adopted person, are not just for childhood but for life. Linden, a parent accessing support through BTC, told us about her recent experience with her daughter who was removed for adoption when she was three, and is now an adult:

> My daughter did get in touch … She didn't want to go down the proper channels, but I did. And when we did speak on the phone, I understood everything more and I couldn't cope. She was wanting money. And I thought, I'm not just gonna hand money to you, because I don't know you that well. Because I don't know you. I would love to get to know you … I would love to see her and talk to her. But she was nasty … because she was on drugs. And she might not be in a better state, I understand that. I'm a bit worried to give it another shot, just in case it turns nasty. (Linden, parent, Power of Words workshop)

Linden's story here is one we do not often get to hear: what happens when an often-longed-for reconnection with children they have lost to adoption does not go well? Behind the scenes of this story are Linden's daughter, for whom adoption was not a happy-ever-after story, and an adoptive family in distress. There is the haunting of potential for the cycle of trauma to be recycled if Linden's daughter has children she is unable to care for. Drayak (2023: 96) reminds us that 'When children in the care of the state age out of that care it is the family who picks up the pieces and supports the child through adulthood and beyond'. For adopted children, this might involve adoptive *and* birth families. Policies, practices and stories around contact need to widen their lens to an entire life, not just the short span of childhood.

So why not make adoption more open? Of course, 'it's always been done this way' is a powerful factor, as is the fear that potential adopters would be deterred. It is also *emotionally* difficult: direct contact, particularly in the early stages when relationships are not securely developed, can be painful for everyone. However, the pain is there, no matter what, and will surface at other times in potentially less healthy or constructive ways. As argued in the previous chapter, more recognition of the fundamentally and unavoidably heartbreaking emotions at the heart of child removal and adoption itself is necessary (Lambert, 2020). Rather than the 'happy ever after' narrative of adoption, acceptance of the flawed and painful realities of child removal might enable different, better experiences and outcomes for children and their families, birth and adoptive.

Conclusion

The evidence and discussion in this chapter amplifies calls for the state, in the form of centralised and localised governmental services, to provide much more and better support, at a short-term minimum in line with the support offered to adoptive families. Evidence and discussion demonstrate that responsibility and blame are misplaced, so that some parents and social care professionals, in different ways, bear weight that should not be on their shoulders. Where children are removed because appropriate care cannot be provided to support the family, official paperwork should reflect this, to deflect blame from parents. These achievable short-term measures should be seen as part of a re-configuration of interdependencies between all families and the state, away from a model of privatised, isolated families whose status is judged according to their levels of need. There are long term social and economic benefits for the state in caring about families in this proactive way, rather than distancing themselves from families until there is a child protection crisis requiring intervention.

Interdependencies between birth and adoptive families have also been revisited. Open adoption offers direct challenge to the feted idea of the self-sufficient family unit. The idea that more open and fluid, intertwined families work together to support a child, and each other, is not new. Staff at BTC, seeing first-hand what damage severance and disconnection cause, have practical insights and suggestions for reforming communications and contact in ways that challenge binary either/or outcomes. Keziah suggests it is okay for people to 'have it all', but only if we 'work together':

> It's okay for the child to know where they're from *and* to have loving adoptive parents. It's okay to say to a birth parent 'you're not a failure. But you're just not able to do this right now. So this [adoption] is a decision that needs to be made, but you're still not a bad person, and we're not going to discard you'. You know, why can't we just all work together? (Keziah, BTC staff interview)

What Keziah nails here is that political reform is about emotional and relational reform; it is about a fundamental shift in our emotional approaches to parents and to children in society. The suggestions made in this chapter work at different interconnected levels, some involving a change of ethical and political will to put into practice, such as social workers being empowered to name state responsibilities and failings and indicate clearly in legal documentation when child removal might be avoided if adequate support were available. Others, such as the provision of potentially life-long support for all families, require radically different visions of social organisation. There is an urgent need to *re/imagine* such visions. Imagining is not separate from practical ideas or concrete examples. Rather, these different levels of praxis infuse and inform each other. Discussion in previous chapters illustrated that attachments and emotions propel people's lives and decisions in material ways. Bhattacharyya's (2023: 112) conceptualisation of heartbreak as 'more than an affective state' connects forms of suffering and sorrow to articulate something moving towards 'shared pains' (p 113). Interconnectedness at affective levels may begin with imagined connection:

> Yes, we do need an affective connection to each other. Perhaps only an imagined affective relation, something like the imagined community of nationhood transposed into dreams of new worlds beyond nations. New ways of marking our kinship and interconnectedness as a shared resource even when the connections remain largely imagined for now. (Bhattacharyya, 2023: 110)

For Bhattacharyya (2023) this is made possible through our emotional capacities to grieve and imagine pain and be willing to allow this pain to form the basis of politics, of imagining otherwise. Grief and pain are at the heart of un/making family through adoption, but they are repressed and regulated via formulations of adoption process and of family itself. However, despite the best communication efforts of the state and private adoption industry, adoption is not a happy story. Despite decades of policy reform, there are no real solutions to the problems of families struggling without adequate support to care for children. Even when individuals manage to thrive, against the odds, adoption itself cannot be recuperated as a happy ending.

Acknowledging our complex and interconnected griefs can be a starting point for collectively imagining (and doing) family differently. Barrett and McIntosh (1982: 159) suggest doing away with current formations of family, not by creating alternatives but by working to 'make the family less necessary, by building up all sorts of other ways of meeting people's needs'. The authors of The Care Manifesto make a comparable argument, putting care 'centre stage' by defining it as 'a social capacity and activity involving the nurturing of all that is necessary for the welfare and flourishing of life ... to put care centre stage means recognising and embracing our interdependencies' (The Care Collective, 2020: 5). Arguing that 'care at the scale of kinship' is all too often 'inadequate, unreliable and unjust', they propose an ethics of 'promiscuous care' as a more capacious and, indeed, profligate conception of 'caring more and in ways that remain experimental and extensive by current standards' (The Care Collective, 2020: 40–41). But, the authors add, this requires building the institutional infrastructures that can support these wider communities of care (The Care Collective, 2020; see also Featherstone and Gupta, 2023). In the day-to-day contexts of family intervention, such approaches are easily dismissed. Dominant conservative and liberal ideologies uphold legislative systems across the world in which the family unit forms the basis of society and the rights and responsibilities of that unit to be independent of state interference are sacrosanct. Such ideologies, in the service of economic power, are resistant to empirical realities. In these contexts, alongside radical imaginings and the development of workable alternatives, how do we better support multiple expressions of family as they are lived? If reframing family itself feels abstract in this moment of intersecting crises, (how) can we reframe the systems that support families? While there is no shortage of motivation based on social justice, socio-political and economic arguments for reframing the relationships between state and families are also compelling and need to be made and remade wherever they can be heard and understood.

The next and final chapter holds onto these divergent approaches, troubling adoption and the wider systems that underpin it in radical terms while re/articulating careful propositions that enable changes to contemporary understanding and practice.

8

A manifesto for change

Introduction

I began writing this chapter at the beginning of Art of Attachment workshops (see Chapter 3). It started out as a document called 'change' which remained open on my laptop to document ideas emerging from the lively workshop discussions. Researching with Breathe, Trust, Connect (BTC) I asked staff and parents 'what would you do to change the current system of child intervention?' We conjured magic wands to imagine things done differently. Their answers went into this document. It is perhaps not surprising that many people had similar complaints about current practice and ideas for reform, echoing findings and recommendations already made in the critical literature. Despite the novelty of the research methods and the original data generated and presented throughout *Troubling Adoption*, the findings and suggestions for reform that emerge are not new. This makes me feel both angry and energised. Angry because a lot of people with expertise, research-based and experience-based, have been saying similar things for a long time, but are ignored or spoken over. The problem is acute: high and increasing numbers of children across the UK on Child Protections Plans; high and rising numbers of removal of children from their families; high and rising numbers of adoptive families in crisis (Ireland et al, 2024; Lyttle et al, 2024; O'Marah et al, 2025). Despite this, austerity has been used as an excuse to further reduce funding for children's services (Sen and Kerr, 2023c). There is a lack of political will and the corresponding financial commitment to make changes which run counter to established orthodoxies. This political neglect is distressing. At the same time as these feelings of anger and frustration, I feel energised that I am not a lone voice; my findings amplify others' cogent arguments and add weight to mounting evidence for adoption reforms. Val Gillies, Rosalind Edwards and Nicola Horsley (2017: 171) suggest that 'There is space here for academics, practitioners and families to exercise the power to disrupt and unsettle'. Although the space may feel restricted, through collaboration with Vincent Dance Theatre (VDT) and BTC, and in the research and writing of this book, I have tried to play a part in exercising power to trouble.

That adoption is not working and needs to change is beyond dispute. The case for change of current adoption discourses, policies and practices has been established in extensive interdisciplinary scholarship, endorsed and extended by empirical evidence, ranging from statistical analysis of datasets to the sensory ethnographic insights presented here. Calls for change may be conservative, such as the policy reforms put forward by the MacAlister Review (2022), circumscribed from the outset by financial limitations and preoccupied with economic implications (Sen and Kerr, 2023c). Or they may be articulated in radical and visionary ways, articulating the impossibility of making adaptations in practice when the wider system is unequal and dysfunctional (such as Selina Thompson's theatre production Twine[1]). These arguments echo and engage with projects working to reform adoption in transnational and other national contexts (see discussion in Chapter 1). Change is also routinely called for in social work practice in the kinds of everyday exchanges shared at the beginning of this chapter. Throughout this research, I have not encountered a single person who is happy with the system as it is.

However, the task of troubling adoption is not straightforward. It is messy, contested work which started long ago, manifests in multiple forms, and must be ongoing. This concluding chapter offers a manifesto to continue the trouble. It takes summary issues from discussion and analysis in previous chapters which point to necessary changes to current adoption practice. The specifics apply to the UK contemporary context but can be adapted and applied as necessary in different or changing contexts. It is a manifesto that grows out of the troubling methodologies deployed throughout, imbued with the spirit of non-linear movement and possibility through which arguments for change have been framed. The manifesto for troubling adoption looks like this:

1. Safeguard everybody
2. Take emotion seriously
3. Challenge and change the stories
4. Support all based on need
5. Re-imagine families
6. Make adoption as open as possible
7. Enable social justice work
8. Make space and time for reflection, dialogues, alliances

Manifestos tend to be assertive and sometimes absolutist in their form. Behind the bossy headlines this manifesto acknowledges complexity and contradiction. It is influenced by what is practicable but also driven by what is necessary. In this way it navigates a space between reforming and abolitionist arguments and energies. This is in keeping with the scalar ambitions of the analysis throughout, weaving connections between conceptual framings, political implementations and the micro politics of daily interactions in social work and creative contexts. At the beginning of the book, I mapped out the conceptual territories of abolition and reform, suggesting that both are necessary and that the dissonance created by bringing them together is part of the politics of meaningful change. The chapter proceeds by briefly revisiting abolition/reform debates to locate and tune into this manifesto's pitch. Following that, each point is considered in more depth, pulling through selective arguments, evidence and discussion from preceding chapters, and suggesting possibilities for both large-scale, longer-term transformation and immediate changes.

Reform and abolition revisited

As we saw in Chapter 1, Dorothy Roberts (2022) takes her arguments for abolition of the family welfare system from the prison abolition movement, specifically from the work of Critical Resistance, an organising collective based in the US. Citing Dylan Rodriguez from Critical Resistance, she defines abolition as 'a practice, an analytical method, a present-tense visioning, an infrastructure in the making, a creative project, a performance, a counterwar, an ideological struggle, a pedagogy and curriculum, an alleged impossibility that is furtively present' (Rodriguez, in Roberts, 2022: 10). Such a definition captures the immanent sense of urgent change which characterises contemporary adoption debates across the globe, and in all their different manifestations (see van Wichelen, 2018; Pösö et al, 2021). As we saw in Chapter 1, Roberts (2022) makes a strong case for abolition of child welfare, or what she calls the family policing system. Her work highlights how the state's removal of children from families is part of a wider carceral complex which disproportionately targets Black and poor families. There are national differences between the US and UK in terms of historical and contemporary family intervention processes, but Roberts makes a fierce and necessary argument articulating entanglements of family intervention in a wider state system of policing of families. Her account is relevant for understanding the material and affective politics of family intervention in the UK, and elsewhere, and for thinking about solutions. My conclusions are not the same as Roberts'. This is not because the case for abolition of all carceral and policing aspects of state governance, to be replaced with a more caring, grassroots system of genuine protection and support, does not resonate in the UK context: it does (see Cottam, 2018; The Care Collective, 2020). However, as evidence and analysis in previous chapters has demonstrated, some of the best available support is currently embedded in state provision. For many parents accessing BTC's service, their case worker was their sole means of support, their only ally: there to walk alongside them as they navigate an adversarial system. We have seen the complicated and often ambivalent negotiations such workers need to make on a day-to-day basis, operating within a deeply imperfect system, to provide the kind of support and outcomes they feel are fair. The research here has demonstrated that social care practitioners who are able to understand, critically challenge and work therapeutically within the system are a powerful resource. At this juncture, they are the people most able to make a material difference in the short term, and their input to what is necessary for more radical change in the future is vital.

Given this commitment to working (for now) with/in the system for change rather than breaking apart the system itself, why not leave 'abolition' to the abolitionists and focus on reforming the adoption system we have? As established in Chapter 1, there is an ethical and epistemological case for reform *and* abolition, refusing to see them as a binary in which choosing one forecloses the other. Kathi Weeks (2023: 434) documents the abolitionist project as comprising both 'systems thinking with a focus on social structures, including institutions and the discursive underpinning that provide their ethical warrants, political rationales and cultural meanings' as well as 'critique that refuses reform as an adequate remedy' (Weeks, 2023: 434). Both components are useful for troubling adoption. As Chapters 2 and 3 argued, to engage critically with contemporary adoption it is necessary to examine the ethical warrants and forms of knowledge which underpin and uphold adoption as a legitimate form of family making. A focus on archival and research practices has highlighted how knowledge constitutes the power to define and enact adoption discourse in cultural, institutional, political and other contexts. Also important in Week's (2023) formulation is the emphasis on time. Abolitionism needs to 'play the long game'. Abolition can be considered 'as a *method* with a distinctive theoretical infrastructure, one that requires scaling up our analyses both spatially and temporally' (Weeks, 2023: 434, original emphasis). We have seen clear evidence that reform is needed *now*. We have also seen that some of the necessary changes require taking a longer temporal lens and a slower approach to address cycles of deprivation and injustice (Fitzpatrick et al, 2023). It is a false separation to see large scale, perhaps even utopian, visions for the future as being incompatible with immediate interventions. Weeks (2023: 448–449) concludes with a valuable list of practical recommendations, suggesting that

> A liveable minimal guaranteed income could provide the economic resources to enable someone to escape an abusive family or to support other household configurations. Shorter working hours, for example a thirty-hour week, without a decrease in pay could provide somewhat more of the time necessary to care for children, the elderly and others, which adequately funded caring services with well paid and highly skilled employees could also supplement. Universal health care delinked from both employment and family membership would give many people more options with regard to waged work, household formation

and the relations between them. Finally, more affordable housing with a range of units that could fit both single residents and a variety of groups could allow some to leave family-based households and support living alone or experimentation with other kinds of domestic arrangements.

Her list is a reminder that at the heart of radical dreams are ordinary demands which should be part of any functional and human social organisation: liveable income, time to care (for self and others), adequate health provision and housing which is affordable and meets the needs of real, rather than imagined, family circumstances.

Another reason why I am unwilling to let go of some commitment to abolition is the weight of evidence *against* adoption in all its (trans/national, historical and contemporary) forms. Transnational adoption scholarship, as reviewed in Chapter 1, exposes the neo-colonialism of adoption discourse and implementation, making it increasingly difficult to defend without colluding with conservative if not right-wing defences of colonial and 'pro-family' entitlements (van Wichelen, 2018). Adoption re/produces social and economic inequalities (Featherstone et al, 2014; Kirton, 2019). Gillies et al (2017: 161) note that 'early years policies in the UK have become detached from basic considerations of human needs and social justice'. There is plenty of evidence that the UK's politics of early intervention as prevention can be unjust (Broadhurst and Mason, 2017, 2020) and that issues of distributional justice mean that poverty and its intersections with racism, poor health, geographical and other circumstances beyond their control, remain central to families' struggles to care for their child/ren (Ireland et al, 2024; Mckay, 2024). Despite adoption's powerful position, regarded by many as the most positive legal option for children unable to live with their families of origin, adoption in its current formations does not break cycles of intergenerational trauma and deprivation but can become part of re/producing them, leading to poor outcomes for many adoptees and their families (Palacios et al, 2019; Lyttle et al, 2024). Even with a lack of adequate data on adoption breakdowns and long-term outcomes (Selwyn, 2023; Thoburn, 2023; AUK, 2024) if we are to take existing evidence seriously, adoption in its current form is not working well. This view is not just held by anti-adoption activists but comes increasingly from within adoption networks. Examples of this are collated in the work of Al Coates.[2] Coates is an adoptive and foster parent, social worker and trainer, who blogs and co-hosts The Adoption and Fostering Podcast, which offers a wide range of perspectives on contemporary adoption.[3] Coates (2018) writes in a blog entry:

> Adoption … is not and never will be a binary issue with a 'correct' position. It reflects the values, politics and perspectives of the society it's based in and it dates really badly. Look back 40 years at adoption

practice and its appalling. You'll look back 40 years from now and be appalled.

When I was interviewing BTC staff, Sylvia similarly reflected:

> I remember watching the film Philomena and saying to a colleague that we're going to look back on our practice in fifty years' time … and we will be just as horrified about adoption as were from Philomena, and everybody looked at me, like, are you crazy? What planet are you on? And that isn't that long ago, and I can already feel some movement … I'm not saying adoption isn't needed. But I think that the system's horrific. And it's not fit for purpose. (Sylvia, BTC staff interview)

Philomena is an award-winning mainstream film made in 2013, based on the true story of a woman in the 1950s in Ireland who was placed in a convent and had her child removed from her and adopted to the US. It offers an example of the critical engagement possible when considering past adoption practices which can be harder to articulate in relation to current practice. These critical insights are not coming from an 'anti-adoption' stance but rather from people who understand the necessity of sometimes removing children from a family with whom they cannot be looked after and finding a safe and secure home for them. In invoking an imaginary judgement from the near future, Coates and Sylvia both express the urgency of doing something *now*. The emotional temporality they draw on here invites us to imagine the future differently. Gil Hochberg (2021: xi) suggests that

> To move away from wounded attachment, loss, and impossibility, and toward a politics invested in future potentiality, is the ability to imagine otherwise – to take a risk and let go of the investment in predefined collectives configured in familiar political categories … in favour of new and still unrecognizable collectives of/for the future.

This risk, a 'letting go', can be enacted by bringing these utopian imaginings into the present. Avery Gordon (2017: x) talks of a way of knowing at the 'utopian margins … in which ideas and actions in the-yet-to-come are sometimes articulated in the present tense, as if they required the power of a narrated story told to you now urgently patiently'. Such an articulation could be regarded as reforming the narratives of adoption, something we have seen enacted in artistic and social practices throughout *Troubling Adoption*. Changing the story, reforming narrative, is a vital early step in making intelligible the possibilities of doing things differently. This narrative action is not an end point. Reform of practical and material aspects of adoption policies and practices can and must also happen now. The future-orientated timeframe of radical re/visioning sits alongside the immediacy of achievable change. Gordon (2011: 8) observes:

> This particular combination of acute timeliness and patience, of there being no time to waste at all and the necessity of taking your time, is what I associate with the abolitionist imaginary, which has guided the worldwide movements to abolish slavery and captivity, colonialism, imprisonment, militarism, foreign debt bondage, and to abolish the capitalist world order known today as globalization or neo-liberalism. Abolition recognizes that transformative time doesn't always stop the world, as if in an absolute break between now and then, but is a daily part of it, a way of being in the ongoing work of emancipation, a work which inevitably must take place while you're still enslaved, imprisoned, indebted, occupied, walled in, commodified, etc.

So, an abolitionist spirit with long-term vision can (and must) sit uncomfortably alongside a reforming agenda. Energised with abolitionary intentions and attentive to the texture and feel of changes to current practice, I take each manifesto demand and consider some detail.

A manifesto for troubling adoption

1. Safeguard everybody

'Safeguarding', like many words and concepts in social care settings, risks becoming somewhat stripped of meaning. It is used widely, and frequently, and has a power which is not always tethered to anything, invoking as it does the emotional necessity of saving and protecting lives. Keeping children as safe as possible remains at the heart of any reform of adoption. Throughout the fieldwork undertaken for *Troubling Adoption*, this primary commitment to children's safety was emphasised repeatedly by professionals from across family services. Safeguarding children can sometimes be deployed against the needs of parents, framed in binary terms where children's needs take precedent. It is possible and necessary to safeguard everyone in the interconnected space of family protection. In Chapter 6, focusing on the daily work of BTC, we saw how creating 'safety' was fundamental to all other work. It was not possible for anybody, parent or professional, to be emotionally regulated, to make important decisions or understand complex situations, if they do not feel safe. We saw how ensuring safety for parents enabled them in turn to look after their children. In Sylvia's example of the mother bottle-feeding her baby incorrectly, Sylvia knew an automatic 'safeguard the child' response could be to intervene and correct the mother's action, or feed the baby herself; however this would lead to a breakdown in the relationship between Sylvia and the mother, a relationship which was essential for enabling the mother to keep her baby in her care. Sylvia noted then how 'the person who needs to know is mum, and she needs to know *safely*'. Sylvia could judge that the longer-term interests of the baby were better met by a regulated, careful and empathetic intervention over time. Against the odds, as I completed my research with BTC, care proceedings were being stepped down and that baby looked set to stay with her mum. The therapeutic focus on safeguarding relationships enabled the best outcome.

Sometimes a baby or child does need to be immediately removed from an unsafe situation. Attention then needs to turn to what is going on for the parent/s from whom they have been removed, and what can be done to support them in their own and the child/ren's interests? Having adequate staffing is vital here, and a front-line social worker, with responsibility for ensuring the timely physical safety of a child, cannot attend adequately to parents' emotional or practical needs. This requires an additional person working therapeutically to look after the parent. Linnea, a member of staff at BTC told me that

> What I would love is *for our service to be offered to every parent*. So every family that gets referred to Children's Services will get a child social worker, because they need to be an independent assessor of the child's situation, but the family gets allocated … a [Breathe, Trust Connect] social worker who could be there for the parent, who doesn't do the assessment, but who is there to really support the parents … non-judgemental, who's just there to walk alongside them through that difficult period in their life … It would impact outcomes. It would impact on the engagement of those parents with any other people, any other service now and in the future … It would … decrease the pressure and the workload for those assessing social workers. (Linnea, BTC staff interview)

Put simply, there needs to be many more services which do the work of BTC and *every* family at risk of losing their child/ren should have a dedicated worker alongside their assessing social worker able to offer the kind of support which we have seen BTC do. Such services need to be trauma-informed, not be time-limited, and not take away women's reproductive autonomy (Geddes, 2021). It is also vital to safeguard social workers. We saw in Chapter 6 that all family social care professionals, whatever service they are working with, are dealing with intensely emotional, sometimes heartbreaking circumstances and must manage these emotions in the context of high caseloads and tight time pressures. An emotionally regulated social worker can make better decisions and support those they are working with. To do this, they need manageable caseloads, therapeutic training and support and supervision. In this way, rather than a hierarchy with competitive need, safeguarding needs to be thought of in more relational terms as an ecosystem.

2. Take emotion seriously

Neglecting or silencing heartbreak 'depletes political imagination' (Bhattacharyya, 2023: 110). Rather than side-lining grief, what becomes possible if we reconfigure sites of trauma, grief and mourning 'as radical spaces to live in, spaces full of possibility, not spaces of shutting down and shame, but places a person can go to claim agency' (Carland and Cvetkovich, 2013: 73)? This approach de-pathologises heartbreak as well as politicising it. We have seen the harrowing grief and loss that follows having a child or children removed. The heartbreaks involved in un/making family through adoption need to be honestly accounted for in adoption narratives. Parents who have their children removed are silenced and their experiences and feelings invalidated: we documented the 'disenfranchised grief' associated with this kind of loss in Chapter 6 (see also Memarnia et al, 2015; Deblasio, 2021; Geddes, 2021; Mason et al, 2023). Enabling their sorrow to be spoken and storied is part of enfranchising such grief, with potential to reduce stigma. As previous chapters have demonstrated, this storying may require creative approaches open to listening to emotional and embodied forms of expression. As well as having their emotions validated, parents are entitled to understand what has happened to them. We saw in Chapter 5 that parents often do not fully understand why or how their child/ren came to be removed, or what can be done about it (Deblasio, 2021). Addressing those questions is far from a straightforward tick box exercise: it requires careful therapeutic work and empathetic and creative approaches to facilitate understanding where words are not enough or do further harm. Emotion is often written out of the scripts at institutional levels, where narratives of adoption are re/produced and authorised, as well as in media reporting, recruitment or training materials, policy documents and political speeches. In all these spaces, there is an ethical imperative for more explicit attention to be paid to what knowledges emotion reveals, and to naming the emotional realities and complexities of adoption.

It is not just heartbreak that had threaded through *Troubling Adoption* but also hope. Eleanor Jupp (2022: 31–32) notes that

> as well as potentially unleashing rage, anxiety and suspicion, it is also worth considering whether different, more progressive emotional registers of hope, possibility, resistance and solidarity might also have space to 'surface', cutting across governance scales and sites within such a landscape, leading to possibilities of progressive transformation and change.

We have seen these emotional registers in action in the cautious steps taken by the four women at the end of Art of Attachment (see Chapter 4) expressing, in Vikki's words '*bits of hope, to cope/ to bend, not break*'. We have seen it in the affirming creative work undertaken by BTC: As Olive put it, 'There's always hope … Can we get in early enough to do this work? You see the movement over time, over the weeks, you see the movement' (Olive, BTC staff interview). This is not the solution-based, happy ever after story that pervades dominant adoption discourse, but a more troubled and troubling form of optimism captured as movement which keeps things – people, bodies, feelings, outcomes – alive with possibility.

3. Challenge and change the stories

Challenging and changing stories is not enough, but it is critical work and underpins other aspects of change. Throughout *Troubling Adoption*, we have seen the power of stories told in new ways. We must engage more critically and creatively with existing archives while developing new archives and archival practices. Building on existing work in feminist, queer and decolonial studies, we must continue to experiment with diverse methods of knowledge production, being willing to work with messy and uncertain knowledges alongside and in critical dialogue with statistical and scientific evidence. The methods developed and shared here are not blueprints but rather an invitation to think with emotion and embodiments when generating accounts of knowledge, whether in social research or cultural and artistic formations. Parents who have had their child/ren removed from them for adoption have little voice (Rushton, 2003; Deblasio, 2021) and storytelling in all its forms needs to include their experiences and knowledges, as well as that of adopted people, adoptive parents, social workers and policy makers. Recognising damage done by knowledge regimes such as state archival and documentary practices, attention needs to turn to doing paperwork with care. As we saw in Chapters 2 and 4, stories recorded in documents can constitute and fix paper or digital identities in damaging ways. Creating different, more inclusive and accessible archives will expand adoption knowledges, facilitating better understanding and dialogue.

Challenging dominant adoption narratives invites apologies for past harms. We have seen national apologies over historical forced adoption in a number of contexts, but not yet in England (Sherwood, 2025). This formal apology is an important part of recognising that adoption is an outcome, sometimes directly, sometimes indirectly, of social wrongs including colonialism, racism, poverty and politically motivated family policies. It is not enough to simply generate or enable the telling of different stories; they also need to be heard and made intelligible in the spaces and times that matter. These include political and policy arenas, media discourse (on and offline), networks of statuary agencies and local government, and everyday spaces of encounter. Drawing on renewed archives of contemporary adoption knowledge, storytelling in all these and other spaces needs to take a variety of forms using all the senses. These tasks will be facilitated by interdisciplinary thinking and action. Collaborations of different kinds bring scholarship and social practice into necessary dialogue, and working with creative practitioners expands the range of media and sensory resources in which we can all think and act.

4. Support all based on need

The research here adds its voice to a weight of evidence that poverty and intersectional structural oppressions contribute to situations in which some people are unable to care for their children without support (Webb et al, 2022). The case for more and better support, for all families, was evidenced in Chapter 7. We have seen what can happen when support is lacking, and what can be possible when it is provided. The political strategy of 'early intervention', critically examined in Chapter 4, should be reframed so that intervention is supportive not punitive. Assessment is not support (Drayak, 2023). If assessment is necessary, support should be provided additionally. Emma Geddes (2021: 16) notes a 'pressing need for good quality post adoption support which does not infringe on women's reproductive autonomy to be made available for first families consistently throughout the country' and the evidence provided throughout this book supports existing calls for such provision at national levels. While this demand has resourcing implications, it makes long-term financial sense, as dedicated work at early stages can prevent children needing state care (Morris and Featherstone, 2010). As a service, BTC are in no doubt that their contribution makes financial sense. As Laurel puts it:

> We are saving ... a significant amount of money ... by preventing adoptions, by having children that have been languishing in care for many years to be able to return home, by working with SGO [Special Guardianship Orders] and preventing placement disruptions, which again will put a cost on the system. So every which way you look at investing in birth parents' support services, you're preventing recurrent care proceedings. And you're hopefully being a part of prevention of intergenerational trauma continuing. (Laurel, BTC staff interview)

This insight resonates with wider research into the value of early interventions to prevent recurrent care proceedings. Although economic benefits here may seem self-evident, they rely on a holistic and long-term perspective that recognises early investments pay off down the line, sometimes in future generations, by resourcing families to care for their own children. They do not make sense in an increasingly short-term and siloed system where decisions are driven by artificial and competitive targets. Interconnections between different services are vital, as observed by social workers in the following discussion:

Participant 1: To get this change, you'd have to change the whole of the approach of safeguarding. You'd have to change the whole thing … CAMHS [Child and Adolescent Mental Health Services] … There'd have to be a whole overhaul of how safeguarding is looked at that includes the history not just the present. There's no *background* [in the current approach] … They deal with the presenting issue but not with what *caused* the wound, with 'how did the wound get there?' … You'd have to get to a *complete change*
Participant 2: a change of the whole social care system!
Participant 3: Is someone writing that down? [all laugh]
Participant 2: But you're right, the whole of the social care system needs to be overturned, ripped apart and started all over again.
Participant 1: Yeah.
(Social workers from Family Drug and Alcohol Court team, Art of Attachment workshop)

Here practitioners reflected on change needing to occur in the whole system and take account of the past and future. There are currently imbalances in therapeutic and practical support allocated to different types of families. All families should be given support that is timely, appropriate and long-term, as necessary. The question driving safeguarding decisions is not 'can this family care for their child/ren without support?' but 'with this support, can they care for their child/ren?' This reframes the relationship between family and state, replacing blame and responsibility on individuals and families and thinking collectively about how care can be provided for those who need it.

5. Re-imagine families

As established at the outset of *Troubling Adoption*, in and across different national contexts, adoption is implicated in deeply unequal patterns of breaking and making families. The terms on which this breaking and making takes place are dictated by a neoliberal capitalist model of 'ideal' families which was examined critically in Chapter 7. Attending to adoption policies and practices exposes the structural organisation of 'family' as flawed. Instead, 'Recognising interdependence as the core of human flourishing would require greater understanding and acknowledgement of the way family and community ties generate crucial resources for children and adults' (Gillies et al, 2017: 166). As well as much greater support for all families based on need from the state, policies and practices which value diverse and interconnected family formations need to be valued and enabled. Isolated family units lacking connections with other families and communities, sets people up to fail, particularly those already in marginalised social positions.

Any reform of adoption needs, as we have seen, to trouble idea/l/s of 'family' and be prepared to fight for different understandings as well as different practices for *doing* and *undoing* family. A radical reimagining of family needs to be at the heart of *any* progressive politics. Idealised forms of family are re/produced to serve narrow political and economic interests. Different models of organisation of resources are possible. Conceptual critiques and alternative visions abound: queer and feminist conceptualisations such as Sophie K. Rosa's (2023) 'radical intimacy', and the abolitionist theories and manifestos of Kathi Weeks (2023), Sophie Lewis (2022) and M E O'Brien (2023) offer recent additions to a long history of such visions. Practical examples are also highlighted in The Care Collective's (2020) Manifesto. Perhaps the most powerful idea is planted by Gordon (2011: 5):

> That real alternatives … are already here, embedded in the practice of subversion and not hiding in some elusive or fantasmatic futurity, is profoundly unsettling: this knowledge makes the present waver, makes it not quite what we thought it was. This living knowledge is a power on its own, the object of a great deal of repressive activity by states and civil societies and families, too.

This insight is a reminder not to simply imagine things differently (although that is important work) but also to do things differently, where possible, and make the 'living knowledge' explicit – in practice; stories, in new archives. The potential for change coming from everyday actions rather than solely through legal and policy reform is also articulated by van Wichelen (2018: 162) in her critical account of transnational adoption, when she writes: 'I do not mean to suggest a legal reform or prohibitions of international adoption. My plea would be instead geared towards the doing and desiring of kinship otherwise'. One such concrete example of this is birth and adoptive families recognising their interdependencies and developing interconnections via more open forms of communication.

6. Make adoption as open as possible

Adoption is not just a relational but a legal severance between a child and the family they are born into. The child is disconnected not just from their parent/s but they also lose their entire network of birth relatives and the culture/s they inhabit, receiving a renewed certificate with their adoptive family's name. Their birth families have no further rights or responsibilities, and until they are themselves legally adults, adopted children have no legal recourse to access information about their birth families. In most cases of a child being removed for adoption, there is not adequate evidence to justify total severance (that is, the legal outcome that is adoption). Attempts at justification include immediate risks that birth families may pose to their children and risks that ongoing connection would destabilise their adoptive family. However, we have seen from the evidence here as well as a range of other research literature, that even when parents are undoubtedly unable to keep their child/ren safe, they love them and wish the best for them (Charlton et al, 1998; Deblasio, 2021; Drayak, 2023). The exceptions to this *are* exceptions. Current practice does not allow for change of any kind. It does not enable birth parents to change; it does not recognise that children grow up and have different needs than those they had at the point of the adoption order. And instead of providing stability, there is evidence that an adopted child's ongoing traumatic experience of loss contributes to destabilisation of adoptive families, particularly as children reach teens and early adulthood (Selwyn and Meakings, 2016; Palacios et al, 2019; Lyttle et al, 2024). This situation is unfair and damaging to birth families and children and sets adoptive families up to fail.

A range of reports and policy recommendations have acknowledged this, with calls to reform contact (MacAlister, 2022; Public Law Adoption Reform Group, 2024). As discussed in Chapter 8, letterbox is the default arrangement for maintaining contact between birth and adoptive parents, usually consisting of an annual or biannual exchange of letters managed administratively by post-adoption or 'keeping in touch' teams at Local Authorities or Regional Adoption Agencies. Calls for this outdated, inadequate system which works for no-one have been loud, clear and consistent from all sources for some time (Neil et al, 2015; Neil, 2018). The empirical insights here add to this appeal. Reforming letterbox will not resolve bigger issues around adoption: it is very much tinkering at the edges. However even small improvements, such as requiring and supporting adoptive parents to write; training and supporting adopters and birth family members with regards to content of communications; facilitating a wider range of communication than just letters, would make a significant difference to parents who wait all year for a letter that never comes, or are told to edit out their appropriate expressions of feelings for their child/ren. Despite being simple, these changes will only work with some cultural changes around how birth families are regarded, removing unfounded or disproportionate fear of risk (Drayak, 2023).

Although there has been significant cultural change in adoption in the past decades, making 'openness' around children's histories an expectation of adoptive parenting, we have seen that in practice this is subject to adoptive parents' willingness and abilities to enable and support knowledge and understanding and connection between their adopted child/ren and their families of origin (MacDonald and McSherry, 2011). While recognising that there may be times when it is necessary to remove a child from their family to keep them safe, and in some cases that removal may need to be permanent, the case for absolute severance is difficult to uphold. In practice, as Sally Sales' (2012) research demonstrates, this difficulty leads to a paradoxical and messy kind of openness in contemporary adoption where 'live' documentary practices in the form of life story work and letterbox correspondence between birth and adoptive families keep a child's first family as an absent presence in their lives (see discussion in Chapter 2). With a lack of genuine openness, traumas of separation, for parents and children, cannot be adequately acknowledged and addressed. Secrecy, fear, lack of belonging and rejection thrive under the cover of maintaining adoptive family as a separate entity. In current practice, the 'legibility' of adoptive families is constructed through acts of severance and secrecy. Kit Myers (2014: 187) notes that

> The violence that is produced and reiterated is not necessarily the explicit and sole work of the adoptive family; rather, the adoptive family grasps onto and employs such signifying strategies because it is the model and the way in which adoption discourse has presented the condition of possibility for the adoptive family, that is, adoption discourse has demarcated definitions of family and presents these guides for legibility.

Myers (2014) calls for greater appreciation of the complexity of adoption with a view to making family legible in different ways. Different modes of legibility can be generated by adoptive families themselves when they pursue connections with their child/ren's birth families and narrate adoption in diverse ways (re/producing different stories and archives). Some adoptive families already reject and subvert these signifying strategies and instead work with a definition and understanding of family and incorporates birth, foster and adoptive family members. Olive told me

> There are adoptive families that will … say this [letterbox contact] isn't good enough for my children …and they take on the social workers … You're talking the exception to the rule. And it's almost, I would say, that's *fought against* [by the Local Authority] … Doing something different, I don't think it's necessarily welcomed. It doesn't fit with what we've always done. It's also the fear of risk almost entrenched into the system. (Olive, BTC staff interview)

Different accounts that make trauma visible and struggle legible can trouble the limited scripts through which adoption is legitimated. There is a much greater role for adoption agencies and post-adoption support services to endorse and amplify different modes of legibility for adoptive families. Making adoption *as open as it can be* is reform that can begin now, making changes over time that could lead to recognising that the family security provided to children via adoption can be achieved with greater support for all and interconnectivity between families rather than severance.

7. Enable social justice work

Olive noted that as a social worker 'you do what you can, with the knowledge you have and the resources you have' (BTC Raw Emotions workshop). Social work professionals need more, and different knowledges, and more, and different resources. The kinds of knowledges and resources they need include those generated and highlighted throughout *Troubling Adoption*; they include emotional and embodied knowledges and therapeutic and creative resources. As we have seen through the experiences of BTC, social worker labour is fundamental to how (adoption) policy plays out. While of course changes at the level of policy making are important, in any context policy makers are dependent on practitioners to translate and implement policy. While mechanisms of 'professionalisation' of social workers' roles and responsibilities seek to control, regulate and standardise their practice, workers are human and interpret and manage their labour in a spectrum of compliant or resistant ways (Pease 2016; Baines, 2017). This agency, together with work towards cultural change within social work services and teams, is where potential for change lies.

Previous chapters have provided insights into the difficult, emotional labour of differently positioned social workers. Social work professionals need to be able to act in children's and families' interests; their work should be recognised as emotional labour in need of proper support. This should take the form of more time, reduced caseloads, and therapeutic supervision. Where possible, support should precede assessment. There are times when assessment is required, and times when that assessment indicates the removal of a child from their parent/s is necessary. The reality that sometimes parents are not able to keep their children safe pervaded this research. It informs the day-to-day practice of family social workers, particularly those with front-line safeguarding roles. For this reason, even if all social workers are enabled to practice in empathetic and trauma-informed ways, there is a need, as already established, for a different support worker who is not an assessing social worker when parents are at risk of losing their child/ren. Resourcing services such as BTC to support front-line colleagues is an action which provides more just outcomes for parents and children and offers the therapeutic support necessary for front-line workers themselves.

Endorsing the current trend of workplaces and services becoming 'trauma informed', it should not be possible to lay claim to this without evidence of workers having adequate time and support to do their jobs in humane and ethical ways. In Chapter 6 we saw the powerful ways in which emotional regulation was key to bringing about different outcomes: for parents in professional settings, for children being cared for by parents and for staff supporting dysregulated parents. 'Relational connection' emerged as being the key factor in terms of positive and fair outcomes for children and families. Relational connection comes with trust, built over time to enable parents to feel safe. At that point of safety, when they can become vulnerable, they can begin to reflect on their lives, their practices, their futures. This is an example of a 'small' change, in the sense of its operational scale in everyday interactions and encounters of relational work. However, to be effective it needs to be practised consistently across a service, over time, and this durational consistency requires the kinds of time and support highlighted above in relation to social workers' labour.

8. Make space and time for reflection, dialogues, alliances

There is need to generate physical and virtual spaces where people, and their opinions and ideas, can come together. It means different media being put to work to re/present and share experiences. It means an expanded archive which can be accessed easily, enhancing people's knowledges and understandings of other perspectives. In the emotional and contested political site of adoption, dialogue is not always easy. To engage in meaningful dialogue, commitment to listening is necessary. Listening, using Julietta Singh's (2018b) formulation, is an active and embodied process, a form of touching and being touched by others. Listening is emotional work. It can be uncomfortable. We saw this repeatedly in the space of Art of Attachment workshops where practitioners encountered trauma, attachment and family intervention in different ways. Thalia Drayak (2023: 86) observes that

> From all angles, we need to rewrite this child protection narrative ... because in the real world, in real life, there are very few monsters and very few baddies. Rather, we have lots of people with good hearts, lots of people who are trying their best and lots of people who are struggling with insurmountable challenges - on every side of the child protection table.

Living with discomfort and ambivalence, even contradiction, needs to be normalised in adoption discussions. On social media platforms people who have been adopted get accused of being 'ungrateful' for being 'rescued' from abortion or a neglectful family if they are critical of adoption. Recognising that everybody has individual experiences, and of course not all adoptive families are experienced in positive ways, a frequent counterargument is that it is possible to love your adoptive parent/s and hate adoption. Many adoptive parents increasingly articulate similar non-binary positions: adoptive parents love their children while recognising the wrongness of adoption. Recognising the multiple ways in which the needs of adoptive families are not met, and the devastating effects on this for so many, Al Coates (2017, 2025) calls for a renegotiation of the 'adoption contract'. Empirical evidence from professionals has highlighted contradictory perspectives from many people working in family services experience. Social workers are far from homogenous in their feelings and opinions about state intervention in families and about the place of adoption. Working within the system as it is, many may feel complicit in practices they are critical of and uncomfortable with. Discomfort is not easy, but it is necessary for change to happen.

Dialogue is not just about people and perspectives (birth and adoptive families, adoptees, social workers, policy makers and so on). It is also about the interdisciplinary connections between theories and practices, and between creative and scholarly formations. It is about the generation of spaces and time for academics, creatives, social care professionals and those with lived experiences and knowledges to come together in mutual learning and exchange resources. Often practice is disconnected from research or draws on a limited and selective evidence base as we saw in Chapter 4 in relation to attachment. Social workers have been shown to rely on normative assertions rather than research-based knowledge (Rosen, 1994; Skivenes and Tefre, 2012). Unusually, social work practitioners at BTC engage with academic research and theory as well as with policy and practice. Their work is influenced by attachment and therapeutic literature, and social research such as Beth Neil's work on contact (see Neil et al, 2015) and the Born into Care research (see Mason et al, 2022). This and other research evidence informs their practice. As a service they are conscious of the privileged insights and understanding they can access because of having time and space to *think* offered by clinical supervision. As Laurel put it, 'We're part of a community of practice, linked to research and practice. So we were trying really hard to make sure that we're in all the right spaces to be able to start making some changes, because that's how change happens, isn't it?' (BTC staff interview). John Radoux (2023: 164) notes how 'thinking and attunement' about the effects of trauma can be 'emotionally uncomfortable' for many professionals. He observes that avoiding 'thinking' may be part of a necessary dissociation strategy when social workers need to make emotional decisions, observing that 'What is required are many more opportunities to reflect, think and feel throughout the entire ecology of the care system' (Radoux, 2023: 165).

Conclusion

One of the BTC social workers Olive told me that 'It doesn't seem to me there's anything in the system that's going to drive that change ... Where's that change going to come from? You know, years down the line, who's going to say, perhaps you could be doing this differently?' In *Troubling Adoption*, I have demonstrated we can be doing it differently. The arguments in this book attempt a nuanced and critical position on a set of debates which are impassioned and can be polarised. Advocates speak with and from experience, sometimes very painful experiences. 'Nuanced and critical' risks pleasing no one: it may be too provocative for a staunchly pro-adoption stance, while being too diluted and full of compromise for abolitionists. Many of the research findings on which the arguments here are based are troubling and uncomfortable, and this is a troubling and uncomfortable manifesto. I am not sure it can be any other way. What is needed right now is hard listening, dialogue across and between differently positioned people, and theoretical, political and emotional commitments to no longer needing adoption in its current form. This commitment needs to be held alongside lobbying and enacting change in practical, incremental ways.

At its heart, *Troubling Adoption* has wrestled with adoption knowledge, addressing how dominant knowledges gain power through archival practices and the circulation of limited discourses. Alongside the generation and maintenance of dominant narratives, alternative and marginalised stories and understandings are blocked, silenced, dismissed. Using creative, affective and embodied methods of knowledge generation, drawing on research traditions in sociology, feminist and queer studies, the preceding chapters have highlighted stories which can be difficult to hear. Not only are these stories emotionally challenging and politically troubling, but they are often communicated without spoken or written words, demanding emotional and embodied engagement to receive, feel and understand them. The knowledge produced through creative and ethnographic research and presented here is not sufficient for achieving change: like all data and analysis, it takes its place alongside and in critical dialogue with other forms of research, policy and experiential information.

Throughout *Troubling Adoption*, the apparently conflicting forces of heartbreak and hope have been held in tension. Of course, they are not in conflict but rather components of the same life-force. Conceptually, and in concrete examples, I have attended to the kind of realistic hope that can manifest out of heartbreak. Heartbreak offers important knowledges about family intervention and adoption. Allowing ourselves to be moved enables us to take steps and, as one participant wrote on a heart made from paper during an Art of Attachment workshop, 'Listen, breathe, feel'.

Notes

Chapter 1
1. Biological families are interchangeably referred to as 'birth' or 'first' family. Where it is necessary to distinguish, I have used the term 'birth family' as that was the term used by parents and staff at Breathe, Trust, Connect (BTC).
2. Details available at https://www.vincentdt.com/project/home-truths-2
3. Details of Art of Attachment available at https://www.vincentdt.com/project/art-of-attachment-film-installation-2024-25-available-from-autumn-2024/
4. BTC changed their name from *Breaking The Cycle* to *Breathe, Trust, Connect*, at around the time I completed fieldwork with them. The change reflected dissatisfaction with the ethics and possibilities of 'breaking the cycle'.
5. See, for example, https://www.thedunbarproject.org.uk/ and https://howtobeadopted.com/
6. See https://www.childrensservices.network/
7. Public law family court Care Proceedings are conducted under Section 31 of the Children's Act 1989, when there is concern about significant (risk of) harm to children from their carer.
8. For example, Support not Separation: https://supportnotseparation.blog/
9. Parents with 'lived experience' of their child/ren being removed and adopted are often involved as advisors and experts on relevant Boards and Commissions, such as *The Independent Review of Children's Social Care* (MacAlister, 2022).

Chapter 3
1. For further information about the Art of Attachment project, see https://www.vincentdt.com/project/art-of-attachment/ and film installation https://www.vincentdt.com/project/art-of-attachment-film-installation-2024-25-available-from-autumn-2024/. The project was a collaboration with Brighton Oasis Project https://www.oasisproject.org.uk/ and was funded by the Wellcome Trust.
2. See https://www.vincentdt.com/project/in-loco-parentis/
3. A map of services offering support to birth parents across the UK is available from Family Rights Group at https://frg.org.uk/birth-families-map/
4. Full ethical approval was granted by the University of Warwick's Research Governance and Ethics Committee: reference HSSREC 15/22-23.

Chapter 5
1. Further information about Theraplay available at https://www.theraplay.org.uk/

Chapter 6
1. 'Counter-transference refers to situations where someone in a therapeutic role transfers emotions based on their past experiences, onto the client. Social care practitioners are humans, just as clients are; they will have their history of hope, love, desire to heal others, as well as their own sadness, attachment issues and relationship issues … supervision and emotional support and systems that support self-awareness and self-care are crucial for social care practitioners' (Sylvia, staff workshop discussion).

Chapter 7

1. There are many good reasons for making 'close matches' along the lines of race, ethnicity, culture and so on (Wainwright and Ridley, 2012).
2. Details of the Adoption and Special Guardianship Support Fund are available at https://www.gov.uk/guidance/adoption-support-fund-asf. For examples of wider resources, see https://beaconhouse.org.uk/.
3. This 'one off' meeting between adoptive and birth parents was dramatised in a 2024 BBC series *Lost Boys and Fairies*, directed by Daf James. This scene provided unusual insight into the emotional complexities of the connections between these parents.

Chapter 8

1. For information about Selina Thompson's play Twine, see https://selinathompson.co.uk/work/twine/
2. Information about Al Coates' blog, training and podcast is available at http://www.alcoates.co.uk/
3. Available at http://www.alcoates.co.uk/p/the-adoption-fostering-podcast.html

References

Adoption UK (AUK) (2022) *Children with a plan for adoption are spending increasing time in care before being adopted*, 17 November. Available at https://www.adoptionuk.org/news/children-with-a-plan-for-adoption-are-spending-increasing-time-in-care-before-being-adopted, accessed January 2023.

Adoption UK (AUK) (2023) *The Adoption Barometer: a stocktake of adoption in the UK*, May 2023. Available at https://www.adoptionuk.org/Handlers/Download.ashx?IDMF=6501ceec-87a1-4f03-ab7a-a5b2bcd62edb, accessed May 2023.

Adoption UK (AUK) (2024) *The Adoption Barometer: a stocktake of adoption in the UK*, May 2024. Available at https://www.adoptionuk.org/the-adoption-barometer, accessed October 2024.

Ahmed, S. (2004) *The Cultural Politics of Emotion*, Routledge.

Ahmed, S. (2012) 'A wilfulness archive', *Theory and Event*, 15(3).

Ahmed, N., James, D., Tayabali, A. and Watson, M. (2022) *Ethnicity and Children's Social Care*, Department for Education.

Ainsworth, M. (1978) *Patterns of Attachment: A Psychological Study of the Strange Situation*, Lawrence Erlbaum.

Allen, G. and Duncan Smith, I. (2008) *Early Intervention: Good Parents, Great Kids, Better Citizens*, Centre for Social Justice and the Smith Institute. Available at https://www.smith-institute.org.uk/book/early-intervention-good-parents-great-kids-better-citizens/, accessed October 2024.

Allen, K. and Osgood, J. (2009) 'Young women negotiating maternal subjectivities: the significance of social class', *Studies in the Maternal*, 1(2): 1–17.

Allen, K. and Taylor, Y. (2012) 'Placed parenting, locating unrest: failed femininities, troubled mothers and rioting subjects', *Studies in the Maternal*, 4(2): 1–25.

Alrouh, B. et al (2022) *Mothers in recurrent care proceedings: new evidence for England and Wales*, Nuffield Family Justice Observatory. Available at https://www.nuffieldfjo.org.uk/resource/mothers-in-recurrent-care-proceedings-new-evidence-for-england-and-wales, accessed October 2024.

Alper, J. (2019) (ed) *Supporting Birth Parents Whose Children Have Been Adopted*, Jessica Kingsley.

Althusser, L. (1972) 'Ideology and ideological state apparatus', in B. Cosin (ed) *Education, Structure and Society*, Penguin, pp 242–280.

Amin, K (2016) 'Haunted by the 1990s: queer theory's affective histories', *WSQ: Women's Studies Quarterly*, 44(3/4): 173–189.

Anderson, B. (2022) 'Forms and scenes of attachment: a cultural geography of promises', *Dialogues in Human Geography*, 1–18.

Back, L. (2007) *The Art of Listening*, Bloomsbury.

Back, L. and Puwar, N. (2012) (eds) *Live Methods*, Wiley-Blackwell.

Baines, D. (2017) (ed) *Doing Anti-Oppressive Practice: Social Justice Social Work*, Fernwood Publishing.

Barrow, M. (2021) 'Privatisation of children's services is bad for children and bad for taxpayers', blog post for *The Transparency Project*, 17 February. Available at https://transparencyproject.org.uk/privatisation-of-childrens-services-is-bad-for-children-and-bad-for-taxpayers/, accessed September 2024.

Barrett, M. and McIntosh, M. (1982) *The Anti-Social Family*, Verso.

Bawden, A. (2025) One in four young people in England have mental health conditions, NHS survey finds, *The Guardian*, 26 June. Available at https://www.theguardian.com/society/2025/jun/26/young-people-england-common-mental-health-conditions-nhs-survey, accessed June 2025.

Behar, R. (2022 [1996]) *The Vulnerable Observer: Ethnography That Breaks Your Heart*, Beacon Press.

Berlant, L. (2011) *Cruel Optimism*, Duke University Press.

Bernard, C. and Harris, P. (2019) 'Serious case reviews: the lived experience of Black children', *Child and Family Social Work*, 24(2): 256–263.

Berry, L. (2023) *The Home Child*, Chatto and Windus.

Bhattacharya, T. (2018) *Social Reproduction Theory: Remapping Class, Recentring Oppression*, Pluto.

Bhattacharyya, G. (2023) *We, The Heartbroken*, Hajar Press.

Bilson, A. and Bywaters, P. (2020) 'Born into care: evidence of a failed state', *Children and Youth Services Review*, 116.

Bilson, A., Featherstone, B. and Martin, K. (2017) 'How child protection's 'investigative turn' impacts on poor and deprived communities', *Family Law*, 47: 316–319.

Bleasby, C. (2023) '"Nobody wants to remove a baby … that's the crux of it": Social Workers' Experiences of Undertaking Pre Birth Assessments', unpublished Doctoral Thesis, University of Dundee. Available at https://discovery.dundee.ac.uk/en/studentTheses/nobody-wants-to-remove-a-baby-thats-the-crux-of-it, accessed February 2024.

Blencowe, C. (2021) 'Family debilitation: migrant child detention and the aesthetic regime of neoliberal authoritarianism', *GeoHumanities*, 7(2): 415–440.

Boddy, J., Hanrahan, F. and Wheeler, B. (2023) *Thinking Through Family: Narratives of Care Experienced Lives*, Bristol University Press.

Bondi, L. (2014) 'Understanding feelings: engaging with unconscious communication and embodied knowledge', *Emotion, Space and Society*, 10: 44–54.

Bowlby, J. (1951) 'Maternal care and mental health', *World Health Organization Monograph (Serial No. 2)*.

Bowlby, J. (1969) *Attachment and Loss: Vol. 1. Attachment*, Basic Books.

Bowlby, J. (1973) *Attachment and Loss: Vol. 2. Separation: Anxiety and Anger*, Basic Books.

Bowlby, J. (1980) *Attachment and Loss: Vol. 3. Sadness and Depression. 2*, Basic Books.

Bourdieu, P. (1999) *The Weight of the World: Social Suffering in Contemporary Society*, Stanford University Press.

Briggs, L. (2012) *Somebody's Children: The Politics of Transracial and Transnational Adoption*, Duke University Press.

Brim, M. and Ghaziani, A. (2016) 'Introduction: Queer methods', *WSQ: Women's Studies Quarterly*, 44 (3/4): 14–26.

Broadhurst, K. and Mason, C. (2013) 'Maternal outcasts: raising the profile of women who are vulnerable to successive, compulsory removals of their children - a plea for preventative action', *Journal of Social Welfare and Family Law*, 35(3): 291–304.

Broadhurst, K. and Mason, C. (2017) 'Birth parents and the collateral consequences of court-ordered child removal: towards comprehensive framework', *International Journal of Law, Policy and the Family,* 31(1): 41–59.

Broadhurst, K. and Mason, C. (2020) 'Child removal as the gateway to further adversity: birth mother accounts of the immediate and enduring collateral consequences of child removal', *Qualitative Social Work: Research and Practice*, 19(1): 15–37.

Broadhurst, K., Mason, C. and Ward, H. (2022) 'Urgent care proceedings for new-born babies in England and Wales – time for a fundamental review,' *International Journal of Law, Policy and the Family*, 36(1): 1–31.

Broadhurst, K., Shaw, M., Kershaw, S., Harwin, S.J., Alrouh, B., Mason, C. and Pilling, M. (2015) 'Vulnerable birth mothers and repeat losses of infants to public care: is targeted reproductive health care ethically defensible?' *Journal of Social Welfare and Family Law*, 37(1): 84–98.

Brockmann, O. and Garrett, P.M. (2022) "People are responsible for their own individual actions': dominant ideologies within the Neoliberal Institutionalised Social Work Order', *European Journal of Social Work*, 25(5): 880–893.

Brodzinsky, D., Gunnar, M. and Palacios, J. (2022) 'Adoption and trauma: risks, recovery, and the lived experience of adoption', *Child Abuse and Neglect*, 130.

Broome, E. (2021) 'A real apology for the mistakes of the past must include action to make sure that the situation has really changed', Coram BAAF. Available at https://corambaaf.org.uk/real-apology-mistakes-past-must-include-action-make-sure-situation-has-really-changed-writes-ellen, accessed November 2024.

Brown, A., Waters, C.S. and Shelton, K.H. (2017) 'A systematic review of the school performance and behavioural and emotional adjustments of children adopted from care', *Adoption and Fostering*, 41(4): 346–368.

Browne, K. and Nash, C.J. (2010) (eds) *Queer Methods and Methodologies: Intersecting Queer Theories and Social Science Research*, Routledge.

Buckwalter, K.D., Reed, D. and Mercer, D. (2017) 'Ghosts in the adoption: uncovering parents' attachment and coping history', *Families in Society*, 98(3): 225–234.

Butler, J. (1997) *The Psychic Life of Power: Theories in Subjection*, Stanford University Press.

Butler, J. (2004) 'Violence, mourning, politics', in J. Butler (ed) *Precarious Life*, Verso, pp 19–49.

Bywaters, P. and Skinner, G. (2022) 'The Relationship Between Poverty and Child Abuse and Neglect: New Evidence', Final Report, University of Huddersfield/ Nuffield Foundation. Available at https://www.nuffieldfoundation.org/wp-content/uploads/2022/03/Full-report-relationship-between-poverty-child-abuse-and-neglect.pdf, accessed November 2024.

Bywaters, P., Brady, G., Sparks, T. and Bos, E. (2016) 'Child welfare inequalities: new evidence, further questions', *Child and Family Social Work*, 21: 369–380.

Bywaters, P., Scourfield, J., Webb, C., Morris, K., Featherstone, B., Brady, G., Jones, C. and Sparks, T. (2019) 'Paradoxical evidence on ethnic inequities in child welfare: towards a research agenda'. *Children and Youth Services Review*, 96: 145–154.

The Care Collective (Chatzidakis, A., Hakin, J., Littler, J., Rottenberg, C. and Segal, L.) (2020) *The Care Manifesto: The Politics of Interdependence*, Verso.

Carby, H. (2019) *Imperial Intimacies: A Tale of Two Islands*, Verso.

Carby, H. (2020) 'The National Archives', *InVisible Culture: A Journal for Visual Culture*, 31. Available at https://www.invisibleculturejournal.com/pub/the-national-archives/release/1, accessed September 2024.

Carland, T.R. and Cvetkovich, A. (2013) 'Sharing an archive of feelings: a conversation'. *Art Journal*, 72(2): 70–77.

Caruth, C. (1996) *Unclaimed Experience: Trauma, Narrative and History*, John Hopkins University Press.

Carp, E.W. (1998) *Family Matters: Secrecy and Disclosure in the History of Adoption*, Harvard University Press.

Caswell, M. (2020) 'Feeling liberatory memory work: on the archival uses of joy and anger', *Archivaria*, 90: 148–164.

Caverero, A. (2000) *Relating Narratives: Storytelling and Selfhood*, Routledge.

Chadwick, R.J. (2023) 'The question of feminist critique', *Feminist Theory*, 25(3): 376–395.

Charania, M. (2023) *Archive of Tongues: An Intimate History of Brownness*, Duke University Press.

Charlton, L, Crank, M., Kansara, K. and Olivia, C. (1998) *Still Screaming: Birth Parents Compulsorily Separated from their Children*, After Adoption.

Chen, M.Y. (2012) *Animacies: Biopolitics, Racial Mattering, and Queer Affect*, Duke University Press.

Cherry, L., Treisman, K. and de Thierry, B. (2023) 'The unintended consequences of the expansion of trauma informed practice', webinar. https://www.eventbrite.co.uk/e/the-unintended-consequences-of-the-expansion-of-trauma-informed-recording-tickets-751532512977, accessed September 2023.

Children's Commissioner (2024) 'Over a quarter of a million children still waiting for mental health support', Children's Commissioner warns. Press Notice. Available at https://www.childrenscommissioner.gov.uk/blog/over-a-quarter-of-a-million-children-still-waiting-for-mental-health-support/, accessed June 2025.

Clapton, G. (2024) '"The past is never dead. it's not even past" (Faulkner, 1919 Requiem for a Nun p. 85): mapping and taking care of the ghosts in adoption', *Genealogy*, 8(2): 7.

Cossar, J. and Neil, E. (2010) 'Supporting the birth relatives of adopted children: how accessible are services?' *British Journal of Social Work*, 40(5): 1368–1386.

Coates, A. (2017) 'Adoption contract', blog post, 20 September. Available at https://alcoates.co.uk/blog%2C-news-%26-articles/f/adoption-contract, accessed June 2025.

Coates, A. (2018) 'Adoption: Pragmatic DNA', blog post, 17 May. Available at http://www.alcoates.co.uk/2018/05/, accessed November 2024.

Coates, A. (2025) 'Renegotiating the adoption contract', blog post, 30 April. Available at https://alcoates.co.uk/blog%2C-news-%26-articles/f/renegotiating-the-adoption-contract, accessed June 2025.

Coates, A., Hughes, J. and Thorley, W. (2020) 'Policing childhood aggressive violent of aggressive behaviour: responding to vulnerable families', CEL&T Training and Development. Available at https://childhub.org/en/child-protection-online-library/childhood-challenging-violent-and-aggressive-behaviour-ccvab, accessed October 2024.

Condit-Shrestha, K. (2018) 'South Korea and adoption's ends: re-examining the numbers and historicizing market economies', *Adoption and Culture*, 6(2): 364–400.

Condit-Shrestha, K. (2021) 'Archives, adoption records, and owning historical memory', in Levison, D., Maynes, M.J. and Vavrus, F. (eds) *Children and Youth as Subjects, Agents, Objects: Innovative Approaches to Research Across and Space Time*, Palgrave Macmillan, pp 155–173.

Connerton, P. (1994) *How Societies Remember*, Cambridge University.

Copeland, V. (2023) 'Editorial: a note on collective experimentation towards abolition', *Abolitionist Perspectives in Social Work*, 1(1). Available at https://apsw-ojs-uh.tdl.org/apsw/article/view/23, accessed November 2024.

Cottam, H. (2018) *Radical Help: How We Can Remake the Relationships Between Us and Revolutionise the Welfare State*, Virago.

Critchley, A. (2020) "'The lion's den': social workers' understandings of risk to infants', *Child and Family Social Work*, 25(4): 895–903.

Cvetkovich, A. (2003) *An Archive of Feelings: Trauma, Sexuality and Lesbian Public Cultures*, Duke University Press.

Dann, M., Fulton, L., Rogers, C. and Harris, A. (2021) 'Why can't orphans play baseball? Writing into the primal wound', *Qualitative Enquiry*, 27(3–4): 465–472.

Davidson, H. (2024) 'US diplomats seeking clarity for hundreds of families in the process of international adoption', *The Guardian*, 6 September. Available at https://www.theguardian.com/world/article/2024/sep/06/china-ending-foreign-adoption-international-intercountry, accessed November 2024.

Davis, A.Y. (2003) *Are Prisons Obsolete?* Seven Stories Press.

Davis, J. and Marsh, N. (2020) 'Boys to men: the cost of "adultification" in safeguarding responses to Black boys', *Critical and Radical Social Work*, 8(2): 255–259.

Deblasio, L. (2021) *Adoption and Law: The Unique Personal Experiences of Birth Mothers in Adoption Proceedings*, Routledge.

Derrida, J. (1995) *Archive Fever: A Freudian Impression*, University of Chicago Press.

Department for Education (DfE) (2020) (authors Boddy, J., Bowyer, S., Godar, R., Hale, C., Kearney, J., Preston, O., Wheeler, B. and Wilkinson, J.) *Evaluation of Pause*, Evaluation Report. Available at https://assets.publishing.service.gov.uk/government/uploads/system/uploads/attachment_data/file/932816/Pause_-_Sussex.pdf, accessed November 2024.

DfE (2024) *Children Looked After in England Including Adoptions*, Department for Education, 14 November. Available at https://explore-education-statistics.service.gov.uk/find-statistics/children-looked-after-in-england-including-adoptions, accessed November 2024.

Dinshaw, C., Barale, M., Goldberg, J., Moon, M. and Sedgwick, E. (1999) *Getting Medieval: Sexualities and Communities, Pre- and Postmodern*, Duke University Press.

Doka, K.J. (1999) 'Disenfranchised grief', *Bereavement Care*, 18(3): 37–39.

Dominelli, L., Strega, S., Callahan, M. and Rutman, D. (2005) 'Endangered children: experiencing and surviving the state as failed parent and grandparent', *British Journal of Social Work*, 35: 1123–1144.

Dorow, S.K. (2006) *Transnational Adoption: A Cultural Economy of Race, Gender and Kinship*, New York University Press.

Drayak, T. (2023) 'Humane social work practice: a more parent friendly system? Hopes and challenges in the 2020s', in R. Sen and C. Kerr (eds) *The Future of Children's Care: Critical Perspectives of Children's Services Reform*, Policy Press, pp 85–100.

Drew, I., Pierre, R. and Sen, R. (2023) 'Exploring and re-imagining children's services in England through a decolonial frame', in R. Sen and C. Kerr (eds) *The Future of Children's Care: Critical Perspectives of Children's Services Reform*, Policy Press, pp 101–121.

Dubinsky, K. (2010) *Babies Without Borders: Adoption and Migration Across the Americas*, University of Toronto Press.

The Dunbar Project (2024) 'Nurturing healing: The imperative of trauma-informed care for adoptees'. Available at https://www.thedunbarproject.org.uk/articles/nurturing-healing-the-imperative-of-trauma-informed-care-for-adoptees, accessed November 2024.

Duschinsky, R. (2020) *Cornerstones of Attachment Research*, Oxford Academic. Available at https://doi.org/10.1093/med-psych/9780198842064.001.0001, accessed June 2024.

Duschinsky, R., Greco, M. and Solomon, J. (2015) 'The politics of attachment: lines of flight with Bowlby, Deleuze and Guattari', *Theory, Culture and Society*, 32(7–8): 173–195.

Edwards, R., Gillies, V. and Gorin, S. (2021a) 'Problem-solving for problem solving: data analytics to identify families for service intervention', *Critical Social Policy*, 42(2): 265–284.

Edwards, R., Gillies, V. and Gorin, S. (2021b) 'Data linkage for early intervention in the UK: parental social licence and social divisions', *Data and Policy*, 3.

Edkins, J. (2003) *Trauma and the Memory of Politics*, Cambridge University Press.

Elliot, A. (2013) *Why Can't My Child Behave? Empathetic Parenting Strategies that Work for Adoptive and Foster Families*, Jessica Kingsley.

Eng, D. (2010) *The Feeling of Kinship*, Duke University Press.

Evans, R., Ribbens McCarthy, J., Bowlby, S., Wouango, J. and Kébé, F. (2017) 'Producing emotionally sensed knowledge? Reflexivity and emotions in researching responses to death', *International Journal of Social Research Methodology*, 20(6): 585–598.

Featherstone, B. and Fraser, C. (2012) 'I'm just a mother. I'm nothing special, they're all professionals': parental advocacy as an aid to parental engagement', *Child and Family Social Work*, 17(2): 244–253.

Featherstone, B. and Gupta, A. (2023) 'Protecting children: a social model for the 2020', in R. Sen and C. Kerr (eds) *The Future of Children's Care: Critical Perspectives on Children's Services Reform*, Policy Press, pp 178–193.

Featherstone, B., White, S. and Morris, K. (2014) *Re-Imagining Child Protection: Towards Humane Social Work with Families*, Policy Press.

Featherstone B., Gupta, A. and Mills, S. (2018) *The Role of the Social Worker in Adoption - Ethics and Human Rights: An Enquiry*, BASW.

Ferguson, S. (2020) *Women and Work: Feminism, Labour and Social Reproduction*, Pluto.

Fitzpatrick, C., Hunter, K., Shaw, J. and Staines, J. (2023) 'Confronting intergenerational harm: care experience, motherhood and criminal justice involvement', *The British Journal of Criminology*, 64(2): 257–274.

Forslund, T. and Duschinsky, R. (2021) (eds) *Attachment Theory and Research: A Reader*, Wiley Blackwell.

Foster, S. (2022) 'Are safe haven laws an adequate replacement for abortion rights?' *CICLR Online*, 57. Available at https://larc.cardozo.yu.edu/ciclr-online/57, accessed January 2023.

Foucault, M. (1969/2002) *The Archaeology of Knowledge*, Routledge.

France, L., McIntosh, S. and Woods, K. (2024) 'An exploration of a Theraplay® informed group as an intervention for adoptive families', *Adoption and Fostering*, 48(2): 223–242.

Frank, A.W. (1995) *The Wounded Storyteller: Body, Illness, and Ethics*, University of Chicago Press.

Fravel, D.L., McRoy, R.G. and Grotevant, H.D. (2000) 'Birthmother perceptions of the psychologically present adopted child: Adoption openness and boundary ambiguity', *Family Relations*, 49(4): 425–432.

Freeman, E. (2010) *Time Binds: Queer Temporalities, Queer Histories*. Duke University Press.

Garrett, P. (2017) 'Excavating the past: Mother and Baby Homes in the Republic of Ireland', *The British Journal of Social Work*, 47(2): 358–374.

Geddes, E. (2021) ' "Some days it's like she has died". A qualitative exploration of first mothers' utilisation of artefacts associated with now adopted children in coping with grief and loss', *Qualitative Social Work*, 21(5): 811–832.

Gill, D. and Lambert, B. (2019) 'Breaking the cycle: an approach to group work with birth mothers', in J. Alper (ed) *Supporting Birth Parents Whose Children Have Been Adopted*, Jessica Kingsley, pp 151–168.

Gillies, V. (2007) *Marginalised Mothers: Exploring Working Class Experiences of Parenting*, Routledge.

Gillies, V., Horsley, N. and Edwards, R. (2017) *Challenging the Politics of Early Intervention: Who's 'Saving' Children and Why?* Policy Press.

Goddard, J., Feast, J. and Kirton, D. (2008) 'A childhood on paper: managing access to child care files by post-care adults', *Adoption and Fostering*, 32(2): 50–62.

Golding, K. and Hughes, D. (2012) *Creating Loving Attachments: Parenting with PACE to Nurture Confidence and Security in the Troubled Child*, Jessica Kingsley.

Golding, K. and Gould, J. (2019) ' "No quick fix": the benefits of longer term counselling for birth parents with complex Histories. Of trauma and abuse: Carrie's story', in J. Alper (2019) (ed) *Supporting Birth Parents Whose Children Have Been Adopted*, Jessica Kingsley, pp 109–131.

Golm, D. (2024) 'Breaking the taboo: let's talk about child-to-parent violence', *Adoption and Fostering*, 48(2): 163–166.

Gordon, A. (2011) 'Some thoughts on haunting and futurity', *borderlands*, 10(2): 1–21.

Gordon, A. (2017) *The Hawthorn Archive: Letters from the Utopian Margins*, Fordham University Press.

Gorin, S., Edwards, R., Gillies, V. and Vannier Ducasse, H. (2024) '"Seen" through records: parents' access to children's social care records in an age of increasing datafication', *The British Journal of Social Work*, 54(1): 228–245.

Grotevant, H.D., Lo, A.Y.H., Fiorenzo, L. and Dunbar, N.D. (2017) 'Adoptive identity and adjustment from adolescence to emerging adulthood: a person-centered approach'. *Developmental Psychology*, 53(11): 2195–2204.

Gunaratnam, Y. (2012) 'Learning to be affected: social suffering and total pain at life's borders', in L. Back and N. Puwar (eds) *Live Methods*, Blackwell.

Gunaratnam, Y. (2013) *Death and the Migrant: Bodies, Borders and Care*, Bloomsbury.

Gunaratnam, Y. and Eisa, A. (2024) 'Foreign bodies: a conversation between Yasmin Gunaratnam and Ali Eisa', *Mortality*, 29(1): 207–221.

Gunsberg, L. (2017) 'The ghost kingdom: the secret narrative of the adoptee's birth and origins', in J.D. Lichtenberg, F.M. Lachmann and J.L. Fosshage (eds) *Narrative and Meaning: The Foundation of Mind, Creativity, and the Psychoanalytic Dialogue*, Routledge, pp 190–214.

Gupta, A. (2017) 'Poverty and child neglect – the elephant in the room?' *Families, Relationships and Societies*, 6(1): 21–36.

Gupta, A. and Blumhardt, H. (2016) 'Giving poverty a voice: families' experiences of social work practice in a risk-averse child protection system', *Families, Relationships and Societies*, 5(1): 163–172.

Gupta, A. and Featherstone, B. (2020) 'On hope, loss, anger, and the spaces in between: reflections on living with/in adoption and the role of the social worker', *Child and Family Social Work*, 25(1): 165–172.

Hagen, R. and Ahmed, A. (2025) *Social Work, Housing and Homelessness*, Routledge.

Hammond, S.P., Young, J. and Duddy, C. (2020) 'Life story work for children and young people with care experience: a scoping review', *Developmental Child Welfare*, 2(4): 293–315.

Harris, N. (2012) 'Assessment: when does it help and when does it hinder? Parents' experiences of the assessment process', *Child and Family Social Work*, 17(2): 180–191.

Harris-Waller, J., Granger, C. and Hussain, M. (2018) 'Psychological interventions for adoptive parents: a systematic review', *Adoption and Fostering*, 42(1): 6–21.

Hartman, S. (2019) *Wayward Lies: Beautiful Experiments*, Serpentine.

Hayden, C. and Jenkins, C. (2014) 'Troubled Families' Programme in England: "wicked problems" and policy-based evidence', *Policy Studies*, 35(6): 631–649.

Haynes, J. (2024) *Birmingham: A Child Poverty Emergency*, Birmingham Live/Reach PLC Data Unit. Available at https://childpoverty.birminghamlive.co.uk/, accessed September 2024.

Henry, R. (2012) 'Gifts of grief: performative ethnography and the revelatory potential of emotion', *Qualitative Research*, 12: 528–539.

Hill, M., Lambert, L., Triseliotis, J. and Buist, M. (1992) 'Making judgements about parenting: the example of freeing for adoption', *British Journal of Social Work*, 22(4): 373–389.

Hill-Collins, P. (1998) 'It's all in the family: intersections of gender, race, and nation', *Hypatia*, 13(3): 62–82.

Hillman, S., Lajmi, N., Steele, M., Hodges, J., Simmonds, J. and Kaniuk, J. (2024) 'Adoptive parents' worries and concerns about their adolescent adopted children', *Adoption and Fostering*, 48(1): 126–148.

Hipchen, E. and Deans, J. (2003) 'Introduction: adoption life writing: origins and other ghosts', *A/b: Auto/Biography Studies*, 18(2): 163–170.

Hochberg, G.Z. (2021) *Becoming Palestine: Toward an Archival Imagination of the Future*, Duke University Press.

Holmes, H. and Hall, S.M. (2020) (eds) *Mundane Methods: Innovative Ways to Research the Everyday*, Manchester University Press.

Holt, A. (2013) *Adolescent-to-Parent Abuse: Current Understandings in Research, Policy and Practice*, Policy Press.

Houliham, B. and Kinder, E. (2024) 'States of apology: the politics of memory, access, and Irish archives administration', in P. Svard and B. Ibhawoh (eds) *Documentation from Truth and Reconciliation Commissions*, Routledge.

Horrocks, C. and Goddard, J. (2010) 'Adults who grew up in care: constructing the self and accessing care files', *British Journal of Social Work*, 40: 2617–2633.

Howard League for Penal Reform and Transition to Adulthood (2015) *You Can't Put a Number on it: a report from young adults in why in criminal justice maturity is more important than age*, The Howard League. Available at https://howardleague.org/publications/you-cant-put-a-number-on-it/, accessed December 2022.

Howe, D. and Feast, J. (2000) *Adoption, Search and Reunion: The Long-Term Experience of Adopted Adults*. Children's Society.

Hughes, D. and Baylin, J. (2012) *Brain Based-Parenting: The Neuroscience and Caregiving for Healthy Attachment*, WW Norton.

Hughes, D., Golding, K. and Hudson, J. (2019) *Healing Relational Trauma with Attachment-Focused Interventions*, WW Norton.

Humphreys, C. and Kertesz, M. (2012) '"Putting the heart back into the record": personal records to support young people in care', *Adoption and Fostering*, 36(1): 27–39.

Ireland, G., Wijlaars, L., Jay, M.A., Grant, C., Pearson, R., Downs, J. and Gilbert, R. (2024) 'Social and health characteristics of mothers involved in family court care proceedings in England', *Nuffield Foundation*, September. UCL Great Ormond Street Institute of Child Health. Report available at https://www.nuffieldfjo.org.uk/news/one-in-15-young-mothers-involved-in-care-proceedings-before-their-eldest-child-is-10, accessed November 2024.

Ivinson, G. and Renold, E.J. (2021) 'What more do bodies know? Moving with the gendered affects of place', *Body and Society*, 27(1): 85–112.

Jensen, T. (2018) *Parenting the Crisis: The Cultural Politics of Parent-Blame*, Policy Press.

Joint Committee on Human Rights (JCHR) (2022) *The Violation of Family Life: Adoption of Children of Unmarried Women 1949–1976*, Third Report of Session 2022–23 Report, together with formal minutes relating to the report, July 2022. Available at https://committees.parliament.uk/publications/23076/documents/169043/default/, accessed November 2022.

Jondec, A.F. and Barlow, J. (2023) 'An intensive perinatal mentalisation-based intervention for women at risk of child removal and the role of restorative relationships', *Child Abuse Review*, 32(1).

Joyce, K. (2013) *The Child Catchers: Rescue, Trafficking, and the New Gospel of Adoption*, PublicAffairs.

Jupp, E. (2022) 'Emotions, affect and social policy: austerity and Children's Centers in the UK', *Critical Policy Studies*, 16(1): 19–35.

Kaba, M. and Richie, A. (2022) *No More Police: A Case for Abolition*, New Press.

Kay, J. (2011) *Red Dust Road*, Picador.

Keddell, E. (2017) 'Interpreting children's best interests: needs, attachment and decision-making', *Journal of Social Work*, 17(3): 324–342.

Keddell, E. (2022) 'Mechanisms of inequity: the impact of instrumental biases in the child protection system', *Societies*, 12(3): 83.

Keller, H. (2013) 'Attachment and culture', *Journal of Cross-Cultural Psychology*, 44(2): 175–194.

Kim, E. (2019) 'My folder is not a person: kinship knowledge, biopolitics, and the adoption file', in S. Bamford (ed) *The Cambridge Handbook of Kinship*, Cambridge University Press, pp 451–480.

Kirton, D. (2019) 'Adoption wars: inequality, child welfare and (social) justice', *Families, Relationships and Societies*, 9(2): 253–268.

Kirton, D., Peltier, E. and Webb, E. (2001) 'After all these years: accessing care records', *Adoption and Fostering*, 25(4): 39–49.

Koch, P. (2024) 'Records of relinquishment: caregiving and emotion in the philanthropy archive', *The Public Historian*, 46(2): 79–103.

Kramer, A.M. (2011a) 'Kinship, affinity and connectedness: exploring the role of genealogy in personal lives', *Sociology*, 45(3): 379–395.

Kramer, A.M. (2011b) 'Mediatizing memory: history, affect and identity in who do you think you are?' *European Journal of Cultural Studies*, 14(4): 428–445.

Lambert, C. (2018) *The Live Art of Sociology*, Routledge.

Lambert, C. (2020) 'The ambivalence of adoption: adoptive families' stories', *Sociology*, 54(2): 363–379.

Lambert, C., Williams, S. and Douglas, R. (2023) 'Sexual cultures in university: an arts-based intervention', *Gender and Education*, 35(4): 348–364.

Leng, K. (2020) 'Fumerism as queer feminist activism: humour and rage in the lesbian avengers' visibility politics', *Gender and History*, 32(1): 108–130.

Letherby, G. (2003) *Feminist Research in Theory and Practice*, Open University Press.

Lewis, S. (2019) *Full Surrogacy Now: Feminism Against Family*, Verso.

Lewis, S. (2022) *Abolish the Family: A Manifesto for Care and Liberation*, Verso Books.

Lifton, B.J. (2009) 'Ghosts in the adopted family,' *Psychoanalytic Inquiry*, 30(1): 71–79.

Lorde, A. (1984) *Sister Outsider: Essays and Speeches*, The Crossing Press.

Lorde, A. (2017) *Your Silence Will Not Protect You*, Silver Press.

Love, H. (2007) *Feeling Backward: Loss and the Politics of Queer History*, Harvard University Press.

Love, H. (2016) 'Queer messes', *Women's Studies Quarterly*, 44(3/4): 345–349.

Lyttle, E., McCafferty, P. and Taylor, B.J. (2024) 'Experiences of adoption disruption: parents' perspectives', *Child Care in Practice: Northern Ireland Journal of Multi-Disciplinary Child Care Practice*, 30(3): 333–352.

MacAlister, J. (2022) The Independent Review of Children's Social Care. Available at https://childrenssocialcare.independent-review.uk/final-report/, accessed January 2023.

MacDonald, M. (2023) 'Post-adoption contact', in N. Lowe and C. Fenton-Glynn (eds) *Research Handbook on Adoption* Law, Edward Elgar Publishing Limited, pp 248–268.

MacDonald, M. and McSherry, D. (2011) 'Open adoption: adoptive parents' experiences of birth family contact and talking to their child about adoption', *Adoption and Fostering*, 35(3): 4–16.

MacDonald, M. and McSherry, D. (2013) 'Constrained adoptive parenthood and family transition: adopters' experience of unplanned birth family contact in adolescence', *Child and Family Social Work*, 18(1): 87–96.

MacKenzie, A. and Roberts, C. (2017) 'Adopting neuroscience: parenting and affective indeterminacy', *Body and Society*, 23(3): 130–155.

Maggio, J. (2007) 'Political theory, translation, representation and Gayatri Chakravorty Spivak: can the subaltern be heard?', *Alternatives*, 32(4): 419–443.

Main, M. and Solomon, J. (1990) 'Procedures for identifying infants as disorganized/disoriented during the Ainsworth Strange Situation', in M.T. Greenberg, D. Cicchetti and E.M. Cummings (eds) *Attachment in the Preschool Years*, University of Chicago Press, pp 121–160.

Mann, J. and Rabin, K. (2024) *The Secret Language of the Body: Regulate Your Nervous System, Heal Your Body, Free Your Mind*, HarperCollins.

Martinez, C. and Mukerjee, R. (2025) (eds) *All This Safety is Killing Us: Health Justice Beyond Prisons, Police and Borers - Abolitionist Frameworks from Clinicians, Organizations and Incarcerated Activists*, North Atlantic Books.

Mason, C., Ward, H. and Broadhurst, K. (2023) 'Giving HOPE and minimising trauma: an intervention to support women who are separated from their babies at birth due to safeguarding concerns', *Child Abuse Review*, 32(1).

Mason, C., Broadhurst, K., Ward, H., Barnett, A. and Holmes, L. (2022) 'Born into care: developing best practice guidelines for when the state intervenes at birth,' Nuffield Family Justice Observatory. Available at https://www.nuffieldfjo.org.uk/resource/born-into-care-developing-best-practice-guidelines-for-when-the-state-intervenes-at-birth, accessed November 2024.

Mason, J. (2018) *Affinities: Potent Connections in Personal Life*, Polity Press.

McElhone, M., Kemp, T., Lamble, S. and Moore, J.M. (2022) 'Defund - not defend - the police: A response to Fleetwood and Lea', *The Howard Journal of Crime and Justice*, 62: 277–282.

McFarlane, A. (2016) 'When nothing else will do', FLBA National Conference Keynote Address, 22 October. Available at https://www.judiciary.uk/speech-by-lord-justice-mcfarlane-nothing-else-will-do/ accessed February 2023.

McGrath, J., Lhussier, M., Crossley, S. and Forster, N. (2023) '"They tarred me with the same brush": navigating stigma in the context of child removal', *International Journal of Environmental Research and Public Health*, 20(12).

Mckay, E. (2024) *Too Little, Too Late: The Multi-Agency Response to Identifying and Tackling Neglect*, NSPCC.

McKee, K. (2019) *Disrupting Kinship: Transnational Politics of Korean Adoption in the United States*, University of Illinois Press.

McSherry, D., Samuels, G. and Brodzinsky, D. (2022) 'An introduction to the adoption and trauma special issue', *Child Abuse and Neglect*, 130: 2.

McQuillan, K. and Taylor B.J. (2014) 'Perspectives of foster parents and social workers on foster placement disruption', *Child Care in Practice*, 20(2): 232–249.

McWilliam, E. (2000) 'Laughing within reason: on pleasure, women and academic performance', in St. Pierre and W. Pillow (eds) *Working the Ruins: Feminist Poststructuralist Theory and Methods in Education*, Routledge, pp. 164–178.

Melville, J. and Bean, P. (1989) *Lost Children of the Empire*, Routledge.

Memarnia, N., Nolte, L., Norris, C. and Harborne, A. (2015) '"It felt like it was night all the time": listening to the experiences of birth mothers whose children have been taken into care or adopted', *Adoption and Fostering* 39(4): 303–317.

Menakem, R. (2017) *My Grandmother's Hands: Racialised Trauma and the Pathway to Mending Our Hearts and Bodies*, Penguin.

Merritt, M. (2024) 'Be grateful or be quiet: confronting the epistemic harms of adoptism', *Feminist Philosophy Quarterly*, 10(3).

Monck, E., Reynolds, J. and Wigfall, V. (2004) 'Using concurrent planning to establish permanency for looked after young children', *Child and Family Social Work*, 9(4): 321–331.

Morgan, H., Nolte, L., Rishworth, B. and Stevens, C. (2019) "My children are my world': raising the voices of birth mothers with substantial experience of counselling following the loss of their children to adoption or foster care', *Adoption and Fostering*, 43(2): 137–154.

Morris, K. and Featherstone, B. (2010) 'Investing in children, regulating parents and supporting whole families', *Social Policy and Society*, 9(4): 557–586.

Morris, K., Mason, W. and Bywater, P. (2018) 'Social work, poverty, and child welfare interventions', *Child & Family Social Work*, 23(3): 364–372.

Morriss, L. (2018) 'Haunted futures: the stigma of being a mother living apart from her child(ren) as a result of state-ordered court removal', *The Sociological Review*, 66(4): 816–831.

Morriss, L. and Broadhurst, K. (2022) 'Understanding the mental health needs of mothers who have had children removed through the family court: a call for action', *Qualitative Social Work: Research and Practice*, 21(5): 803–808.

Murphy, C. (2023) '"Rising demand and decreasing resources": Theorising the "cost of austerity" as a barrier to social worker discretion', *Journal of Social Policy*, 52(1): 197–214.

Murphy, C., Turay, J., Parry, N. and Birch, N. (2024) 'What do child protection social workers consider to be the systemic factors driving workforce instability within the English child protection system, and what are the implications for the UK Government's reform strategy?' *Journal of Social Work Practice*, 38(2): 205–220.

Myers, K.W. (2014) '"Real" families: the violence of love in new media adoption discourse', *Critical Discourse Studies*, 11(2): 175–193.

Myong, L. and Bissenbakker, M. (2021) 'Attachment as affective assimilation: discourses on love and kinship in the context of transnational adoption in Denmark', *NORA – Nordic Journal of Feminist and Gender Research*, 29(3): 165–177.

Nayak, S. (2020) 'For women of colour in social work: black feminist self-care practice based on Audre Lorde's radical pioneering principles', *Critical and Radical Social Work*, 8(3): 405–421.

Neary, M. and Saunders, G. (2016) 'Student as producer and the politics of abolition: making a new form of dissident institution?', *Critical Education*, 7(5).

Neil, E. (2013) 'The mental distress of the birth relatives of adopted children: 'disease' or 'unease'', *Health and Social Care in the Community*, 21: 2.

Neil, E. (2018) 'Rethinking adoption and birth family contact: is there a role for the law?', *Family Law*, 48: 1178.

Neil, E., Beek, M. and Ward, E. (2015) *Contact After Adoption: A Longitudinal Study of Post Adoption Contact Arrangements*, CoramBaaf.

Neil, E., Morciano, M., Young, J. and Hartley, L. (2020) 'Exploring links between early adversities and later outcomes for children adopted from care: implications for planning post adoption support', *Developmental Child Welfare*, 2(1).

Neil, E., Rimmer, J., Rawcliffe, C. and Copson, R. (2024) *Evaluation of the Letter Swap Pilot: Final Report*, UEA Centre for Research on Children and Families.

Neil, E.C. and Howe, D. (2004) *Contact in Adoption and Permanent Foster Care: Research, Theory and Practice*, BAAF.

Nolte, L. and Forbes, C. (2023) 'Building relational trust and hope: the experiences of counsellors in a service for birth relatives whose children have been adopted or taken into care', *Adoption and Fostering*, 47(1): 77–93.

Nuffield Foundation (2021) *The Lifelong Health and Well-being of Care Leavers*, Policy Briefing, October. Available at https://www.nuffieldfoundation.org/wp-content/uploads/2021/10/The-lifelong-health-and-well-being-of-care-leavers.-Nuffield-Foundation-and-UCL-policy-briefing.-Oct-2021.pdf, accessed October 2024.

Oaks, L. (2015) *Giving Up Baby: Safe Haven Laws, Motherhood, and Reproductive Justice*, New York University.

O'Brian, M.E. (2023) *Family Abolition: Capitalism and the Communizing of Care*, Pluto Press.

Office for National Statistics (ONS) (2022) 'The education background of looked-after children who interact with the criminal justice system'. Data released 5 December 2022. Available at https://www.ons.gov.uk/peoplepopulationandcommunity/educationandchildcare/articles/theeducationbackgroundoflookedafterchildrenwhointeractwiththecriminaljusticesystem/december2022, accessed January 2023.

O'Marah, R., Hodge, S. and Machin, L. (2025) 'Caring for traumatized children: a systematic review exploring experiences of secondary trauma and compsassion fatigue among adoptive and foster parents', *Adoption Quarterly*, 1–31.

ONS (2023a) 'Children looked after in England including adoptions'. Available at https://explore-education-statistics.service.gov.uk/find-statistics/children-looked-after-in-england-including-adoptions/2023, accessed June 2025.

ONS (2023b) 'More adults living with their parents', May 2023. Available at https://www.ons.gov.uk/peoplepopulationandcommunity/populationandmigration/populationestimates/articles/moreadultslivingwiththeirparents/2023-05-10, accessed June 2025.

Osborne, T. (1999) 'The ordinariness of the archive', *History of the Human Sciences*, 12(2): 51–64.

Oswin, N. and Olund, E. (2010) 'Governing intimacy', *Environment and Planning D: Society and Space*, 28(1): 60–67.

Paine, A.L., Fahey, K. and Anthony, R.E. (2021) 'Early adversity predicts adoptees' enduring emotional and behavioral problems in childhood', *European Child and Adolescent Psychiatry*, 30: 721–732.

Page, C. (2022) 'Mother-and-baby homes: One of the greatest scandals', *BBC News*, 2 January. Available at https://www.bbc.co.uk/news/uk-northern-ireland-64087190, accessed January 2022.

Page, T. (2017) 'Vulnerable writing as a feminist methodological practice', *Feminist Review*, 115: 13–29.

Palacios, J., Rolock, N., Selwyn, J. and Barbosa-Ducharne, M. (2019) 'Adoption breakdown: concept, research, and implications', *Research on Social Work Practice*, 29(2): 130–142.

Parker, J. (2019) 'Integrative arts and the art of attachment', *Art/Law Network*, 15 January. Available at https://artlawnetwork.org/integrative-arts-and-art-of-attachment-by-joanna-parker/, accessed October 2024.

Paton, K. and Jackson, E. (2025) 'Introduction to Live Methods Revisited: the roots and conjuncture of Live Methods', *The Sociological Review*, 73(5): 941–952.

Patterson, O. (1982) *Slavery and Social Death: A Comparative Study*, Harvard University Press.

Pattinson, R., Broadhurst, K., Alrouh, B., Cusworth, L., Doebler, S., Griffiths, L. et al (2021). *Born Into Care: Newborn Babies in Urgent Care Proceedings in England and Wales*, Nuffield Family Justice Observatory.

Pease, B. (2016) (ed) *Doing Critical Social Work: Transformative Practices for Social Justice*, Routledge.

Penner, J. (2023) 'Post-adoption service provision: a scoping review', *Adoption Quarterly*, 27(4): 319–348.

Perks, B. (2024) *Trauma Proof: Healing, Attachment and the Science of Prevention*, Ithaca.

Peterson, I., Peltola, T., Kaski, S., Walters, K.R. and Hardoon, S. (2018) 'Depression, depressive symptoms and treatments in women who have recently given birth: UK cohort study', *BMJ Open*, 8: e022152.

Philip, G., Yousanamouth, L., Bedston, S. et al (2020) '"I had no hope, I had no help at all": insights from a first study of fathers and recurrent care proceedings', *Societies*, 10(4): 89.

Pink, S. (2015) *Doing Sensory Ethnography* (second edition), Sage.

Plummer, K. (2019) *Narrative Power: The Struggle for Human Value*, Polity Press.

Pösö, T., Skivenes, M. and Thoburn, J. (2021) (eds) *Adoption from Care: International Perspectives on Children's Rights, Family Preservation and State Intervention*, Policy Press.

Posocco, S. (2022) 'Harvesting life, mining death: adoption, surrogacy and forensics across borders', *Catalyst: Feminism, Theory, Technoscience*, 8(1): 1–19.

Poulis, K. (2025) 'The consequentiality of absences in social settings: a sensemaking perspective', *Sociology*, 59(1): 107–125.

Public Law Working Group (2024) 'Recommendations for best practice in respect of adoption', Interim report, November 2024. Available at https://www.judiciary.uk/guidance-and-resources/wholesale-reform-to-adoption-process-is-needed-says-public-law-working-group/, accessed November 2024.

Pugh, G. and Schofield, G. (1999) 'Unlocking the past: the experience of gaining access to Barnardo's records', *Adoption and Fostering*, 23(2): 7–18.

Purtell, J., Mendes, P. and Saunders, B.J. (2021) 'Where is the village? Care leaver early parenting, social isolation and surveillance bias', *International Journal on Child Maltreatment: Research, Policy and Practice*, 4: 349–371.

Quinn, J. (2023) *Invisible Education: Posthuman Explorations of Everyday Learning*, Routledge.

Radoux, J. (2023) 'Caring for children and young people in state care in the 2020s', in R. Sen and C. Kerr (eds) 'The future of children's care', *Critical Perspectives on Children's Services Reform*, Policy Press, pp 161–177.

Redden, J., Dencik, L. and Warne, H. (2020) 'Datafied child welfare services: unpacking, politics, economics and power', *Policy Studies*, 41(5): 507–526.

Rees, C. (2024) 'The right to identity: the effects and consequences of restricting adoptees' access to birth records', The Dunbar Project. Available at https://www.thedunbarproject.org.uk/articles/the-right-to-identity-the-effects-and-consequences-of-restricting-adoptees-access-to-birth-records, accessed November 2024.

Rees, J. (2009) *Life Story Books for Adopted Children: A Family Friendly Approach*, Jessica Kingsley Publishers.

Ridge, T. (2013) '"We are all in this together?' The hidden costs of poverty, recession and austerity policies on Britain's poorest children', *Children and Society*, 27: 406–417.

Richardson, L. (1990) Narrative and sociology, *Journal of Contemporary Ethnography*, 19(1): 116–135.

Roberts, D. (2022) *Torn Apart: How the Child Welfare System Destroys Black Families - and How Abolitions Can Build a Safer World*, Basic Books.

Roberts, L., Meakings, S., Forrester, D., Smith, A. and Shelton, K. (2017) Care-leavers and their children placed for adoption, *Children and Youth Services Review*, 79: 355–361.

Rosa, S.K. (2023) *Radical Intimacy*, Pluto.

Rose, H. and Rose, S. (2016) *Can Neuroscience Change Our Minds?* Polity Press.

Rose, R. (2012) *Life Story Therapy with Traumatized Children: A Model for Practice*, Jessica Kingsley Publishers.

Rosen, A. (1994) 'Knowledge use in direct practice', *The Social Service Review*, 68(4): 561–577.

Rundle, K. (2011) 'Improbable agents of empire: coming to terms with British child migrants', *Adoption and Fostering*, 35(3): 30–37.

Rushton, A. (2003) 'The adoption of looked after children: a scoping review of research', Social Care Institute for Excellence, University of Bristol.

Rutter, N. (2023) 'Rupture, repair, the loss and reconstruction of identity: seeking support in situations of adolescent-to-parent violence and abuse', *Frontiers in Health Services Research*, 3.

Rutter, N. (2024) 'Explosive and harmful impulses: a subset of child and adolescent-to-parent violence and abuse', *Journal of Interpersonal Violence*, 39(23–24): 4722–4747.

Sacker, A., Lacey, R., Maughan, B. and Murray, E. (2022) 'Out-of-home care in childhood and socio-economic functioning in adulthood: ONS Longitudinal study 1971–2011', *Children and Youth Services Review*, 132.

Said, E. (1984) 'Permission to narrate', *Journal of Palestine Studies*, 13(3): 27–48.

Sales, S. (2012) *Adoption, Family and the Paradox of Origins: A Foucauldian History*, Palgrave.

Sales, S. (2018) 'Damaged attachments and family dislocations: the operations of class in adoptive family life', *Genealogy*, 2(4): 55.

Samuel, M. (2024) 'Social work morale has fallen since 2020, finds study for regulator', *Community Care*, 21 March. Available at https://www.communitycare.co.uk/2024/03/21/social-workers-less-likely-to-have-high-morale-or-to-recommend-profession-than-in-2020-finds-study/, accessed June 2025.

Saunders, C. (1964) 'Care of patients suffering from terminal illness at St Joseph's Hospice, Hackney, London', Nursing Mirror, 14 February, pp vii–x.

Scarry, E. (1985) *The Body in Pain: The Making and Unmaking of the World*, Oxford University Press.

Schore, A. (2000) 'Attachment and the regulation of the right brain', *Attachment and Human Development*, 2(1): 23–47.

Selman, P. (2023) 'The rise and fall of intercountry adoption 1995–2019', in N. Lowe and C. Fenton-Glynn (eds) *Research Handbook on Adoption Law*, Edward Elgar Publishing Limited, pp 321–345.

Selwyn, J. (2023) 'Outcomes for children adopted from care in the UK', in N. Lowe and C. Fenton-Glynn (eds) *Research Handbook on Adoption Law*, Edward Elgar Publishing Limited, pp 228–247.

Selwyn, J. and Wijedasa, D. (2011) 'Pathways to adoption for minority ethnic children in England-Reasons for entry to care', *Child and Family Social Work*, 16(3): 276–286.

Selwyn, J. and Meakings, S. (2016) 'Adolescent-to-parent violence in adoptive families', *The British Journal of Social Work*, 46(5): 1224–1240.

Selwyn, J., Wijedasa, D. and Meakings, S. (2014) 'Beyond the Adoption Order: challenges, interventions and adoption disruption', DfE research report. Available at https://assets.publishing.service.gov.uk/media/5a74b507e5274a3f93b4825b/Final_Report_-_3rd_April_2014v2.pdf, accessed August 2025.

Sen, R. and Kerr, C. (2023a) (eds) *The Future of Children's Care*, Policy Press.

Sen, R. and Kerr, C. (2023b) 'Introduction: critical perspectives on children's services reform', in R. Sen, and C. Kerr (eds) *The Future of Children's Care*, Policy Press, pp 1–13.

Sen, R. and Kerr, C. (2023c) 'Reclaiming social work, the social work complex and issues of bias in children's services', in R. Sen, and C. Kerr (eds) *The Future of Children's Care*, Policy Press, pp 60–84.

Sharpe, G. (2015) 'Precarious identities: "young" motherhood, desistance and stigma', *Criminology and Criminal Justice*, 15: 407–422.

Sherwood, H. (2025) 'Time running out' for UK to apologise over forced adoptions, *The Guardian*, 9 February. Available at https://www.theguardian.com/society/2025/feb/09/forced-adoptions-time-running-out-for-uk-to-apologise, accessed June 2025.

Shepherd, E., Hoyle, V., Lomas, E., Flinn, A. and Sexton, A. (2020) 'Towards a human-centred participatory approach to child social care recordkeeping', *Archival Science*, 20(4): 307–325.

Shuttleworth, P. (2023) 'Kinship care for England and Wales in the 2020s: assumptions, challenges and opportunities', in R. Sen and C. Kerr (eds) *The Future of Children's Care: Critical Perspectives on Children's Services Reform*, Policy Press, pp 122–144.

Siegel, D.J. and Bryson, T.P. (2012) *The Whole-Brain Child: 12 Proven Strategies to Nurture Your Child's Developing Mind*, Robinson.

Singh, J. (2018a) *No Archive Will Restore You*, Punctum Books.

Singh, J. (2018b) *Unthinking Mastery: Dehumanism and Decolonial Entanglements*, Duke University Press.

Sissay, L. (2019) *My Name is Why: A Memoir*, Canongate.

Skinner, G.C.M., Bywaters, P.W.B. and Kennedy, E. (2023) 'A review of the relationship between poverty and child abuse and neglect: Insights from scoping reviews, systematic reviews and meta-analyses', *Child Abuse Review*, 32(2).

Skivenes, M. and Tefre, Ø.S. (2012) 'Adoption in the child welfare system - A cross-country analysis of child welfare workers' recommendations for or against adoption', *Children and Youth Services Review*, 34(11): 2220–2228.

Smolin, D. (2023) 'The legal mandate for ending the modern era of intercountry adoption', in N. Lowe and C. Fenton-Glynn (eds) *Research Handbook on Adoption Law*, Edward Elgar, pp 384–407.

Social Work England (2024) The Social Work Workforce. Available at https://www.socialwengland.org.uk/about/publications/the-social-work-workforce/, accessed June 2025.

Solomon, R. (1997) 'Beyond ontology: ideation, phenomenology and the cross cultural study of emotion', *Journal for the Theory of Social Behaviour*, 27(2–3): 289–303.

Spivak, G. (1988) 'Can the subaltern speak?', in C. Nelson and L. Grossberg (eds) *Marxism and the Interpretation of Culture*, Macmillan Education, pp 271–313.

Spratt, V. (2023) 'Vulnerable homeless people forced to move hundreds of miles away by councils due to housing crisis', *i-news*, 25 August. Available at https://inews.co.uk/news/vulnerable-homeless-people-move-hundreds-miles-councils-housing-crisis-2570781, accessed January 2023.

Squire, C. (2020) *Stories Changing Lives: Narratives and Paths Toward Social Change*, Oxford University Press.

Stanley, E. (2015) 'Responding to state institutional violence', *British Journal of Criminology*, 55: 1149–1167.

Steedman, C. (2001) 'Something she called a fever: Michelet, Derrida, and Dust Author(s)', *The American Historical Review*, 106(4): 1159–1180.

Stoler, A. (2002) 'Colonial archives and the arts of governance: on the content in the form', in C. Hamilton, V. Harris, J. Taylor, M. Pickover, G. Reid and R. Saleh (eds) *Refiguring the Archive*, Kluwel Publishing, pp 83–102.

Stones, L. (2023) (ed) 'Adoption crisis: the jarring reality of adoption'. Available at https://www.ourpatch.org.uk/wp-content/uploads/2024/03/The-Jarring-Reality-of-Adoption.pdf, accessed September 2024.

Syrstad, E. and Slettebø, T. (2019) 'To understand the incomprehensible: a qualitative study of parents' challenges after child removal and their experiences with support services', *Child and Family Social Work*, 25(1): 100–107.

Tepe-Belfrage, D. and Wallin, S. (2016) 'Austerity and the hidden costs of recovery: Inequality and insecurity in the UK households', *British Politics*, 11(4): 389–395.

Thoburn, J. (2023) 'Understanding adoption breakdown: a socio-legal perspective', in N. Lowe and C. Fenton-Glynn (eds) *Research Handbook on Adoption Law*, Edward Elgar, pp 269–284.

Triseliotis, J. (1973) *In Search of Origins: The Experience of Adopted People*, Routledge and Kegan Paul.

Tyler, I. (2020) *Stigma: The Machinery of Inequality*, Zed Books.

Van der Kolk, B. (2014) *The Body Keeps the Score: Mind, Brain and Body in the Transformation of Trauma*, Penguin.

van Wichelen, S. (2018) *Legitimating Life: Adoption in the Age of Globalization and Biotechnology*, Rutgers University Press.

Verrier, N. (2009) *The Primal Wound: Understanding the Adopted Child*, BAAF.

Vincent, C. (2023) 'Reflecting on the collaborative practice and socially engaged principles underpinning the making of Vincent Dance Theatre's Art of Attachment', unpublished PhD Thesis, Canterbury Christ Church University School of Creative Arts and Industries. Available at https://www.vincentdt.com/charlotte-vincents-phd/, accessed October 2024.

Wainwright, J. and Ridley, J. (2012). 'Matching, ethnicity and identity: reflections on the practice and realities of ethnic matching in adoption', *Adoption and Fostering*, 36(3–4): 50–61.

Wastell, D. and White, S. (2017) *Blinded by Science: The Social Implications of Epigenetics and Neuroscience*, Policy Press.

Webb, C., Bennett, D. and Bywaters, P. (2022) 'Austerity, poverty, and children's welfare and public services', *Social Policy and Society*, 1–22.

Webb, C., Bywaters, P., Scourfield, J., Davidson, G. and Bunting, G. (2020) 'Cuts both ways: ethnicity, poverty, and the social gradient in child welfare interventions', *Children and Youth Services Review*, 117: 105–299.

Weeks, K. (2020) 'Anti/Post feminist politics and a case for a basic income', *Triple C: Journal for a Global Sustainable Information Society*, 18(2): 575–594.

Weeks, K. (2023) 'Abolition of the family: the most infamous feminist proposal', *Feminist Theory*, 24(3): 433–453.

Williams, P., Shepherd, E. and Sexton, A. (2024) 'Working with care leavers and young people still in care: ethical issues in the co-development of a participatory recordkeeping app', *Archive Science*, 24: 41–60.

Woodcock, J. (2003) 'The social work assessment of parenting: an exploration', The *British Journal of Social Work*, 33(1): 87–106.

Index

References to figures appear in *italic* type. References to endnotes show both the page number and the note number (188ch7n3).

A

abandonment of babies, decriminalisation of 5
abolition 9, 170–174
 and reform 19–21
abortion 110
acceptance 121–122, 133, 134
access to care records and support for people 32
accommodation 122
accounting for lack of support 151
activist and therapeutic alliances 18
addiction 89, 90
adoption
 attachment theory and 73–95
 contexts of 5–6
 crisis in 4–5
 critical stance towards 16–17
 distress caused to birth mothers by 113
 emotional complexities of 116–139
 globalisation of 7
 knowledges and ways of knowing 46–72
 making as open as possible 180–183
 manifesto for change 168–186
 narratives, role of archives in 26–45
 nature of 1–25
 policies and practices, interdependence in 140–167
 positive representations of 14
 prioritisation of 156
 in the UK 9–13
Adoption Act (1976), section 51 32
Adoption and Children Act (2002) section 52b 10
The Adoption and Fostering Podcast 173
Adoption Barometer 15
adoption contract 185
adoption court records, access to 33–34
Adoption Order 10, 157
adoption stories and storytelling 3–4, 17–18, 23, 26, 34, 65, 71 *see also* archives
 telling of in new ways 96–115
Adoption UK 15
adoption wars 5
adoption workers 147
adoptive families 13, 14–16, 24, 141, 163, 164, 181–182
adoptive family life, absent-presence in 162
adoptive parents 15–16, 161, 163, 164, 185, 188ch7n3
adultification of young people 138, 155
affirmations 159–160
After Adoption 61
agency, lack of 33
Ainsworth, Mary 74, 75
alcoholism 91
anger 136
Annette 70, 82, 85–88, *86*, 92, 94, 99, 100, 101, 103, 106
anti-adoption argument 17
anxiety 110, 121
Arcadia Gallery in Coventry, workshops held at 53, 54, 58, 66
archaeon 28
archaic fever 29
archival turn 27
archives
 and archival practices 22, 177–178
 role of in adoption narratives 26–45, 97, 161
Art of Attachment
 film installation and workshops 2–3, 22–23, 30, 43, 47, 49, 52–60, *55*, 62, 63, 64, 66–72, 72–73, 74, 79, 82–85, *83*, 87, 88, 91–94, 97, 98–99, 100–103, 106, 108, 111, 113, 115, *128*, 136, 161, 168, 177, 179, 184, 186
 scripts 85–88, 89, 90, 91–92, 101, 102
artwork 108
Ash 122
assessment 134, 178, 183
assessment documentation 38
attachment 23, 70–71
 and brain science 74–77
attachment theory
 and adoption 73–95
 critical responses to 77–79
attachments
 ambivalence of damaged 88–91
 desire for absent 85–88
Attenborough Centre for Creative Arts, Brighton 52
Australia, forced emigration of poor children to 11
authority 33, 70

Index

Avarez, Anna 88, 90, 92
Ayla 118, 121, 122

B

Barnardo's Children: The Largest Family in the World (television documentary) 32
basic survival needs 120–121
basic tasks and support 121–122
behaviour, modelling of 118–119, 153–154
being with 121–122
biological families *see* birth families
Birmingham, poverty in 5
Birmingham Children's Trust 61
birth certificate 35
birth families 102, 141, 147, 162, 163–164, 181–183
birth mothers 103–106 *see also* Elowen
birth parents 38, 102, 112, 114, 136, 147, 156, 161, 188ch7n3
birthing 91
Black families 170
Black populations 7
Black women in New York, counter-narrative of 42–43
Black young people at increased risk 138
blame and stigma 77, 141, 143, 148
Bowlby, John 74, 75
brain science *see* neuroscience
Breaking The Cycle 61, 187ch1n4 *see also* Breathe, Trust, Connect
Breathe, Trust, Connect (BTC) 3, 11, 23, 24, 27, 47, 60–62, 64, 65, 66, 70, 71, 72, 93, 94, 95, 97, 98, 102–103, *104*, *105*, 106, *107*, 107–110, *108*, 111, 112, 113, 114, 115, 117, 118–120, 121, 122, 123, 124, 124–126, 127, 128, 129, 130, 131–139, 140, 141, 144, 145, 147, 148, 150–159, 161, 162–164, 165–166, 168, 170, 173, 174, 175, 177, 178, 182, 183, 185, 186
  ethnography with 62–63
  use of creative methods at 66–70, *68*
Brighton Oasis Project 3, 52, 53, 54, 70, 82, 84, 90, 91
BTC *see* Breathe, Trust, Connect
bureaucracy and emotion 83–84
burn-out, effects of on staff well-being 132

C

CAMHS *see* Child and Adolescent Mental Health Services
Canada, forced emigration of poor children to 11

CAPVA *see* Child or Adolescent to Parent Violence and Abuse
care
  at the scale of kinship 167
  babies born into 12
  dependence on 152
  ethics of promiscuous 167
  monopolisation of 143
  privatisation of 142
  responsibility for 154–155
  services 127
The Care Collective 8, 152, 180
care-experienced people 11
The Care Manifesto 167, 180
care proceedings 11, 13
  risk of being subject to 11
care records and support for people 32
caseloads, high 85, 122, 123
Child and Adolescent Mental Health Services (CAMHS) 13, 179
Child or Adolescent to Parent Violence and Abuse (CAPVA) 151
Child Permanency Reports 30, 145, 161, 162
child poverty 76
care proceedings 178
child protection 151, 184
Child Protection Conference 118–119, 127
child protection encounter 121
child protection orders 127
Child Protection Plans 168
child protection policies 141
child protection system 12–13, 38
child removal 136, 151, 161
child sexual abuse 69–70
Child Sexual Exploitation (CSE) 69
child welfare system 8, 170
children at risk 152–153
Children's Act (1989) 36
  Section 31 187ch1n7
Children's Services 132, 152, 153, 154–155, 175
Children's Services Assessment 121
choices, poor 91
Circle of Security Parenting course 120
citizens, law-abiding 76
claims about impact of neglectful/abusive parenting 78
Clark, Robert (Rob) 88, 90, 92
clinical supervision for staff 129, 131–134, 138
Coates, Al 172–173
colonial legacies and the adoption-industrial complex 6–9
commencement and commandment 28, 29
community care networks 8

211

community forms of caring 143, 167
compassion 138
concurrent planning 13
connection 133, 134
  and integration service 120
  of adoptive and birth families 144
conservative political agenda 76–77, 172
Constitution of the United States 5
contact
  agreement 38
  between birth and adoptive parents *see* letterbox contact
  between birth parents and children 162–163
  post adoption, direct 163
contact sessions, 'goodbye' 133–134
contact via letters 157 *see also* letterbox contact
contract 38
control over archival access 35
coping strategies, modelling of 119
counter-narratives 17–18, 161
counter-transference 132, 187ch7n1
court proceedings 102, 161
court room scenes 135
craft-based activities 55–56, *56*, *57*, 58, 66–67, 103, *104*, *105*, *107*, *108*, 113–114
creative activities/tasks and approaches 67–68, 100, 103, 107
Critical Resistance 170
cruel optimism 33
CSE *see* Child Sexual Exploitation
cultures of support 151–152

D

damage and transformation 98
data generation and analysis 2–3
datafication 31
DDP *see* Dyadic Developmental Psychotherapy
decision-making 125, 136, 137
Derrida, Jacques 26–27, 28, 29
dialogue 184, 185
digital self 31
disorganised/ disoriented 74
distancing and dissociation 135–136
domestic adoption 6, 10–11
drop boxes 5, 10
drug addiction 109–110
duty, dereliction of 155
Dyadic Developmental Psychotherapy (DDP) 62, 65, 138, 147
dysfunctional base 76, 142, 143

E

ear 111–112 *see also* listening
early development 13

early intervention 12, 13, 76, 178
early investments 178
early permanence 13
economic benefits 178
Eisenhower, President Dwight D 8
Elowen 108–111, 159–160, *160*
emergency action to remove babies at risk, legal sanctioning of 12
emotion 176
emotional burn-out 137
emotional connections 121–122
emotional demands 134
emotional dynamics and politics 20–21, 24, 69, 101–102 *see also* heartbreak
emotional economy 43
emotional registers 177
emotional regulation 119–120
  and relational connection 126–131, 184
emotional support 139
emotions, taking of seriously 176–177
empathy, role of 134–138
empirical research and methodologies 47
epistemic generosity 50
epistemic violence 64
ethical approval and concerns 64
ethical processes 63
ethics of human interdependence and social and political responsibility 81
ethics of promiscuous care 167
ethnographic work 3, 23
evidence 78, 106
  of actual harm 77
expert advice 145

F

families 140
  correspondence and contact between adoptive and birth 38–40
  monopolisation of care within 143
  power and responsibility of ideal 141–144, 179
  re-imagining of 179–180
  and the state 140–141, 167
  structural organisation of 179
  unsupportable 148
family care services 127
Family Drug and Alcohol Court team 179
family history 34, 44–45
family intervention 130–131, 139, 167, 170
family need, re/conceptualisation of 152
family of origin, legal severance from 157
family policing systems 7–8, 170
family poverty 14
family support systems 144–147
fear 13, 38, 110, 121, 161, 181, 182
feeding methods, teaching mother 129–130

Index

film 54–55, 58, 70, 71, 82–93, *83*, *86*, 95, 103
First Minister of Scotland, apology by for forced adoptions 17
fixing problems 127
Floyd, George 8
foster care and foster carers 10, 30, 85, 104, 126, 130, 133–134, 144
foster-industrial complex 8
foster-to adopt 13
Foucault, Michel 26, 28
Freedom of Information requests 31
front-line work/labour 125–126
 conditions of 137
 supporting colleagues doing 134–138
fund, centralised support 146
future biopsychosocial profile 77
future harm 12, 77

G

gate-keeping behaviours of record keepers, unethical 33
genealogical services 32
generational harm, cycles of 14
ghost archive 35–36
global adoption *see* transnational adoption
global politics 5
government agendas 76
grief 114, 116, 117, 139, 166, 167, 176 *see also* heartbreak; sadness
Grove, Antonia (Toni) 85–86, *86*, 91, 92, 94
guilt 156

H

haunting 35–36
Hazel 122, 151–152
heartbreak 20, 46, 49–50, 115, 116, 117, 139, 176, 186 *see also* grief
help, asking for 151–152
Hill, Carys 58
historical materials 41, 42
Holly 125–126, 154, 155–156
hope 93–94, 108–111, 176, 186
hopelessness 156
Houses of Commons and Lords JCHR *see* Houses of Commons and Lords Joint Committee on Human Rights
Houses of Commons and Lords Joint Committee on Human Rights (JCHR) enquiry 17
housing 122–123
Houston, Wendy 3, 86, 87–88, 92, 99
Hughes, Dan 65
hysterectomy 112

I

identity formation 81
ideologies, dominant conservative and liberal 167
Idra 136, 141–142, 162, 163–164
In Loco Parentis 53, 54
independence 140, 155
industrial complex 4, 7–8, 9
inequalities, social, racial and gendered 77
insecure-avoidant 74
insecure-resistant/ ambivalent 74
institutional control 38
institutional infrastructures 167
interconnection and dependencies between birth and adoptive families 156–165, 166
interconnections between different services 179
inter-country adoption *see* transnational adoption
interdependence in adoption policy and practice 140–167, 179–180
interdependencies 114
interdisciplinary framing 44
intergenerational state harms 153, 155
international adoption *see* transnational adoption
interventions 12, 77, 146, 148
interviews
 semi-structured 62, 64–65
 staff 118–120, 121, 122, 123, 124–127, 131–132, 136, 137, 145, 146, 147, 148, 152, 154, 155, 156–157, 158, 159, 161, 162–164, 166, 173, 175, 177, 178, 182, 185
Irish Prime Minister, apology in Parliament for illegal adoptions 17
Ivy 103–106, *107*, 145, 148, *149*, *150*

J

James, Daf 161n3
Jasmine 151–152
judgements 125, 137
 absence of 118, 134

K

Keziah 124–125, 162–163, 166
kinship or Special Guardianship Orders 9
knowledge
 living 180, 185
 pain-as- 113
 and truth 39
 withholding of 33
knowledge production 2, 19, 26, 43
knowledges
 dominant 186
 embodied 45, 183
 emotional 41, 98, 117
 exchange of 2, 17
 experiential 43, 177
 power of 28, 35
 sensory 42

sources of 27
and ways of knowing, developing 22–23, 43, 46–72
Korean adoptees, difficulty of in accessing files 33

L

labelling 135
landmark decisions 5
language 51, 69, 71, 101, 112–113
and knowledges 1
sanitised 102
later life letters 37–38
Laurel 119–120, 132, 137, 138, 145, 146, 147, 156–157, 161, 178, 185
Leah 23, 52, 70, 82, 91, 92, 94, 99, 100, 101, 103, 106, 108
legal documents in adoption 35
legibility of adoptive families 182–183
legislative process and systems 102, 167
letterbox contact 162, 181, 182
liberatory memory work 27
life events 102
life stories 106
life story (book) and letterbox 27, 37–38, 157–160
Linden 111, 112, 113, 114, 159, 164–165
Linnea 131–132, 148, 154, 155, 158, 175
listening 50–51, 184 *see also* ear
Local Authorities 10, 30, 37, 53, 146
Local Authority Children's Services 47, 60 *see also* Breathe, Trust, Connect
Long Lost Family (television show) 32
'Looked After' status, children with 11
loss(es) 102, 114, 116–117, 120, 176
Lost Boys and Fairies (BBC series) 188ch8n3
Louise 23, 52, 70, 82, 88–91, 94, 99, 100, 103
love 110

M

MacAlister review of children's social care system in England 18–19, 152, 169
manifesto for change 168–186
manifesto for troubling adoption 174–185
material preoccupations 121
Maxwell, Jules 89
meaning 100, 102
medical evidence 76
memoirs 31–32
memory 28
manifesto for troubling adoption 24
memory 113
mental health needs 145, 148
methodologies and methodological framing 2–4, 20, 47–51
mother and baby homes 17, 33
mother and baby units 12

mothering 87, 91
mothers, criminalisation of care-experienced 153
mothers perceived as potential risk 77
movement 93, 95, 98, 115
-based and embodied ways of telling stories 111–114

N

narrative, refusal of 40–41
narrative action 98, 173
narrative of risk 161
National Coalition for Child Protection Reform 8
need, support for all (families) based on 144–147, 178–179
neglect 90
neo-colonialism 172
neoliberal capitalist states and models/policies 8–9, 24, 78, 140, 142, 174, 179
neuroscience 73, 74–77
neurosexism 77
New Zealand, forced emigration of poor children to 11
non-discriminatory practice 137
non-judgemental practice 137
Non-Violent Resistance (NVR) 147
nuclear domestic unit 143
NVR *see* Non-Violent Resistance

O

observational (field-)notes 58, 62, 63, 64–65
Olive 69–70, 121, 123–124, 125, 126–127, 131, 135, 136, 145, 146, 148, 149–150, 151, 158, 159, 161, 177, 182, 183, 186
open adoption practices 37, 162–165, 181–182
openness around a child's origins 157, 181–182
optimism 81–82, 88, 94, 177
ordering and reordering 99, 100
origin narratives and stories 27, 28, 29, 34, 36
oxygen mask theory 132

P

PACE approach *see* Playfulness, Acceptance, Curiosity and Empathy approach
pain 128–129, 133, 135, 136, 165, 166
distancing and dissociating from 135–136
total 112–113
pain-as-knowledge 113
paper self 30–31
paperwork and people 29, 85

Index

parental neglect 156
parenting 75–76
  inadequate 153
  state 156 *see also* role of state as corporate *under* parents
parenting pathway 120
parents 3, 111
  as advisors and experts on Boards and Commissions 187ch1n9
  cherishing of 119
  impact of child removal on 103–106
  interviews with 65
  recounting of in workshops 103, 104–105, 111, 112, 114, 144, 145, 148, 158, 159, 164 *see also names of participants in, e.g.* Willow
  at risk 11, 136
  role of state as corporate 152, 153, 154–155, 156
  wording used by professionals dealing with 103
parents' advocate 13
Parker, Jo 84
partnership and contact 36
pedagogy of repetition 102
permanency medical 102
Philomena (film) 173
physical space and set-up 133–134
Planned Parenthood v. Casey (1992) 5
Playfulness, Acceptance, Curiosity and Empathy (PACE) approach 62, 65
policy making 183
political neglect 168–169
politics and power 78, 80, 97, 116, 166, 172–173
positive words 106
post adoption contact system, constructive 163
power
  and emotions 63–66, 118
  and ownership, unethical discourse of 33
  and stories 96, 97, 103
Power of Words (workshops) 63, 64–65, 67, *68*, 70, 71, 97, 103–108, *104*, *105*, *107*, *108*, 111, 112, 144, 145, 148, 158, 159, 164
practical support 120, 139
pre-birth assessments 12, 30, 121
predictive analytics purposes 31
pre-judgement and expectations 137
Prenatal Theraplay 110, 111, 120
prevention of future harm to children 12
primary dependency 80
privatisation of care 142
problem lists 161
problem solving 126
professional jargon 102
professionalisation 183

provision for adoptive/birth families 147
PRUs *see* Pupil Referral Units
psychological burden, damaging 148
public law family court Care Proceedings 187ch1n7
Public Law Working Group report (2024) 19
Pupil Referral Units (PRUs) 13

R

race and class-based factors 77
Random Controlled Trials (RCTs) and evaluations 48
Raw Emotions (workshops) 63, 67–70, 71, 127, 135, 183
RCTs and evaluations *see* Random Controlled Trials and evaluations
reconnection with adopted children 164–165
recurrent care proceedings 178
reductive opposition 36
reform 9, 27, 40–44, 45, 71, 116, 117, 166
  and abolition 19–21, 170–174
reforming agenda for adoption 148
relational approaches 65
relational care 118
relational dynamics 133
relationship/al-based practices 132, 138
relationship building, practical 120
removal of babies/children from mothers 77, 84, 148
replacement family 162
reports
  and files, production and maintenance of 30, 31–32
  wording of 103, 110
reproductive rights 5
research workshops 2–3
resources 65, 70, 71, 148, 183–184
  therapeutic parenting 146
responsibility 154–155
  for care 143
rhythm and pace 123–126
right to abortion 5
risk assessments 12
risk in families 150, 160–161
risk of (future) harm 77, 136, 160, 187ch1n7
risk to children 162, 187ch1n7
Roberts, Dorothy 4, 7–8
role models 108
Rowan 123, 134, 146–147, 157

S

sadness 127
safe boxes 5
Safe Haven movement and laws 5, 10

safeguarding
  of colleagues 138
  of everybody 174–176, 179, 183
safety at Breathe, Trust, Connect, establishing
  for parents 117–123, 139
  for staff 131–132, 139
safety of children 160
Samaritans 109
Sara 120–121
script, alternative 99–100, 107
secure 74
security, physical and emotional 117
self-preservation, need for 137
sensory regulation and methods 58, 100, 118–119
separation between birth parents and their adopted children 159
severance from birth family 163–164, 180–181
sexual abuse 85
SGO *see* Special Guardianship Orders
sitting with parents 126–127, 129
social care system 179
social dysfunction 76, 77
social intervention 139
social justice 102
  work, enabling 183–184
social model 148
social norms 138
social organisation 166
social problems 121
social services 103, 144
  personnel 125, 158
social suffering 112
social work complex 9
social workers and social work staff, labour of 1, 2, 5, 15, 23, 24, 29, 30, 34, 37, 38, 56–57, 58, 60, 61, 70, 85, 89, 96, 100, 102, 103, 122–123, 124–125, 126, 130, 132, 133, 134, 135, 136, 138, 139, 151, 152, 154–155, 156, 157, 163, 166, 169, 170–171, 175, 179, 183–184, 185, 186, 187ch6n1
South Africa, forced emigration of poor children to 11
space and time for reflection, dialogues, alliances, making 184–185
Special Guardianship Orders (SGO) 178
stabilisation 120
staff recruitment and retention 132
staff workshop discussion 187ch6n1
state, impact of as poor parent on families and social workers 152–156
state archives 43
state-as parent 153
state interference 167
state intervention 141, 143
state support, inadequate levels of 148
stay-and-play session 120–121
stigma and guilt 34, 148, 151
stories, challenging and changing 177–178
stress 132
structural injustices and individual experiences 112
substance abuse 86, 91
suicidal feelings 109
support
  absence of adequate 167
  interconnections between emotional and practical 117–123
  social model of unsupportable families or failures in provision of 148–152
support workers 158, 183
supportive services 148
Sure Start Centres 21
survival instincts 80
Sylvia 68–69, 118–119, 128–131, 133, 138, 173, 174–175, 187ch6n1
systemic failure 155

T

tactile distractions 56, *56*, *57*, 58
team
  building safety as 131
  for family time or contact, dedicated 163
Team Leaders 60
technical terminology 102
temporalities and approach to time 35, 66, 71, 117, 125, 131, 139
therapeutic approaches 138
therapeutic input 145
therapeutic interventions 120, 147
Therapeutic Life Story Work 120, 121, 147, 163
therapeutic practice 138
therapeutic service and responsibilities/support 125–126, 131–134
therapeutic support 156
Therapeutic Support Workers 121
therapeutic understanding 138
therapy, accessing of 145–146
Theraplay 110, 111, 120, 128–129, 133, 147
Thompson, Selina 169
threats 160–161
time and space 123–126, 171
touch, fundamental dependence on others' 81
transference and counter-transference 132
translating and trans/forming stories 98–101
transnational adoption 6–9, 10–11, 33, 172, 180
trauma 41–42, 48–49, 60, 64, 69, 73–74, 90, 101, 102, 114, 183
  generational 112

of separation 13, 14–15, 84, 116–117, 129, 182
and violence 34, 182
trauma informed 131, 184
trauma pain 112, 113
triggers 11–12
troubling 35
trust 120, 125, 129
Twine (theatre production) 169

U

understanding 102, 106–107, 138
United Kingdom
  access to adoption records in 34
  open practices in 36
United States, access to adoption records in 34
University of Warwick 64
US Supreme Court
  Dobbs v. Jackson Women's Health Organization, 2022 5

V

VDT *see* Vincent Dance Theatre
Vikki 23, 52, 68, 69, 70, 82, 85, 89–90, 91, 92, 93, 94, 99, 100, 101, 103, 106, 114, 177

Vincent, Bosie 52, 73, 108
Vincent, Dr Charlotte 2, 3, 47, 51, 52, 53, 54, 73, 82, 89, 90, 92–93, 98, 99, 100, 103, 108, 113
Vincent Dance Theatre (VDT) 2–3, 22–23, 43, 47, 51–53, 54, *55*, 59, 60, 62, 63, 64, 67, 70, 71, 72, 73, 79, 82, 85, 86, 88, 95, 98–99, 106, 113, 115, 161, 168
  premises in Brighton 53, 54
vulnerability 80, 119, 131
vulnerable mums-to-be 11
vulnerable research 63

W

walking alongside parents 121, 123, 139
Wellcome Trust funding application 91
Who Do You Think You Are? (BBC documentary) 32
Williams, Sian 62
Willow 103, *105*, 111, 144–145, 157–158
words that get in the way 101–103, 148
working together 166
workshops 65 *see also* Power of Words; Raw Emotions

www.ingramcontent.com/pod-product-compliance
Lightning Source LLC
Chambersburg PA
CBHW051541020426
42333CB00016B/2047